INTERCULTURAL STUDENT TEACHING

A Bridge to Global Competence

Edited by
Kenneth Cushner
Sharon Brennan

Published in partnership with the
Association of Teacher Educators

Rowman & Littlefield Education
Lanham, Maryland • Toronto • Plymouth, UK
2007

Published in partnership with the
Association of Teacher Educators

Published in the United States of America
by Rowman & Littlefield Education
A Division of Rowman & Littlefield Publishers, Inc.
A wholly owned subsidiary of The Rowman & Littlefield Publishing Group, Inc.
4501 Forbes Boulevard, Suite 200, Lanham, Maryland 20706
www.rowmaneducation.com

Estover Road
Plymouth PL6 7PY
United Kingdom

British Library Cataloguing in Publication Information Available

Library of Congress Cataloging-in-Publication Data
Intercultural student teaching : a bridge to global competence / edited by
Kenneth Cushner, Sharon Brennan.
       p. cm.
  "Published in partnership with the Association of Teacher Educators."
  Includes bibliographical references and index.
  ISBN-13: 978-1-57886-579-6 (hardcover : alk. paper)
  ISBN-10: 1-57886-579-4 (hardcover : alk. paper)
  ISBN-13: 978-1-57886-580-2 (pbk. : alk. paper)
  ISBN-10: 1-57886-580-8 (pbk. : alk. paper)
   1. Student teaching. 2. Teachers–Training of. 3. Education and globalization. I.
Cushner, Kenneth. II. Brennan, Sharon. III. Association of Teacher Educators.
  LB2157.A3I57 2007
  370.71'1–dc22   2006037346

⊗™ The paper used in this publication meets the minimum requirements of
American National Standard for Information Sciences—Permanence of Paper for
Printed Library Materials, ANSI/NISO Z39.48-1992.
Manufactured in the United States of America.

CONTENTS

FOREWORD

As an educator of teachers, are you preparing professionals who can effectively educate any child anywhere in the world, now and for the next forty years?

If your answer is yes, then you are one of few educators—along with the authors of this text—who recognize the realities of our global teaching profession in the twenty-first century. You understand that teachers whose life experiences are primarily within a sixty-mile/hundred-kilometer radius of their homes can no longer be offered to schools of the world.

And you understand why we must cause all persons who seek to enter our global profession of teaching to move beyond their comfort zones, develop their talents in communities that are different from those which they know, and demonstrate their abilities to guide the learning of any young person.

Achieving these goals will not be easy, in that teacher educators around the world focus on preparing teachers for schools of today in their local communities, ignoring current realities of our global community and the future of the teaching profession and schools worldwide.

As teacher educators, we have two fundamental responsibilities: to help select and begin the process of preparing individuals who will, throughout their forty-year careers as professional educators, effectively prepare students for the world in which they will live—the world of seventy to over a hundred years in the future.

The process of preparing educators begins with determining who will be offered entry to the global teaching profession, and it continues throughout each educator's career. Successful educators continually recognize and adapt to evolving characteristics of our global community and the expectations of the communities within which they work. They question practice and change actions in response to the unique needs of each student for whom they are responsible.

Ensuring the continued professional development of educators requires effective modeling of expectations and approaches throughout initial teacher preparation. These include implementing procedures through which every prospective educator/teacher candidate can experience life beyond his or her comfort zone to learn to enter a global, not local, profession with responsibility for helping to shape the world in which future generations will live.

One strategy is to implement policy that requires teacher candidates to complete student-teaching requirements in a community that is different from that which they know. Through this experience, candidates become parts of schools and communities that are new to them and through which their understandings of teaching and of themselves grows significantly.

Replicable models of this experience are described in this text and demonstrate that desired outcomes can be achieved through student-teaching assignments in another country and culture or a different economic, social, and/or cultural setting within the student's home country.

But teacher candidates are rarely offered or required to complete student teaching in a different community. Too often, the beginning process of educating educators emphasizes the candidate's past educational experience and current concerns of local schools, leaving them unprepared for changes they will face in the future beyond the local context.

Why is it that candidates, when considering where to complete student teaching, can only imagine doing it in their local community and no other, even though this requirement is completed in almost every community in the world? The answer lies in the beliefs and actions of their teachers, who say

- "We have standards that cannot be gained or demonstrated through student teaching in another community." Bring educators from different locales together and quickly one finds a common core of beliefs about purposes of education and characteristics (standards) of effective educators that can be and are developed in every educational setting.

- "We are assessed by state and national agencies and dare not stray from the program we have implemented." The fear of change within teacher education offers reason for others to implement alternatives that respond to real needs of the profession—and they will. Instead, teacher educators must challenge the rare cases in which state, provincial, or national policies limit broadening of professional preparation.

- "We have a wide range of diversity in our community through which goals can be achieved." It is one thing to work in a school—even a school that is new to the student teacher within one's community—and quite another to move from that community to live and work in another setting. For example, the student in an urban setting will gain significantly more from the experience by being personally and professionally challenged to student teach in a rural school, just as the student from a rural community would gain from student teaching in an international or domestic urban setting.

- "Our students must be prepared to work with the cultures currently residing in our community." All communities evolve and the cultures served by educators change over time. The premise we, as teacher educators, must act upon is that "multicultural" applies to all cultures in our global community, not simply within our local or national settings.

- "Students will not learn the same things if they student teach in a school in another community." A primary purpose of this text is to help readers recognize that students will greatly expand their professional knowledge through teaching experience in other settings. The lessons learned from international student teaching are often the most fundamental in guiding future action—learning alternative approaches to curriculum development and teaching, understanding strengths and weaknesses in each society's educational system (including their own), and forming core philosophical beliefs through comparing educational alternatives.

- "Student teaching in another country would be too different." The variation among schools across national and cultural boundaries is fundamentally no greater than the difference among schools within a local geographic area. Every school has its own culture, sense of community, and intent and approach to preparing students for their future.

- "We are preparing teachers for our community and region—they need experience here, not outside our area." The marketplace for teachers is global, with opportunities around the world and within all regions of each country. While there are contradictions in current policies—difficulty in teachers prepared in the United States moving from one state to another while teachers prepared elsewhere in the world are teaching in every state—the direction of change is clear. Teachers prepared at any institution in the European Union can seek employment in any other EU country and have their qualifications accepted. Soon this may be the case in the United States and other regions of the world as well. In any case, we do not necessarily want, nor can we expect, our graduates to all find jobs in our local area and to remain there for their forty-year career.

- "If our students do not student teach in our local schools they will not find employment; and anyway, student teaching elsewhere is too expensive." Ask students why they choose to student teach in the local community and you will often find their answer has nothing to do with becoming a more effective professional educator. Instead, they are encouraged by their teachers not to leave the comfort of home, to fear loss of job opportunity, and to believe it will cost too much (which is simply not true), affirming the current parochial nature of teacher education. In reality, they do themselves and the profession a disservice, which school administrators are recognizing as they seek to employ educators with broader professional and life experience.

All children in the world have a right to a basic education on which they can build their lives. Equally, they have the right to teachers who have professional and life experience through which they can guide students to achieve their full potential for life in our global community. It is our responsibility to ensure every child has such teachers.

This text is a valuable resource for creative curriculum and program development, written by educators who understand the responsibilities of our profession within a global context. The authors share their experiences to help you utilize resources of the world in preparing teachers for the future by providing rationale for international and cross-cultural experience, guides for curricular and programmatic change, examples of effective practice, and strategies for program revision that, when implemented, will result in educators who are more effective and bring a global perspective to their professional decision making.

Use it well to ensure we fulfill the highest expectations of our profession.

Craig Kissock,
Professor of education,
University of Minnesota, Morris
Director, Global Student Teaching

PREFACE

As we put the finishing touches on the manuscript for this book, we are aware that the world remains in a precarious situation. Conflict in the Middle East continues to challenge all of us, placing many who live in the Muslim world increasingly at odds with the West. Countless ethnic conflicts are currently being waged within nations around the world—many more than currently exist between nations. Major environmental concerns cross national borders. And we stand on the brink of major health catastrophes ranging from HIV-AIDS to the potential bird-flu pandemic. It is no wonder that many would prefer to stick their heads in the sand and "go about their daily business."

But this is our daily business from which we cannot hide, especially those of us who guide and support the education of others. Educators play a critical role in facilitating a greater understanding of the conditions under which we all live. We also play a vital role in enhancing the skills of individuals so they are better prepared to collaborate with others in the resolution of our global problems.

In many ways, that is what this book is all about. We recognize that the majority of teachers as well as teacher educators have relatively limited knowledge and experience living and working with people significantly different from themselves. It is precisely with this in mind that we have been devoted to creating opportunities for preservice teachers to have extended immersion experiences living and teaching outside their home cultures. This book is our attempt to share the organization, administration, experiences, and outcomes of those who are engaged in such work. We hope you find inspiration and value in the book as you consider the role you and your institution can play in advancing a global and intercultural perspective in the preparation of the next generation of teachers.

We are very grateful to the chapter authors who shared ideas and information about how to further global education initiatives. We are also grateful to many other colleagues who helped us bring our ideas to fruition. We regret that space constraints prevent us from publicly acknowledging them here. We particularly wish to thank two individuals who were instrumental in bringing the book together in the final stages. Heather Scarlett, undergraduate student at Kent State University, collected and analyzed a number of research articles that were used in several chapters. Julie Cleary, program coordinator and overseas student-teaching advisor at the University of Kentucky, worked meticulously on the final edit of the manuscript.

May the ideas put forth in this book support all those involved in helping teachers expand their views and their practices toward increasing global understanding.

Kenneth Cushner and Sharon Brennan

1

THE VALUE OF LEARNING TO TEACH IN ANOTHER CULTURE

Kenneth Cushner
Sharon Brennan

The key to the formation of global citizens is the educator, bearing out the concept that the teacher is the most important element in the educational environment. Within the interaction between teacher and learner, the enormous potential hidden in the deepest realms of life may be fully developed.

—D. Ikeda (2005, xi)

Globalization refers to an increase in the scope and magnitude of human contact, with its subsequent escalation of interaction and interdependence. In his recent book *The World Is Flat*, Thomas Friedman (2006) traced this phenomenon back to the time when Columbus traversed the globe more than five hundred years ago. As Friedman and others have pointed out, recent advances in communication and transportation technologies have resulted in a rapidly shrinking world that has increased contact—sometimes forced—among people from diverse cultures.

Living in the "flat" world that Freidman depicts poses many challenges that transcend cultural, ethnic, and national boundaries. Life in the twenty-first century requires that those who are striving to work together in various endeavors around the globe develop understanding of and sensitivity to the views of others as well as a sense of connectedness that taps into common values and goals. In today's world, global citizens must be able to communicate and collaborate with those whose attitudes, values, knowledge, and ways of doing things differ significantly from their own. Building bridges across cultural boundaries will require a high degree of flexibility, a tolerance for ambiguity, and an understanding of the role culture plays in shaping thinking and behavior. Since these traits are not necessarily innate and consequently need to be developed, education can and must play a key role in facilitating the bridge-building process.

PRINCIPLES FOR DEVELOPING SKILLS IN INTERCULTURAL COLLABORATION

For decades, scholars in the field of cross-cultural psychology and education have examined factors associated with successful collaboration across cultures (Brislin 1981; Cushner and Brislin 1996; Landis, Bennett, and Bennett 2004; Stephan and Vogt 2004). A number of principles successfully used in programs to develop or enhance skills in intercultural or international collaboration have been identified. They include:

1. Developing perspective consciousness, or as Hanvey (1982) stated, an understanding that other people hold deep perspectives that may be significantly different from one's own
2. Transcending traditional ethnocentrism to build an ethnorelative orientation toward others
3. Developing a capacity to communicate effectively across cultures, in verbal as well as nonverbal modes
4. Acquiring interpersonal skills to work effectively across cultures
5. Understanding the adjustment or "culture shock" that accompanies international transitions

Although there is evidence to suggest that intercultural education programs based on these principles lead to increased effectiveness in the intercultural and international arenas, the skills needed for collaboration across cultures may not be easily acquired. In presenting a model of intercultural sensitivity, Milton Bennett has characterized some of the challenges associated with this kind of learning.

> Intercultural sensitivity is not natural. It is not part of our primate past, nor has it characterized most of human history. Cross-cultural contact usually has been accompanied by bloodshed, oppression, or genocide. Education and training in intercultural communication is an approach to changing our "natural" behavior. With the concepts and skills developed in this field, we ask learners to transcend traditional ethnocentrism and to explore new relationships across cultural boundaries. This attempt at change must be approached with the greatest possible care. (1993, 21)

EXPERIENCE AND CULTURAL LEARNING

Despite the challenges described by Bennett (1993) and the research highlighting the important role experience plays in learning about other cultures, the dominant delivery system for most educational programs remains predominantly cognitive and abstract. Universities, for example, often rely on such methods as lecture, reading, and discussion to help their students learn about other cultures and culture contacts. And, all too frequently, those international programs at the university level that do include a study-abroad component, place students in self-contained "island" programs where they travel to another culture but live together, segregated from the local community. Unfortunately, there is very little correlation between acquiring knowledge this way and developing the skills needed to facilitate adjustment and increase intercultural understanding. As is readily apparent with language learning, experience solidifies understanding. Effective cultural learning comes about with a significant experiential component where the learner is situated in another culture ideally for an extended period of time. International programs that successfully foster this type of learning immerse students in a local community so they can reap the full benefit. Living within the community provides rich opportunities for meaningful interactions with a cross-section of the host society and in equal-status contexts. Since these types of experiences engage students in a holistic way, they have the potential to influence their cognitive, affective, and behavioral domains. Immersion experiences are particularly relevant for students enrolled in teacher-education programs since experience is at the heart of learning to teach.

PREPARING CULTURALLY COMPETENT TEACHERS

There are several compelling reasons for teacher-education programs to include field experiences in intercultural or international settings in the preservice curriculum. Schools of education today are preparing professionals to teach in a world that is much flatter, interconnected, and more complex than in the past—and these professionals will serve an increasingly diverse population of learners. Therefore, graduates of education schools must be equipped to address a range of needs in their classrooms, and they must have the necessary disposition, knowledge, and skill to prepare their pupils to function in a global society. In other words, they must be culturally competent. But are they?

Some have criticized teacher education for insufficiently preparing teachers for work with diverse populations (e.g., Gay 2002; Ladson-Billings 1999), and others have questioned whether education schools adequately address global issues (Jennings 2006). In a recent issue of *AACTE Briefs*, Jennings points out that "Americans, throughout their school years especially . . . do not study about other people in the world, people whose beliefs, cultures, and status will directly impact their own lives in ways that were not even imagined a generation ago" (2006, 2). These admonitions remind us that, as education schools endeavor to help their candidates develop pedagogical competence, they must also consider cultural competence as part of the curriculum package. Teaching in the twenty-first century involves helping learners function in and contribute to life in a global society, or as Jennings has suggested, deal with "complicated issues in both local and global communities" (2006, 2).

Professional associations are beginning to recognize the need to address the global dimension of teaching and learning. Indeed, the National Council for the Accreditation of Teacher Education (NCATE) now requires teacher-education programs undergoing accreditation reviews to show evidence of how the curriculum addresses such perspectives. Standard 4—Diversity states, "Regardless of whether they live in areas with great diversity, candidates must develop knowledge of diversity in the United States and the world, dispositions that respect and value differences, and skills for working in diverse settings" (NCATE 2006, 31). It continues, "One of the goals of this standard is the development of educators who can help all students learn and who can teach from multicultural and global perspectives that draw on the histories, experiences, and representations of students from diverse cultural backgrounds" (31).

In response to the changing global climate as well as the growing recognition in the teacher-education community of the need to focus on the cultural competence of their candidates, universities worldwide are increasingly adding a global dimension to their teacher-education programs. They have done so through a variety of means, including encouraging the study of foreign languages, creating internationally focused courses, and offering extracurricular activities that include international experiences. However, as with the university programs we described earlier, these offerings are often rather limited and restricted. Although these efforts undoubtedly offer some benefit in terms of increasing cultural awareness, they are not sufficiently linked to practice to influence the professional lives of participating candidates in a lasting way.

CULTIVATING CULTURAL COMPETENCE THROUGH STUDENT TEACHING

One way to prepare teachers to address the challenges associated with teaching children in a global age is through carefully structured, intercultural field experiences where candidates are immersed in another culture. Since student teaching requires candidates to show they can translate theory into practice over an extended period of time, this capstone event is ideally suited for strengthening candidates' intercultural understanding. Placements in other cultures open tremendous opportunities for student teachers to learn about another's view of the world from an insider's perspective, and thus become more global in their thoughts and actions. The curriculum, material, and approach to teaching are all likely to be different from what they would experience in a local placement. Imagine, for example, the possibilities for growth when a teacher candidate from an American university, who is student teaching in Germany or England, is asked to teach about World War II, or when an American student teacher in South Africa is asked to teach about race relations.

Student teaching in other cultures also enables teacher candidates to simultaneously strengthen their practice and personally stretch beyond their traditional zone of comfort—away from support networks provided at home, in school, or by friends—and to develop interpersonal relationships with host nationals. In addition, unlike many study-abroad experiences where participants spend most of their time with others from their own country, student teachers abroad are generally on their own, where increased self-efficacy becomes possible. Finally, opportunities exist for student teachers to broaden their cultural knowledge, develop a global perspective, and increase their understanding of the value of multicultural education through interaction with children, other professionals, and adults from varying cultural backgrounds.

SUCCESSFUL INTERCULTURAL INITIATIVES IN TEACHER EDUCATION

Three long-standing initiatives illustrate the benefits of long-term, carefully structured, intercultural immersion experiences for teacher candidates. The Consortium for Overseas Student Teaching (COST), the International Teacher Education Program (ITEP) in the California State University System, and the cultural immersion projects at Indiana University have each coordinated and sustained structured intercultural field experiences for student teachers for many years. Cited as one of the oldest organizations facilitating international student-teaching placements (Heyl and McCarthy 2003), the Consortium for Overseas Student Teaching (COST) was established as a formal organization in 1973 through an alliance of faculty from six universities located in neighboring states who served together on teams conducting accreditation visits at independent/international K–12 schools in Central and South America. While working together, these like-minded colleagues had many opportunities to share ideas and identify high-quality placement sites. Archival records suggest the founders of COST established the program out of concern that students who attended their institutions had little or no intercultural experiences; many, in fact, had never traveled beyond the region in which they lived. COST founders sought to remedy the situation. They made reducing cultural barriers and increasing global understanding as overarching program goals (Anderson and Self 1983). Since its inception, COST has placed thousands of teacher candidates in international settings. Participant reports suggest that they find the experience both personally and professionally transformative (Cushner and Mahon 2002).

The cultural immersion project and overseas student-teaching project, both offered at Indiana University, give teacher candidates opportunities to broaden their intercultural horizons with placements in international as well as domestic settings. For the past thirty years, candidates have been afforded opportunities to student teach on Native American reservations in the Southwest as well as in various international locations. Using the motto "Education unites the world," the overseas project aims to foster the development of world-minded teachers. This project, which is affiliated with the Wisconsin-based Foundation for International Education, has been recognized for excellence by the American Association of Colleges for Teacher Education, the Goldman-Sachs Foundation, and the Asia Society. A considerable amount of research data has been collected over the years about the efficacy of these programs (Stachowski and Visconti 1997; Stachowski and Chleb 1998).

California State University's International Teacher Education Program was established in 1994 to provide bilingual student-teaching experiences in neighboring Mexico. Today, it is in partnership with Mexico's State Department of Education and is the only international credential program in California that is approved by the California Commission on Teacher Credentialing.

There are many similarities between Indiana's cultural immersion projects, COST, and ITEP, including the careful structure and monitoring systems that are in place, attention to orientation and preparation prior to departure, close supervision during the placement period, and structured debriefing sessions upon return. Evaluation data from these programs reported in subsequent chapters in this volume suggest that students improve their cultural and instructional competence through participation.

ORGANIZATION OF THIS BOOK

The purpose of the book is to show ways that international and domestic intercultural field experiences, especially student-teaching opportunities that immerse candidates in another culture for a sustained period of time, can help refresh and reshape teacher-education programs while addressing significant global concerns. The authors featured in this edited volume all participate in intercultural programs, managing and monitoring the progress of teacher candidates. Each author addresses a unique aspect of the intercultural student-teaching experience. The book is presented in distinct sections. Chapters 1 through 4 address foundational aspects of this work. Chapters 5 through 9 provide a case-study approach, with each chapter addressing a specific dimension of the programmatic experience. Chapter 10 offers a way of looking at this work in light of critical pedagogy.

In chapter 2, Jennifer Mahon and Gretchen Espinetti share their expertise in establishing and managing international student-teaching programs. Between them, they have more than a decade of experience administering the COST program on two different campuses. In addition, Mahon shares her experiences of establishing such a program in a new university context.

Essential to achieving the goals of any intercultural experience is effective preparation and planning. In chapter 3, two experienced intercultural educators, Mary Anne Flournoy and Angene Wilson, share insights into the orientation and preparation of students through courses they designed for teacher candidates prior to their overseas sojourn. Offering guidelines to others planning such experiences, they argue for intense and comprehensive preparation on the part of all overseas participants.

Educators have long wondered about the impact an international experiences has, both on personal as well as professional development. In chapter 4, Jennifer Mahon and Kenneth Cushner survey the research that looks at the impact of an international experience in general, but more specifically, report on an ongoing investigation into how such an experience affects the personal and professional development of teachers.

Laura Stachowski has been a driving force behind the cultural immersion project at Indiana University (IU) for many years, offering students the opportunity to student teach both in a variety of overseas settings as well as on Navajo reservations in the United States. In chapter 5, she describes the program at IU that enables student teachers to live and teach on Navajo Indian reservations in the Southwest and shows how teacher competencies and intercultural effectiveness can be derived from powerful domestic experiences.

In chapter 6, Reyes Quezada and Cristina Alfaro describe the ITEP program that sends candidates who are seeking bilingual teaching certification in Spanish and English to teach in Mexico. The authors discuss key aspects of the program in the context of theoretical constructs and research findings. They also provide a series of questions for program developers to consider when planning global teacher-education programs.

In chapter 7, Sharon Brennan and Julie Cleary trace the evolution of the overseas student-teaching program that has been in place at the University of Kentucky for more than three decades. They describe a methodology recently developed to improve reflection and guide and monitor the growth of their candidates, and they discuss preliminary results gleaned from the initial implementation and offer ideas for research and program development using this methodology.

In chapter 8, Neil Andersen brings the host site experiences to the forefront. Over many years of hosting COST student teachers in New Zealand, he has collected anecdotes and stories of host families, teachers, and administrators. His insights into the impact the student teacher can have on host communities offers much for us to consider as we work to better prepare teacher candidates.

In chapter 9, Rosalie Romano takes the reader on a journey exploring the power of initial curiosity in new teachers, ignited by the imagination of a lifetime dream of going overseas—and then the terror of it all. She tactfully examines the space between the act of applying to teach abroad, the final departure, and ultimately the students' responses to their overseas experience. Romano relays the intersection when terror or extreme anxiety meets the wave of curiosity, which combine to produce extraordinary growth as individuals become remarkable teachers.

In the final chapter, Rosalie Romano and Kenneth Cushner link the international experience with the essential work of Paulo Freire—bringing educational practice into question and challenging one to not accept the status quo but to become aware of the possibilities in life. They reflect on the role that the international experience plays in enabling students to become one with their students and shift their paradigm, arguing that an intercultural student-teaching experience provides opportunities for new teachers to become critical reflective thinkers, to assume their subjectivity within classrooms through meeting new cultures, and to learn to navigate as part of that culture. It is through this encounter that personal and professional growth can occur.

This book is built on the premise that teacher-education programs need to prepare candidates who are not only pedagogically competent but also culturally competent. We have argued here, as our coauthors do in subsequent chapters, that cultural competence, which we believe includes a global dimension, is an integral part of what it means to be an effective teacher. Teachers who are culturally competent understand cultural traditions that extend beyond the borders of the United States, can communicate across cultures, and have the expertise to prepare learners for living and working in the global community. The book provides ideas and examples of how teacher-education programs can prepare teachers to be culturally competent and who can help learners in their classrooms succeed in the "flat" world of the twenty-first century. In the chapters that follow, authors show how long-term, sustained immersion experiences outside familiar cultural terrain can help enhance the cultural competence and global mindedness of their candidates in ways that will ultimately not only affect the content they bring to the classroom but also foster global thinking in their learners. We welcome you on this journey.

REFERENCES

Anderson, C., and J. Self. 1983. Consortium for Overseas Student Teaching: History, development, and operations. Unpublished document, University of Alabama, Tuscaloosa, AL.

Bennett, M. J. 1993. Towards ethnorelativism: A developmental model of intercultural sensitivity. In *Education for the intercultural experience*, ed. R. M. Paige, 21–71. Yarmouth, ME: Intercultural Press.

Brislin, R. 1981. *Cross-cultural encounters: Face-to-face interaction*. Needham Heights, MA: Allyn & Bacon.

Cushner, K., and R. Brislin. 1996. *Intercultural interactions: A practical guide*. Thousand Oaks, CA: Sage.

Cushner, K., and J. Mahon. 2002. Overseas student teaching: Affecting personal, professional and global competencies in an age of globalization. *Journal of Studies in International Education* 6, no. 1:44–59.

Freidman, T. L. 2006. *The world is flat: A brief history of the twenty-first century*. New York: Farrar, Straus & Giroux.

Gay, G. 2002. Preparing for culturally responsive teaching. *Journal of Teacher Education* 53, no. 2:106–16.

Hanvey, R. G. 1982. An attainable global perspective. *Theory into Practice* 21, no. 1:162–67.

Heyl, J., and J. McCarthy. 2003. International education and teacher preparation in the U.S. Presentation at the national conference entitled Global Challenges and U.S. Higher Education: National Needs and Policy Implications, Durham, NC, Duke University, January.

Ikeda, D. 2005. In *Educating citizens for global awareness*, ed. N. Noddings, xi. New York: Teachers College Press.

Jennings, C. 2006. Teacher education: Building a foundation for the global workforce. *AACTE Briefs* (April 24).

Ladson-Billings, G. 1999. Preparing teachers for diverse student populations. *Review of Research in Education* 24:211–48.

Landis, D., M. Bennett, and J. Bennett. 2004. *Handbook of intercultural training*. Vol. 3. Thousand Oaks, CA: Sage.

NCATE. 2006. *NCATE: Professional standards for the accreditation of schools, colleges and departments of education*. Washington, DC: National Council for Accreditation of Teacher Education.

Stachowski, L., and J. Chleb. 1998. Foreign educators provide feedback for the improvement of international student teaching experiences. *Action in Teacher Education* 19, no. 4:119–30.

Stachowski, L., and V. Visconti. 1997. Adaptations for success: U.S. student teachers living and teaching abroad. *International Education* 26:5–20.

Stephan, W. G., and W. P. Vogt. 2004. *Education programs for improving intergroup relations: Theory, research, and practice*. New York: Teachers College Press.

2

ESTABLISHING AND MAINTAINING AN INTERNATIONAL STUDENT-TEACHING PROGRAM

Jennifer Mahon
Gretchen L. Espinetti

Overseas student-teaching (OST) programs through college and university campuses take enormous energy, resources, and individual/institutional commitment, compatibility, respect, ongoing conversations, and relationships. Programs must continually assess benefits as well as tensions: What works? What doesn't? How do program assessments indicate changes that need to be made on individual and institutional levels? How do we move forward with providing this valuable opportunity for our teacher candidates in the twenty-first century? What impact does this overseas student-teaching experience have on our teacher candidates when they return to the United States and secure their first teaching positions? Does it matter? If so, in what ways?

We carry out our international teacher-education work within a system of higher education where a philosophy of global and multicultural education must be central to a college of education's mission. Student teaching overseas gives teacher candidates the opportunity to discover new cultures, explore new ways of teaching and knowing, use new languages and dialects, and experience and complete research on global issues. Teacher candidates gain multiple perspectives on the role of schooling, a different educational system and educational policies, and unique opportunities for professional and personal development. Works found in this volume and throughout the literature (e.g., Mahan and Stachowski 1990; Mahon and Cushner 2002; Stachowski and Visconti 1998) enumerate the valued outcomes of student teaching overseas such as cultural learning, increased personal competencies, and preparation for diversity in the classroom.

Yet in order to enable our students to achieve such learning, we must first create a program within our own realities, that is, one that fits the current operational procedures of our institutions. This chapter offers recommendations for those who are considering beginning an OST program at their institution as well as those making changes to existing programs.

Other chapters in this text show the research base that supports the value of overseas student teaching. Building on the research base and to provide a rationale for our discussion, we briefly reference existing literature, which discusses programmatic issues related to study abroad, in an effort to broaden the resources available to the potential program director. While many resources can be found on internationalizing the campus or on large-scale international program administration (for example, via NAFSA: Association of International Educators, or the Council for International Educational Exchange [CIEE]), a few are offered here as general reference. Sevigny (2001) authored a very comprehensive guide for all aspects of international education programs, from student exchange to the admissions of foreign students. While some chapters in his guide extend beyond the scope of what is needed to establish an international teaching program, the chapter on the development of study abroad and legal issues can serve as an excellent resource. Fung and Filippo (2002) also offer helpful suggestions as they consider faculty involvement and describe approaches for becoming involved in existing university programs or setting up one's own. Briscoe (1991) offers a case study of one Midwestern university's attempt to internationalize the campus. Hatton (1995) and Campion and Bostic (1993) discuss program issues specific to community colleges. And Beach (1995) discusses administrative strategies to link departments and entities focusing on international and intercultural efforts across campus in some way.

Other publications address points related to overseas teacher education. Merryfield, Jarchow, and Pickert (1997) edited a work covering various aspects of overseas training for teachers. Pike (2000) describes the establishment of a major course of study in international education in the Canadian context, including overseas student-teaching experiences. Landerholm, Gehrie, and Hao (2004) discuss the comprehensive facets included in globalizing an elementary education program that includes overseas study. Baker and Giacchino-Baker (2000) discuss not only a U.S.–Mexico partnership but one that was undertaken by three U.S. universities working collaboratively. Specific guidelines are included for organizing field experiences and documenting program effectiveness. Taken together, these works demonstrate that there are numerous considerations needed to establish and maintain an international student-teaching program. In this chapter, we address various issues related to developing a program, external pressures and tensions, internal concerns, types of placements, determining host institutions, marketing the program and addressing student concerns, the application process and candidate selection, information to be returned to the program director, candidate placement logistics, and candidate orientation and reentry.

DEVELOPING A PROGRAM

There are several frameworks in which an OST program can be developed and then marketed. The options to consider include (1) a consortium of multiple universities pooling resources together; (2) a university/campus-led effort through a main office and/or a well-established international study office; or (3) a program housed in a college or school of education.

In general, a consortium provides placement opportunities that one university alone cannot offer; however, issues around institutional commitment, marketing of candidates, rules of operation for members, and resources can become concerns, especially as the program grows. For instance, in a smaller institution with relatively few, if any, international partnerships, such a leap to membership in a large consortium, while providing numerous opportunities to students, may add an unnecessary obstacle for program compatibility. In the case of a centralized university program, exact procedures and requirements may exist for the nature of a study-abroad program. This can be helpful because it offers structure and support, but it may also create limitations—including regulations on supervision, payments, and site locations. A program housed in a school or college generally offers the most flexibility and autonomy. However, as all programmatic responsibilities may fall on one or two people who generally have additional responsibilities, resources and staffing become critical concerns.

In making the decision as to which framework is best, it is important to anticipate the aspects of an international program that may bring about concerns on the part of other members of the organization in order to ensure their commitment. Examples of these follow.

EXTERNAL PRESSURES AND TENSIONS

Clearly, there are legitimate concerns to consider in adopting any framework, yet to facilitate change, it is also often necessary to ask critical questions when obstacles arise. One of the most challenging aspects of starting an OST program may be to demonstrate how the international context will not compromise programmatic integrity, departmental mission, particular philosophies of teacher education, and concerns born of external pressures such as state licensure, legislative mandates, and accreditation.

Perhaps the place to begin a discussion of program development is examining state requirements. Some states mandate that student teaching must be completed in the state, thus seemingly ending any possibilities for an overseas program. In these cases, discussions about the program internationalization must take place at the legislative level unless the domestic experience is augmented with an international opportunity. In other states, requirements may be described in terms of weeks to be completed, or days or hours of field contact. Given that a host site may be on a very different academic calendar (for example, in the southern hemisphere), this can mean some sites simply do not work. Additional requirements may exist regarding time spent at different age/grade levels or in content areas, such as an eight-week experience at the upper elementary level followed by another eight weeks in the lower levels. The various content areas in regard to secondary education majors can also become an issue if a particular host country cannot accom-

modate such needs. And special education placements are characteris-
tically difficult to make due to the variety of differences in state requirements and host school programs. Federal background checks as
well as extensive visa applications for some countries have added an entirely new level of complexity and security, complicating application
lead-time and preparation issues.

INTERNAL CONCERNS

One common objection often raised at the home campus is the belief
that to be a well-prepared public school teacher in the United States,
one must student teach in an American public school. It may be difficult
for some faculty members to imagine the possibility that pedagogical
skills practiced in an overseas school can be used to address problems
and parameters of schooling in the United States. Furthermore, some
critics argue that since the majority of these teachers will return to seek
jobs in the United States, lack of domestic student-teaching experience
may harm their employment potential. This objection may also arise in
places where through accountability measures colleges/schools of edu-
cations are pressured to produce data showing that their graduates are
finding jobs.

Merryfield (2000) argues that the relative paucity of faculty diversity
as well as limited global knowledge and lack of significant cross-cultural
experience on the part of most faculty at universities in the United
States represent salient obstacles to international placements. Where
faculty lack international experience, we must acknowledge that such
objections about the suitability of the international context may, on occasion, be construed as evidence of ethnocentric beliefs (e.g., the
United States is the best or only place to receive teacher training). Individuals who have invested much time into crafting a teacher-preparation
program may believe the international context simply does not offer the
same quality or philosophy of teaching. Thus, questions of context often
lead to quality concerns.

Clearly, it is wise to assess a host institution and to assume that quality differences may exist. However, the institutional change literature
adds another perspective to this decision by explaining the anatomy of

resistance. According to Clark (1980), resistance is created by subcultures based on things such as disciplinary affiliation or roles within the system, which present a set of beliefs or practices likely to be incompatible with change efforts. Kashner (1990) adds that subcultures may be the genesis of "sphere of ownership," which becomes especially problematic because a change is perceived as a threat to their rights of possession. Where issues of quality arise, it would be necessary to consider what elements of quality must be demonstrated by an overseas institution and how that will be assessed.

Supervision

Of all the concerns raised by faculty or administrators, questions regarding the supervision and selection of cooperating teachers are most likely to be present. Initially, questions arise about supervisor and teacher qualifications. What backgrounds will overseas supervisors and cooperating teachers have? What is the frequency and type of evaluation, and what differences exist in significance of values on student-teaching assessments? Will the supervisors use home-country evaluation forms or will the university accept the host's format? What happens if state or university regulations require that the institution's faculty member complete direct evaluations of the candidate? In other cases, individuals may believe, given the nature of the institution's training for supervisors and teachers, that the process is so highly specialized that it cannot be replicated by others.

Another issue surrounds documentation and action research. In order to ensure that the candidates complete the same program requirements as their domestic colleagues, faculty may require overseas candidates to complete a student-teaching seminar course while overseas or to complete frequent written assignments that document certain required program competencies. The reality of the student-teaching experience is that it is a busy, stressful time, with weekends and evenings spent preparing lessons, grading papers, and preparing program portfolio requirements rather than getting to know the local community. This flies in the face of culturally relevant pedagogy (Ladson-Billings 1994) that emphasizes the absolute necessity of knowing and using the community to ensure successful student-learner outcomes. In addition, the overseas experience also requires adjusting to and learning about the culture. Cultural adjustment is a skill found throughout the literature on culturally relevant teaching (Hollins and Guzman 2005). Faculty should be aware that requiring candidates to send or e-mail large assignments to the home institution may present a challenge to the host cooperating teacher and supervisor, as they may be concerned with their lack of familiarity with the assignment as they try to assist the candidate, or of having the candidate's focus taken away from the student-teaching day and the cultural experience.

In order to finalize decisions about placements, the types of supervision desired and available must be considered. In all cases, it is assumed that a university contact serves as a regular contact/communication point, and that the supervision of the cooperating teacher is undertaken by one or more of the following: (1) a host university education faculty; (2) a school administrator, for example, in locations where no formal university partnership exists, such as American International or Department of Defense Education Activity (DoDEA) schools; or (3) a home-country evaluator, for example, when sabbaticals, research studies, or other funds allow for travel or stay in the host country. As accountability and accreditation pressures continue to increase in the United States, it may be common for a college or university to have candidates complete a data-driven assignment documenting their ability to effectively plan for, implement, assess, and differentiate instruction, and measure the impact of their teaching on learning. Such documents may be unknown in the host country, and though not impossible, would require more communication with the U.S.-based instructor/supervisor or coordinator, and necessitate consideration of local laws regarding collection of student work in schools.

Candidate Support

Candidate support is essential. When candidates complete their student teaching within the United States, they often have a solid framework of support to call upon during the experience. They have a cooperating teacher in the school, a university supervisor, colleagues and administrators within the building, and sometimes even a cohort of fellow candidates working together through the trials and tribulations of the semester. While student teaching overseas has a very similar framework to student teaching in the United States, some subtle differences do exist that deepen the challenge for candidates to maintain the support they need in order to be successful. Obviously, the distance between the home university and the host site means that a candidate is removed from the familiarity of fellow candidates, former professors, family, friends, and frequent observations/visits from the university supervisor. The advent of technology means that faxes, e-mails, and video-conferencing are available to shorten this distance; however, the fact is that for the candidate, no matter how frequent the e-mails, a distance still remains.

Perhaps most unique to the overseas student-teaching experience is the reversal of the unfamiliar. For example, in the United States, teacher candidates are most anxious about navigating the new environment of the school and find comfort when they go home. On the other hand, overseas candidates may be surprised that school becomes the place that provides the most comfort. At the end of the day, when they leave their school, student teachers enter a different and unfamiliar world. They may find getting to their residence challenging as they learn how to navigate in a community they don't know and/or have to rely on public transportation for the first time. Similarly, they may have to adapt to living with a family who does not share the same language and culture.

All of this adds up to the necessity of recognizing that because it will take time for students to develop host-country support networks, providing support from home, especially in the first weeks of the experience, may be required. Two of many options seem to create this kind of support: communication triangles between the university supervisor at home, the host supervisor, and the candidate, or a communication quadrangle in which the candidates create a support network for themselves, regardless of location. This rapport and relationship could begin during orientation prior to departure and the support is continued while the student teacher is abroad through e-mail, telephone, or newer Internet communication technologies such as Skype, a free voice-over Internet provider (VoIP) computer communication system.

The opportunity for enhanced international relationships returns us to the issue of requirements. There is no doubt that the necessities of a U.S. teacher-education program demand that certain requirements are fulfilled, but this should not be rationale for duplicating a domestic student-teaching program overseas, or worse, not establishing one at all. Rather, arriving at some commonality for the candidate's benefit requires conversations, commitments, and a great deal of mutual respect on many levels. Developing relationships and maintaining these connections with our international partners involves mutual respect and trust built over time and is essential in sustaining any OST program.

TYPES OF PLACEMENTS

Although placements can be arranged in many different ways, we have found that placements are usually secured through either a partner university abroad or directly with an overseas school. Furthermore, we have found instructional delivery in partner schools seems to fall into one of three categories: (1) instruction in English with a U.S.-based curriculum; (2) instruction in English with a non-U.S. curriculum; and (3) non-English instruction.

Instruction in English with a U.S. curriculum at an international American school is a popular option. These schools, which often cater to U.S. expatriates, have similar standards and requirements as U.S. public schools. Department of Defense Education Activity schools, which serve U.S. military personnel and their families overseas, also represent this category.

The second option that exists is instruction in English with a non-U.S. curriculum. In this case, candidates are placed in public or private schools in English-speaking countries. In non-English speaking countries, this may include settings such as Canadian, British, South African, or Australian schools that cater primarily to their expatriates abroad.

Finally, there is non-English instruction. In cases where a teacher candidate may have second-language fluency or be working toward a modern language license, two options are possible—placement in public schools in non-English-speaking countries or in international schools with foreign language or bilingual programs. Usually, these schools require an advanced level of fluency in the foreign language.

DETERMINING HOST INSTITUTIONS

Determining host institutions usually begins with investigating personal and professional contacts that faculty, the college, or university may have overseas. This is the best way to investigate host institution interest and to reduce the amount of rapport building necessary to establish a partnership. Other options are to visit international schools or schools of education while traveling overseas or while presenting at international conferences. Finally, the university's international admissions office may have well-established links with overseas high schools. Given the current trend of increasingly tight university budgets, individuals may be asked to show that their program does not duplicate efforts of other departments or programs on campus. In general, the fact that students will be completing specialized work pertaining to their degrees usually answers this query. However, some universities may hold to policies that different programs may not be offered in the same locations. This may also have to do with the conditions of preexisting international partnership arrangements.

MARKETING THE PROGRAM AND ADDRESSING STUDENT CONCERNS

Once an institution has decided which framework to pursue, marketing the overseas student-teaching opportunity on campus becomes paramount. This can be overwhelming for one person to accomplish on top of other full-time responsibilities, but without "getting the word out," the program will not get off the ground or continually grow. Some examples of successful strategies to inform students of the opportunity include (1) posting flyers throughout buildings on the campus, (2) distributing information through the international study office, (3) holding informational meetings to address potential candidates' questions and concerns, (4) making class presentations in specific program areas, and (5) making presentations at freshman orientations. We cannot emphasize enough the importance of distributing information repeatedly over time to potential candidates, from the time they enter the university and throughout their teacher-education programs, or the important role faculty play in encouraging this option to students.

In addition to marketing international offerings, any viable program must take into consideration pressures experienced by today's students. There are financial considerations for potential candidates, and no discussion of setting up an OST program is complete without considering the overall costs for candidates to fulfill their culminating experience in their teacher-education program. What will candidates pay for this semester abroad? Clearly, they pay tuition and fees at the home institution just like any other semester. In addition, candidates will need a passport, money to cover visa fees (if required for their host country), medical and professional liability insurances, background check processing through the FBI, orientation materials, and possibly other institutional fees. For the overseas experience, the two major costs for candidates are round trip airfare (to and from their home country to the host site) and room and board. Other costs may include local travel (in host country), additional fees by the host site, and miscellaneous expenses. Generally, we have found that the cost of the overseas student-teaching experience per candidate, in addition to tuition, is approximately $4,000–6,000.

In addition to the financial concerns expressed by the candidates, issues of safety, availability of teaching positions and job prospects (upon returning to the United States), and perceptions of an overseas student-teaching experience by prospective school employers are pressures felt by the candidates as well as their parents. The inclusion of parents in the conversations of overseas experiences must be addressed. Marjorie Savage (2003) and many other authors (Mitchell 2006; Daniel and Ross 2001) are writing about what many of us in higher education are experiencing—an increase in parental involvement in college students' lives (sometimes what appears to be overinvolvement) and the consequent impact on international programming and opportunities for our candidates.

In general, program directors should give careful thought to safety and health concerns that may arise in particular host countries. To stay abreast of these concerns, program directors should monitor the advisories issued by the U.S. Department of State, as well as the Canadian Department of State. In addition, the U.S. Centers for Disease Control and the World Health Organization can alert program directors to the most pressing health precautions. These press releases and lists enable universities to exclude countries where there may be a clear and present danger to candidates. On occasion, concerned individuals will mention safety concerns raised by the media regarding certain countries not on any warning list. It is helpful to find ways to tactfully remind people that when opening a U.S. newspaper, for instance, one can regularly see national reports of murder, abuse, rape, natural disaster, gang violence, institutional corruption, and unfortunately, post-9/11 terrorist activity and alerts. Safety concerns are applicable to any country in the world. If care is taken to pay close attention to various sources of warning, and if adequate predeparture orientation is conducted, these risks can be minimized. You are also advised to work closely with your institution's international office concerning such matters. In most cases, they will have resources to assist you.

In addition, emergency contact procedures must be in place at the college and/or university levels in the rare instances when a candidate needs immediate medical attention not available in the host country or in the event of death. Each college and/or university will have unique and specific protocols for handling such matters.

APPLICATION PROCESS AND CANDIDATE SELECTION

An application process for student teaching is a common practice, but we feel that in the case of overseas student teaching, the selection process takes on even greater significance since teacher candidates serve as ambassadors of their universities and the United States. We recommend that about seven months to one year prior to the semester of student teaching, candidates complete and submit an extensive application. There are a number of reasons for such a long lead time. Candidates may need that time to earn the money to pay for their expenses, to complete additional course work, and sometimes to pursue specific language training. A longer lead time, on occasion, also serves as an additional check and balance in the program; individuals who may be tentative about going overseas may decide that they, in fact, would rather remain home, thus averting possible problems overseas. While the lead times and particulars change depending upon the aforementioned international program framework that is chosen, the recommendations detailed here apply, in some way, to all cases.

INFORMATION TO BE RETURNED TO THE PROGRAM DIRECTOR

Prior to developing the application, the program director will need to determine minimum eligibility requirements. For example, to participate in the Consortium for Overseas Student Teaching (COST) program, teacher candidates must have earned an overall grade point average (GPA) of 3.0 on a four-point scale. Other considerations may include the GPA in the candidate's major, reports of misconduct, minimum grades in certain courses, and so forth.

We recommend that applicants provide the following information. The initial part of the application includes biographical data—including permanent and local addresses, as students may move during the application period. Candidates should indicate housing preferences (e.g., apartment, dormitory, or housing with family, which is frequently referred to as homestay). Dietary requirements may also be included, especially in the case of a homestay. Additional information on health conditions such as allergies may also be included. Although the U.S. Right to Privacy Act precludes an organization from directly asking about health information, any conditions voluntarily shared by the candidate will make it easier to guarantee an optimum experience, especially in the case of homestay.

In the COST program, we ask that three references attesting to a candidate's work with children, academic abilities, and character be completed by individuals such as a cooperating teacher, faculty member in the program area, and a previous or current employer. A copy of the candidate's passport and an FBI clearance report must be submitted, as well as proof of both medical and professional liability insurance. In the case of the latter, some universities will carry blanket coverage for students; therefore, the university legal office may need to be consulted by the program director to secure a copy to be used in all future applications. Next, the candidate should include a transcript, an essay, and a listing of course work completed with field contact hours. Since the candidate may be applying to universities in many different countries that have different types of teacher-education programs, the latter should be written out and detailed in such a manner that it provides the host coordinator the clearest possible indication of the candidate's experiences in the classroom. Also, program candidates should be instructed to write an essay that details why they want to student teach overseas. In many cases, candidates write essays that explain *either* their curiosity for culture and travel *or* their dedication to teaching. Through this essay, overseas hosts can gain a good understanding of *both*—that is, of the person who will work with their students for the duration of the program. They want a clear picture of the candidate in terms of why he or she wants to take on the challenge of teaching in an overseas context, what he or she will bring to the host site, as well as what he or she hopes to learn. We recommend that candidates refrain from remarks that are site (country) specific since the essay may be sent to several different sites before a placement is secured.

We advise program directors to have the university legal office review the application form before it is distributed to ensure all legal issues have been addressed and that appropriate risk and release forms are included in the application packet. By signing this form, candidates attest to the fact that they will follow all university rules just as they would if they remained on campus; they must also abide by the laws of the host nation. We cannot stress enough that candidates must clearly understand that their failure to abide by these rules overseas may not only result in coming home early, thereby answering to any monetary or legal issues caused as a result, but also being required to repeat a semester of student teaching (at home) or, in the worst scenarios, in being removed from the home university program altogether. Any doubt about university policies in this regard should be cleared through the university legal office well before a program begins.

Finally, we recommend the program director and/or a selection committee conduct a face-to-face interview with the candidate depending on institutional size and requirements once the application has been reviewed. This is one of the best ways to gauge if the candidate truly understands the commitment he or she is about to make and also to ensure that the application is complete. The interview helps determine the level of seriousness about teaching abroad and may indicate the candidate's level of cultural sensitivity. Candidates must realize that they are being expected to value teaching as their first priority while overseas and not to view this experience as an opportunity for an extended "travel holiday."

Information for the Candidate

We recommend including information for the candidate such as detailed instructions about how to complete the application, including a FAQ section or link to a website where those questions may be answered, and information on what happens after the application is submitted. When the waiting period begins for the candidate, it is often a very trying time, testing their flexibility and value systems. Candidates are informed that their placement confirmations may occur any time from the date of submission of the application to up to sixty days prior to departure. In smaller programs, this date may be as short as thirty days prior to departure; however, issues with flight arrangements and necessary documentation such as visas may become very difficult with such a short lead time. Program directors will want to determine how they will handle the student who continually asks about his or her application despite being told of this variable notification period. In some cases, this may indicate that a student is having second thoughts about the program, and a meeting might be necessary to alleviate both the candidate's as well as the program director's concerns. In cases where candidates know the country where they will be placed (or if it is a choice between one or two destinations), culture-specific resources may also be included to begin the orientation process. Additionally, immunization and health information may also be included, especially in a known location where inoculations against some illnesses require attention to time factors. Finally, the program director may wish to include a letter to the candidate's parents, either now or after the placement location has been determined. This letter goes a long way in helping parents recognize that there is someone they can communicate with when they have questions or to dispel their own anxiety.

CANDIDATE PLACEMENT LOGISTICS

As OST programs are publicized to candidates and the day arrives when more than one candidate is truly committed, the choice must be made whether to allow placement of two or more candidates together at the same host institution. Placing students together can have its advantages. This makes issues such as communication, logistics, and orientation much simpler, and may be the best option for small, developing programs. However, the disadvantages are great, and should be considered carefully. Candidates may become insular, in essence living their U.S. life in another country. When this happens, it defeats one of the most basic objectives of an overseas experience: increasing intercultural interaction.

If one candidate becomes disgruntled, openly critical, or constantly complaining about the country, this may infect others' attitudes as well (and possibly create a living, walking mass embodiment of the "ugly American" persona). Secondly, the candidates may have serious personal conflicts that are further exacerbated by the emotional and cognitive complications of life in a foreign country. It is challenging enough to student teach in another country without adding roommate issues to the mix. While one may argue this could happen if they are placed in a dorm with a host country national, the fact remains that when candidates go together, an expectation of companionship—"we're in this together, and we are Americans so we stick together" may exist on someone's part. Finally, it is not uncommon to expect that when a group of U.S. candidates goes together, they may take it upon themselves to make crucial decisions—such as moving to another apartment or going away for the weekend—without bothering to notify or consult their host or U.S.-based supervisor (creating a legal nightmare when parents, for instance, do not know how to reach them).

ORIENTATION AND REENTRY

There are various types of orientation experiences available to students, including (1) courses for credit that can be designed at institutions where flexibility in credits exist; (2) noncourse credit, where there is a commitment (and requirement) to attend a set number of predeparture sessions; and (3) international study-abroad orientations, already established as a structured program/course for students, but these orientations may leave out crucial considerations pertinent to the teacher-education candidate.

Chapter 3 examines in much greater detail how two universities in the COST program have successfully developed orientation courses on their campuses. We provide a brief description of considerations for orientation sessions to add an additional perspective. A predeparture orientation is essential for all overseas student-teaching candidates because structured sessions help candidates to prepare and deal with the challenges and opportunities of living, teaching, and traveling abroad. Often, these programs may be focused exclusively on the host country and its culture, cross-cultural contrasts, intercultural adjustment, and other aspects to consider in an overseas experience, such as the homestay or language issues (even in English-speaking countries). Some additional topics to consider including in any orientation are:

1. Orientation of the United States in relation to the host country in the world. The orientation should include current events that reflect how the United States is viewed by the host country, as well as official views the U.S. government may hold or positions it may take toward the host country. The overseas student-teaching experience enables candidates to examine the United States from a different perspective via their interactions with their hosts, and to challenge the candidate's preexisting understandings of the orientation of the United States in relation to other nations.

2. Orientation toward a philosophy of education and teaching/learning. Having almost come to the end of their formal preparation in education, candidates often leave for their overseas placements with very specific ideas in mind about pedagogical "best practices." Having been socialized into the field from the time they were in preschool/kindergarten, these ideas are often very solidified for candidates. The overseas experience introduces candidates to different ways of approaching subject matter, different philosophies about the purpose of education, and different ways of looking at students and learning. Candidates may return to the United States with an entirely different way of doing things in the classroom, and for the first time they may be presented with a way of teaching in the United States that does not reflect all that they know.

3. Personal value systems orientation. A significant portion of the orientation needs to concentrate on helping the candidate understand his or her value systems in relation to the value systems of the host country. The overseas experience can present numerous challenges for candidates. Things that candidates take for granted, from the elements of everyday life such as transportation, ready access to technology, and language, to understanding what it means to be an American or to how classrooms work each offers a point of tension and potential conflict.

There are many articles and texts that are useful for candidates to read and discuss during these orientation sessions. Examples we have used include Cushner's (2004) *Beyond Tourism: A Practical Guide to Meaningful Educational Travel*, which relates numerous examples of cross-cultural teaching and learning; *Making the Most of Your Time Abroad* by Kappler and Nokken (1999); and *Maximizing Study Abroad* (Paige et al. 2002), which is especially useful for candidates traveling to countries where English is not the first language.

Reentry to the Home Culture

Equally important as a predeparture orientation is the debriefing or exit interview in the reentry phase for the candidates. In other words, after completing their student teaching overseas, reflecting on the benefits of the experience and providing feedback on the orientation is an essential element of culture learning. Some candidates return to graduate immediately, "walk in the ceremony," and begin their search for local teaching positions. Others decide after being home a short time to pursue out-of-state teaching positions, or in some cases, overseas positions in a variety of industries in addition to teaching. We highly recommend that institutions require candidates to participate in an exit interview/debriefing when they return from the overseas placement. This debriefing serves to not only ease reentry for the candidates but also enables the program director to gather perceptual data about participation.

CONCLUSION

Research findings (e.g., Cushner and Mahon 2002; Mahon and Cushner 2002; Baker 2000) consistently show that the overseas experience enables candidates to grow in the way they support themselves. That is, they begin to be much more confident in both their personal and professional abilities. Candidates also report a growing global awareness. Whether it was learning to connect to different ways of life in their host countries or having conversations about current events with their new friends and colleagues, overseas student teaching enabled them to support this growing global awareness that first sparked their desire to travel overseas.

We began this chapter with several questions we believe should be addressed for those wishing to establish and maintain strong overseas student-teaching programs. What we have offered in the chapter is our current thinking about how to address these questions based on our programmatic experiences and existing literature on the topic. We do not suggest we have found the best way of setting up or maintaining overseas student-teaching programs. In the final analysis, creating a sustainable overseas program is an endeavor that is highly specific to an institution. We believe we must continually ask questions in order to create and develop the kinds of programs that change and grow as our institutions do. In this way, we hope to enable our teacher candidates to engage in learning experiences that will not only broaden their present but also their future, and the future of the many students who will enter their classrooms.

REFERENCES

Baker, B. R. 2000. Moving beyond our education community: Student teaching abroad. Paper presented at the annual meeting of the Association for Childhood Education International, Baltimore, MD, April 17–20.

Baker, F. J., and R. Giacchino-Baker. 2000. *Building an international student teaching program: A California/Mexico experience.* ERDS ERIC Document No. ED449143.

Beach, R. 1995. *Multicultural learning at home and abroad.* EDRS ERIC Document No. ED415791.

Briscoe, K. 1991. Broadening horizons: Institutionalizing an international perspective. *Educational Record* 72:62–64.

Campion, W. J., and D. Bostic. 1993. *Manual for building an international education program in the community college.* EDRS ERIC Document No. ED361013.

Clark, B. R. 1980. *Academic culture.* New Haven, CT: Higher Education Research Group, Yale University Institute for Social and Policy Studies.

Council on International Educational Exchange (CIEE). n.d. Publications Center. At www.ciee.org/publications_center.aspx (accessed May 24, 2006).

Cushner, K. 2004. *Beyond tourism: A practical guide to meaningful educational travel.* Lanham, MD: Scarecrow Education.

Cushner, K., and J. Mahon. 2002. Overseas student teaching: Affecting personal, professional and global competencies in an age of globalization. *Journal of International Studies in Education* 6, no. 2:44–58.

Daniel, B. V., and S. B. Ross, eds. 2001. *Consumers, adversaries, and partners: Working with the families of undergraduates.* New Directions for Student Services 94. San Francisco: Jossey-Bass.

Fung, S., and J. Filippo. 2002. What kinds of professional international opportunities may be secured for faculty? *New Directions for Higher Education* 117:57–62.

Hatton, M. J. 1995. Internationalizing the community college. *Community College Journal of Research and Practice* 19, no. 5:453–70.

Hollins, E., and M. T. Guzman. 2005. Research on preparing teachers for diverse populations. In *Studying teacher education: The report of the AERA panel on research in teacher education*, ed. M. Cochran-Smith and K. M. Zeichner, 477–548. Mahwah, NJ: Lawrence Erlbaum.

Kappler, B., and K. Nokken. 1999. *Making the most of your time abroad.* Minneapolis: International Student and Scholar Services, University of Minnesota.

Kashner, J. B. 1990. Changing the corporate culture. In *Managing change in higher education*, ed. D. W. Steeples, 19–28. New Directions for Higher Education 71. San Francisco: Jossey-Bass.

Landerholm, E., C. Gehrie, and Y. Hao. 2004. Educating early childhood teachers for the global world. *Early Child Development and Care* 174, nos. 7–8:593–606.

Ladson-Billings. G. 1994. *Dreamkeepers: Successful teachers of African-American children.* San Francisco: Jossey-Bass.

Mahan, J. M., and L. L. Stachowski. 1990. New horizons: Student teaching abroad to enrich understanding of diversity. *Action in Teacher Education* 12, no. 3:13–21.

Mahon, J., and K. Cushner. 2002. The overseas student teaching experience: Creating optimal culture learning. *Multicultural Perspectives* 4, no. 3:3–8.

Merryfield, M. M. 2000. Why aren't teachers being prepared to teach for diversity, equity, and global interconnectedness? A study of lived experiences in the making of multicultural and global educators. *Teaching and Teacher Education* 16:429–43.

Merryfield, M. M., E. Jarchow, and S. Pickert, eds. 1997. *Preparing teachers to teach global perspectives: A handbook for teacher educators.* Thousand Oaks, CA: Corwin Press.

Mitchell, B. A. 2006. *The boomerang age: Transitions to adulthood in families.* New Brunswick, NJ: Aldine Transaction.

National Association of Foreign Service Advisors (NAFSA). n.d. Publications. At www.nafsa.org/publication.sec/education_abroad_students (accessed May 24, 2006).

Paige, R. M., A. D. Cohen, B. Kappler, J. C. Chi, and J. P. Lassegard. 2002. *Maximizing study abroad: A student's guide to strategies for language and culture learning and use*. Minneapolis: Center for Advanced Research on Language Acquisition, University of Minnesota.

Pike, G. 2000. Preparing teachers for global citizenship: The impact of the specialization in international education. *Exceptionality Education Canada* 10, nos. 1–2:95–106.

Savage, M. 2003. *You're on your own (but I'm here if you need me): Mentoring your child through the college years*. New York: Simon & Schuster.

Sevigny, J. 2001. *The AACRAO International Guide: A resource for international education professionals*. AACRAO Professional Development and Education Series. Washington, DC: American Association of Collegiate Registrars and Admissions Officers.

Stachowski, L. L., and V. A. Visconti. 1998. Service learning in overseas nations: U.S. student teachers give, grow, and gain outside the classroom. *Journal of Teacher Education* 49, no. 3:212–19.

3

PREPARATORY COURSES FOR STUDENT TEACHING ABROAD

Angene Wilson
Mary Anne Flournoy

The writing of the research paper on the educational system put me on good footing when I arrived. I felt that I could ask intelligent questions and understand what was going on more quickly.

—Ohio University teacher candidate

Having a conversation partner has made much of what we talked about in class come to life through a real example. It was nice to see a person who has taken the risk to come to a new place and hear her talk about the experience.

—University of Kentucky teacher candidate

Teacher-education programs in the United States prepare candidates both academically and practically to complete student-teaching placements in domestic settings. We believe programs should also take care of preparing candidates who will student teach overseas in another country and culture. Ohio University and the University of Kentucky have long required students who participate in overseas student-teaching (OST) programs to take preparatory courses. As designers and longtime instructors of these courses, we have learned a great deal about what candidates need before they begin an overseas placement.

Our purpose in this chapter is to share what we have learned from our course work with those who are interested in establishing or modifying programs at their institutions. In the chapter, we first explain the commonalities of our courses. Then, each of us describes her course in some detail to highlight unique features. As a way to stimulate thought about future program efforts—ours and others'—we close with questions that occurred to us as we wrote this chapter. We also provide a list of annotated references; the references are organized by type and include the sources for activities in our classes such as the "Tree of Life" and "Where I'm From," which are from Merryfield, Jarchow, and Pickert (1997).

COMMONALITIES

As will be evident from the descriptions that follow, our courses have similar aims, although the amount of emphasis on a topic may differ. In addition, we sometimes use different strategies to meet the same objective, as we choose from a wide variety of activities (such as cross-cultural simulations and interviews) and resources (such as short stories by returned Peace Corps volunteers and current newspapers here and in other countries).

Both courses focus squarely on the concept of culture, wanting students to be familiar with their own cultural framework, to understand cultural differences, to learn how to learn in and from another culture, and to consider how one adapts to and functions effectively in other cultures.

Both courses help students think about who they are. Through such strategies as completing an activity on American values and writing a reaction paper to a book written about the United States by a foreigner, we also challenge our students to consider "What is an American?"

Both courses also ask students to learn about a specific country, hopefully the one where they will student teach. To meet that goal, one of us assigns a research paper on another educational system and the other a country portfolio. We both require our students to read online newspapers of a target country.

At the heart of both courses are personal cross-cultural encounters. For University of Kentucky students, that encounter is through an amigo or conversation partner experience over the semester. For Ohio University students, that encounter comes from interaction with international student cultural consultants and participation in the simulation Albatross (Gochenour 1993).

We have organized the course descriptions that follow around these commonalities to illustrate questions addressed in courses including "Culture," "What Is an American?" "Learning about a Specific Country," and "Encounter with the 'Other.'" Each description begins with a brief background sketch explaining how the course evolved.

UNIVERSITY OF KENTUCKY

Background/History

The University of Kentucky has required a course for student teaching overseas, in connection with the Consortium for Overseas Teaching (COST) program, for about thirty years. The course was first offered by a comparative education professor in the foundations department for variable credit (one to three hours) because it included some instruction in Spanish for students who had not previously taken Spanish. The language was important since COST placements in the 1970s and early 1980s were all in binational schools in Mexico, Central America, and South America.

For the past twenty years, the course has been taught by the coauthor of this chapter, now professor emerita in the Department of Curriculum and Instruction, and for six years associate director of international affairs at the University of Kentucky. I (Wilson) have had extensive international experience, both teaching/living and traveling overseas, and my major research area has been the impact of international experience on students, teachers, and schools.

For the past six years, the course has been listed at the 500 level, meaning it can be taken by undergraduate and graduate students. The undergraduate students are in the elementary and middle-school programs; the graduate students are usually in the secondary master's with initial certification program. Occasionally, other students—practicing teacher graduate students, for example, who have already had international living and/or teaching experience or who want that experience eventually—take the class. The size of the class ranged from eight to fifteen students for many years. In 2004, twenty-eight students took the class and in 2005, twenty took the class. The class meets one night a week for the fifteen-week semester for two and a half hours.

Culture

As the basic concept for the class, culture looms large in the course and specifically in the course objectives, which include

- Learning concepts and theories of intercultural communication and cross-cultural adaptation, and applying them in reflective writing in reading logs and in an essay about a conversation partner experience.
- Demonstrating understanding in class of cultural differences and the building blocks of culture through workbook exercises, role-playing, simulations, dialogues and critical incidents, and other activities.

Two texts, Kohls' (2001) *Survival Kit for Overseas Living* and Storti's (1999) *Figuring Foreigners Out*, offer good definitions of culture that we look at as we begin to learn about what Storti calls building blocks of culture. Students deal with culture in their weekly logs, which require them to reflect on assigned reading by answering questions such as "In what ways are you an individualist and what advice could you give a person coming to the United States from a collectivist culture?" Often, we share our logs: visuals of the concept of culture, cartoons imagining life overseas without a car, or examples of miscommunication with conversation partners.

We also write stories about pictures to illustrate what is universal, what is personal, and what is cultural. We discuss how and why differences in Arab and American value systems may be important in understanding Iraq. We brainstorm characteristics of cross-cultural effectiveness. We do simulations like Barnga (Thiagarajan 1990) and debrief them. We share our reviews of cross-cultural films. We read short stories that illustrate positive cross-cultural communication. We read cross-cultural dialogues and critical incidents and analyze them.

Students learn about cultural differences in education systems as well. A tradition is a visit by teachers from Glasgow, Scotland, who bring students on exchange to one of our local high schools each fall. Other comparative education learning occurs when we have, depending on the year, a visiting professor from Australia or South Africa or faculty members originally from Germany or China, who explain their school systems. In fall 2005, four students in the class with previous international experience did presentations on the school systems of France, Japan, Russia, and South Korea. As a returned Peace Corps volunteer, I usually invite recently returned Peace Corps volunteers to talk about cross-cultural adaptation. That session is open to other students who might be interested in later Peace Corps service.

Another assignment related to culture is a global education project of the student's choice. For instance, in fall 2005, three students attended International Night organized by international students on campus. One student wrote, "I attended this festival by myself as an attempt to understand the feeling, although minimized, that goes along with being in a culture other than my own without a friend as a buffer." She was particularly struck by a pamphlet on the *hijab* at a booth explaining Islam and was impressed by a young Indonesian girl performing a traditional dance.

A second student agreed that going to the International Night enabled her to understand how it felt to be by herself. "For the first time in my life, I was a minority. I thought of this as being a preview of how I will need to interact when I go to student teach overseas." She also learned about the *hijab*, and she got her first henna tattoo. The third student to attend the International Night was a resident hall director. She also got a henna tattoo, and the positive reaction of others to her tattoo gave her the idea to work with one of her hall advisors from India to organize a program on traditional body art that drew forty girls.

The final take-home exam also focuses on culture. For example, one question asks students to read the short story "Cross-Cultural Dialogue," written from the Peace Corps teacher's perspective followed by the Guinea Bissau student perspective. It serves as a model for the students to write their own dual-perspective stories. Often the students' stories are from their experiences with their conversation partner. Another question asks students to give examples of three of Storti's (1994)

"Seven Lessons." Again, the question requires students to use their class and life experiences to offer examples for such lessons as "Don't assume sameness," "Familiar behaviors have different meanings," and "You don't have to like or accept 'different' behavior, but you should try to understand where it comes from."

A final question challenges students to imagine their way through a future international experience, using one of the several models of cross-cultural adjustment presented in the course. In a second paragraph, they describe the personal traits and skills they think will help them make the adjustment. In a third paragraph, they describe what changes they expect to see in themselves and their lives—personal and teaching—because of the "lived" international experience. That question also relates to their learning about one culture or country specifically.

What Is an American?

Early in the course, each student writes a poem entitled "Where I'm From," based on a poem of that name by George Ella Lyon, a Kentucky author. Directions and models come from an article by an English teacher (Christiansen 2001) about how to encourage the writing of such poems; the article includes samples of poems written by her high school students. As we share our poems (I have written one, too), we begin to understand our own varied cultural backgrounds and to get to know each other.

During that same class period we complete, in pairs or small groups, several exercises on American culture and diversity from *Culture Matters: The Peace Corps Cross-Cultural Workbook*, and then discuss our responses as a class. One is called "Sources of American Culture" and asks students to categorize American traits by defining features of American culture, such as American geography and the nature of the American immigrant. Another is called "The Things We Say—Culture in Casual Expressions" and asks students to figure out what value or belief is reflected in each group of expressions. For example, one set of expressions includes "Talk is cheap," "Put your money where your mouth is," "He's all talk and no action."

These exercises serve as an introduction to a chapter on American and contrast cultural assumptions and values in Bennett's (1998) *Basic Concepts of Intercultural Communication*, one of our texts. After looking especially at American assumptions and values in terms of such areas as activity, social relations, motivation, worldview, and perception of self, I make several points about the danger of generalizations: cultures change, cultures are complex, and our culture is not only European American. Questions that are often raised include "Are there regional as well as ethnic U.S. cultures—for example, differences between the Northeast and the South?" "Are we the only Americans in North, Central America, and South American—should we call ourselves U.S. Americans rather than just Americans?" "Is it our Constitution that is the common value in our multicultural nation?"

Then we watch excerpts from two movies—*The Long Walk Home* about the Montgomery bus boycott and *Mississippi Masala* about Indian immigrants from Uganda—to remind students that culture crossing has happened and is happening in the United States. I have also read excerpts from some of the 100 diverse reflections in *Being Scottish* (Devine and Logue 2002) so students recognize that people in other countries also struggle with questions of national identity.

Learning about a Specific Country

Most of the preparatory course focuses on learning about such topics as cultural differences and cross-cultural interaction in general, although the examples in texts and other readings may be country specific. As well, the conversation partner is obviously from a particular country, though almost never from the country where the student will be going for student teaching.

The country portfolio, on the other hand, gives the students an opportunity to learn about one of the specific countries they have listed on their application for student teaching abroad. Although the country of eventual assignment is sometimes not the country the student has studied, the portfolio pieces still offer ways to learn about any country. A semester-long project, the portfolio includes weekly reports of news about the country (in recent years, students have read most of their articles in online newspapers from the country); an annotated bibliography of at least twelve varied and recent sources, including books of all kinds (from children's books to guidebooks to cookbooks), magazine articles, and websites; a report on an interview with someone from the country or someone who has lived in or traveled extensively in the country; and two lesson plans about the country written for teaching students in Lexington.

Students seem to find keeping up with news from the country particularly interesting. I encourage them to look at articles about world events to see an Australian or Irish perspective on the war in Iraq, for instance. They also find articles on education and learn a little about other topics such as politics and sports. Websites have become an increasingly important part of bibliographies, of course, and occasionally students will do an interview through e-mail. Interviewees are sometimes study-abroad or COST returnees, and sometimes on-campus faculty and staff whose nation of origin is where the student is going.

The lesson plans give students an opportunity to learn some specific information about the country; they actually teach one lesson in abbreviated form to the class. Students have taught many primary lessons about Australian animals over the years, but they have also taught creatively about language, music, history, and art. For instance, a student in the 2005 class who applied to go to Scotland brought her guitar and taught us a song. For fall 2006, I am considering asking students to develop a lesson plan that would deal with a topic comparatively—in the United States and in the country where they will do their student teaching.

Encounter with the "Other"

As a strong believer in the importance of reflected-upon intercultural experience in the United States and overseas as a way to gain a more global perspective, I initiated a conversation partner program in my secondary social studies methods class in the late 1970s and then brought it to the preparatory course for student teaching abroad. For what we call the "Amigo Experience" (Wilson 1993a), a teacher-education student and an international student conversation partner in our university's English as a Second Language (ESL) program are paired and expected to meet about once a week or at least six to eight times over the semester for an hour or so. We also plan an event for all of us, sometimes a Halloween party, sometimes a reception at the end of the semester.

Through this experience, the future teachers have the opportunity to be helpful hosts and friends to someone who is learning English as a second language and discovering how to negotiate American culture. They also see firsthand and the other way around how the stages of cross-cultural adaptation work. The ESL students come from all over the world, currently more often from Asia than from the Middle East. Partners for fall 2005 were from Armenia, Burkina Faso, France, Indonesia, Japan, Mexico, Peru, South Korea, Taiwan, and Thailand. Reflective papers, due at the end of the semester, ask students to include what they learned about the amigo's culture and what they learned about cross-cultural experience as related to concepts learned in class.

Some years ago, I analyzed thirty-six reflective papers from several classes as part of research on our conversation partner program. Curious to know how students could benefit from an on-campus cross-cultural experience, I based my analysis on categories of impact of international experience that I had developed: substantive knowledge, perceptual understanding, personal development, and interpersonal relationships. Personal development was not evident in the papers, but the other categories were.

I found that students gained substantive knowledge about many topics: schooling and family and male/female relations were most often mentioned. For example, a student wrote, "We discussed so many things: from religion to hairstyle, and from weddings to weather."

Second, students gained perceptual understanding. For instance, one student wrote that her amigo from Taiwan had taught her to look at things in her everyday life in a new way. "I too readily accepted everything as the way it was and did not think to understand life's whys. . . . I believe I am now less judgmental, more open-minded, and very accepting." Of course, that wasn't easy. A student realized at his last meeting with his partner that he had been trying to impress him with Kentucky rather than learn about Spain, and another wrote about overcoming stereotypes such as "All Asians look alike."

Third, I found that students learned how to develop cross-cultural interpersonal relationships, getting past the scary part of communicating across different languages by learning how to use pictures and doing activities together. A student paired with an Indonesian student went hiking for a day with his partner's Indonesian friends and asked them to speak Bahasa Indonesia the whole day so he could have that experience. Another student pointed out that he had to learn to curb his instinct to finish his partner's sentences for him, "a habit which is both insulting and infuriating to the person trying to speak."

In the fall 2005 semester, students were still writing about schooling, family, and male/female relations. One student learned about education in Armenia and also her amigo's favorite holiday, Water Day. A married student was asked by her Japanese partner which set of parents she and her husband lived with. Another student with a Japanese partner learned about the history of U.S. military in Okinawa. In terms of perceptual understanding, some students applied Storti's building blocks of culture, so a student paired with a woman from Burkina Faso, for example, wrote about differences in individualist and collectivist cultures and in monochronic and polychronic cultures.

Students continue to learn how to develop cross-cultural interpersonal relationships, especially recognizing the stumbling block of different languages but also understanding similarities with their amigos and considering how much culture matters. A student from the 2005 class summarized,

> Many of our identity groups were similar and therefore we were able to connect on that level. We both are college students who have too much to do and live for those extra minutes to grab a bite to eat and just hang out and chat. We both are Kentucky Wildcats [fans] and enjoy watching the football and basketball teams play. We both are women and love to shop, listen to music, and gossip. Because we were able to identify with each other in these different ways, culture didn't matter. It didn't matter that her home is across the Pacific Ocean and that she speaks a language that I don't understand. We had enough in common where we could be friends and have a good time together. Furthermore, we were willing to work with the stumbling blocks we faced in order to communicate on a level that was enough to get by, enjoy each other's company and learn about each other's lives.

Another student concluded more generally about the value of the amigo experience:

> Having a conversation partner has made much of what we talked about in class come to life through a real example. It was nice to see a person who has taken the risk to come to a new place and hear her talk about the experience. I think that the whole [process] is beneficial to both parties. It

gives the person who has come here someone to talk to and to ask questions of while allowing someone like me to gain a greater appreciation of what studying abroad might be like.

OHIO UNIVERSITY

Background/History

Since 1992, Ohio University has sent more than 100 teacher candidates abroad through the Consortium for Overseas Student Teaching (COST). Since 1994, all COST students have been required to take two courses in order to participate: Learning from Non-Western Cultures and Teaching Strategies for Cross-Cultural and International Understanding. The latter, at the 400 level, is the orientation course for their international sojourn and was designed by the coauthor of this chapter (Flournoy) and has been taught by her since its inception.

I am the associate director emerita of the Center for International Studies at Ohio University as well as an adjunct faculty member in educational studies with a background in social studies and global education. I have extensive experience teaching and traveling overseas as well as coordinating international outreach to the schools from Ohio University. My research has focused on the impact of international experience on faculty, teachers, students, and institutions.

The purpose of the course is to prepare students for their sojourn abroad. For the past four years, enrollment has been from fifteen to twenty-three students with concentrations in early childhood, middle childhood, integrated language arts, social studies, mathematics, science, music, and art. Upon completion of the course, students will

- be familiar with their own cultural framework and how that affects their adaptation to a different culture;
- develop a set of skills that will help them interpret situations and interact appropriately in another culture;
- learn about the educational system in one of the countries in which they wish to teach;
- become knowledgeable about current issues in the United States that they may have to interpret while abroad and explore some of

the criticisms currently being leveled by other countries about the
United States;

- develop a plan for bringing their overseas experience home and incorporating it into their professional life. (From my Fall 2005 syl-
labus.)

At the heart of the course is a deep encounter with the "Other,"
both intellectually and personally, in which the Other becomes personal and distinguishable, not abstract. I have found over the years
that this is "learning that goes to the soul" (teacher participant, 1995
Summer Institute on Teaching about Africa and Africans from an
African Perspective at Ohio University). In order to have this happen,
students have to be regularly challenged to think and act outside of
their comfort zones.

Culture

We begin our class with an overview of the tenets of culture and an
examination of the assumptions that shape our values as individuals and
as Americans. Kohls' *Survival Kit for Overseas Living* (2001) is the basic text for the course. During the first class, we do the "Tree of Life
Exercise" in which students examine their own cultural values, especially the roots of their perceptions about and encounters with the
Other, however they might define that. They also do an assessment of
their preparedness for and burning questions about the COST experience, focusing on preparing for the experience and which they revisit
at the last class.

I lecture on the benchmarks of culture: concept of self, personal versus societal responsibility, concept of time, locus of control, and styles of
communication. I use as many cross-cultural comparisons as possible in
explaining these concepts. For instance, I use the South African constitution to contrast notions of personal and societal responsibilities and
rights with those in the U.S. Constitution. We look at critical incidents
from the Trompenaars' book *Riding the Waves of Culture* (2000) and
utilize a number of reflections from Peace Corps volunteers, all of which
help COST participants integrate a global perspective into their teaching practice.

The first assignment involves interviewing an international student about his or her experience coming to the United States and reflecting upon the experience. Students look for nonverbal as well as verbal cues. The interaction must address what assumptions the interviewee had about the United States before coming here, whether and how his or her assumptions changed after arrival, and what he or she finds challenging about life in the United States. The discussion should include content that points to similarities and differences in values in the two cultures.

The interview becomes the first entry into an analytic journal that is kept during the quarter and via e-mail during student teaching. This reflective practice is at the heart of a successful international experience, as well as good teaching. As one of our teachers in South Africa wrote, "I remember learning on the history channel about a man who was stuck on an island for a long time. He had to read the Bible out loud every day so he would not forget how to speak. This is the same for these reflections, I will have to read them at least twice a year to never forget what I came, saw, and experience [sic] when I was in Africa" (2006).

What Is an American?

Once we have established a framework for looking at culture, we take an in-depth look at the culture of the United States. Unfortunately, I have found that many teacher candidates at Ohio University are woefully ignorant about politics and world affairs. If they are to understand what it means to be an American, especially in the eyes of the world, they must be able to converse intelligently about the United States. For that reason, students have a quarter-long assignment of reading either the *New York Times* or the *Christian Science Monitor*. I have chosen these two newspapers because they are national newspapers with long traditions of excellence, they have extensive coverage of international news, and they are potential resources for the students when they have their own classrooms. The students develop a "compelling question" that they wish to answer about their country and look for articles during the quarter that speak to this question. Questions from 2005 focused on issues such as the value Americans place on children, the ethics of our level of consumption of world resources, and the imperatives of education for the twenty-first century. After students have chosen a question, they write an answer to it based on their current knowledge. Their final exam consists of writing a second answer informed by the reading they have done. We use the final exam time to share the insights each gained from doing this research. During fall 2005, the sharing took the form of designing and teaching a lesson that introduced the compelling question at an appropriate level of sophistication for the students they intend to teach.

Small-group presentations on "What is an American?" conclude this segment of the course. In 2005 four groups focused on environmental questions, social issues, education, and U.S. parochialism. Presentations must show evidence of a grasp of the benchmarks of culture and awareness of the multiple cultures in the United States and how those groups see American identity. The students do extensive reading, including a folder of current articles collected from various publications. Each one chooses a book written by a foreigner about the United States to read, and writes a two-page reaction essay. Some of the books make them mad. Some make them appreciate their country's finer qualities. Others call into question U.S. foreign policy. Some make them aware of gaps in their historical knowledge. All of these activities help the students to understand their own perceptions, challenge their own assumptions, and examine U.S. culture from multiple perspectives.

Being challenged to "see ourselves as others see us" has proved to be beneficial as the students complete their overseas assignment. A student in Ireland who was berated loudly on a bus for being from the United States remarked, "I remembered that we had talked about this kind of thing in class. I just listened and used it as an opportunity to learn why he was upset. I didn't take it personally" (2003).

Another student in Ireland whose compelling question had dealt with the parochialism of the United States found this played out when he traveled to Scotland.

A friend and I walked into a hostel and met some Australian who made a very interesting comment to another English guy in the room. He said in a sarcastic manner, "Look, Americans with passports." Like we are a joke but it's funny because it's true. . . . I now notice how trapped we are in our giant nation. No one ever leaves and sees the world outside . . . only a couple of us really do travel outside our borders. . . . It is very popular and customary for college aged people (here) to go to Laos, Australia, New Zealand, Africa and America. . . . We are so isolated and I never really saw that until now. . . . Here on basic television they have 4 news channels from Ireland, then the BBC channel, and usually Fox or CNN. This right here gives them at least three different views on world events. We have one view. . . . Their television gives an interesting view on life that I'd never see. I saw a documentary about Fidel Castro that was extremely positive and full of praise. . . . Only when we leave can we see what it means to be an American. (2006)

Another part of the "What is an American?" segment involves designing culture kits that represent some aspect of American life at an appropriate level for their students abroad. While they usually do not finish the kits until they are near their time of departure, the students develop a theme and a plan for the kit, bring in several appropriate physical objects to include in it, and get feedback from their peers to expand their ideas. These kits are to be portable enough to take with them overseas and leave as a gift in their host classroom. They are also a model for a way in which the students can "bring the world home" to their classes in the United States. We have had kits on every possible theme: patriotic symbols, holidays, baseball, my hometown, popular culture, and education, among others. One COST participant in Ireland who prepared a video of her practicum school in Athens County (Ohio) urged others to make one as well.

My students and teacher LOVED, LOVED, LOVED the video I made. They got such a kick out of the students talking and showing them around the school! They have watched it about 10 times since I have been here. . . . The kids love to see REAL pictures of what America looks like. . . . It just starts you off on the right foot with the students and your teacher. (2001)

Encounter with the "Other"

Encountering the Other involves exploring similarities and differences with cultural consultants from several countries, readings such as *Sacred Rac and Body Ritual of the Nacirema*, structured observations designed to make the familiar strange, and participation in the simulation Albatross (Gochenour 1993). We take advantage of visitors on campus such as the Cape Town, South Africa, COST coordinator, as well as returned COST participants. Interactions with Ohio University international graduate students focus on their educational systems and how the United States is viewed in their country. Perhaps the most powerful of these came in fall 2005 from a woman from Laos, who worked for a nongovernmental organization that locates and disarms unexploded ordinances left behind in the "Secret War" carried on there by the United States during the Vietnam War. My students knew nothing of this period of their history, and were shocked to learn of the promises made to the hill tribes who aided the United States and of the subsequent feeling of betrayal when the promises were not kept. That same evening a Ghanaian presented a very positive view of the United States framed by his experience in a school supported by missionaries from the United States. Multiple perspectives abounded.

As a challenge to students to step out of their comfort zones, they go on a guided observation to a part of the campus with which they are quite familiar. They may not talk to anyone for one hour, attempt to suspend any knowledge they already have of this place, and record only what they see and hear. In their journals they respond to such questions as "Is there anyone in charge here?" "How can you tell?" "What seems to be the correct behavior?"

Sometimes I utilize the Martian Anthropology Exercise (Gochenour 1993) as a follow-up or a substitute for the campus observations. In that exercise, students pretend they are a team of Martian anthropologists who come to Earth to learn about the social and cultural norms in order to prepare a high-ranking delegation for their first visit to Earth. Students go in groups of two or three to such places as a bowling alley to study religion or a downtown bank to study the education system.

The most intense class session is the Albatross simulation developed for the Experiment in International Living. We carry out the simulation at my home, followed by a meal of a cuisine with which the students are not familiar (usually Indian or Indonesian). We invite the cultural consultants who have visited class earlier to join us.

The students are told only that they will meet some Albatrossians and later share a meal with them. The simulation involves two Albatrossians, one male and one female, dishes or bowls for hand washing, a liquid to drink, and food to eat. We darken the room, light incense and candles, and play some unfamiliar music in the background. Students enter, take off their shoes, and go immediately downstairs to see a male seated in a chair and a female seated beside him on the floor, barefooted, at one end of the room. What follows is a ceremonial greeting and offering of hospitality performed by the two members of this imaginary culture. No words are spoken and there are long periods of silence. The students are offered unfamiliar food and drink. After each part of the ceremony, the Albatrossian woman returns to her seat on the floor beside the male and he pushes her head to the floor.

During the critical debriefing, students reflect first on what happened and how they felt about it, and then venture what they "know" about this culture. Gradually they begin to realize how their observations are colored by their own cultural blinders and how they personally react to something unfamiliar or unexpected. One student wrote in his journal,

When the guy from Albatross came up to me and started rubbing my leg with his knee, I froze. I thought he was coming on to me and that was just not acceptable. So I backed away and wouldn't let him touch me any further. Now I realize how conditioned I am to what kinds of touch are acceptable, how close someone you don't know can get to you. This has really caused me to think about my personal boundaries. (2003)

When we discuss how the students felt about what was happening, they always mention how uncomfortable the silence was. "I realize how jittery silence makes me feel. I felt like I needed to be doing something or I was doing something wrong or I needed to say something. . . . I'm never quiet when I'm with a group of friends" (2004). When the students are allowed to question the Albatrossians about their culture, they discover that many of their assumptions about what was going on were false.

Seeing that Albatrossian guy push that woman's head to the floor all the time really made me uneasy. I thought he probably expected us to do that to the women sitting next to us but I knew that if I did, those women would punch me out. Boy, was I amazed that their culture believes that women are closer to the earth, which is sacred, and that the only way the man could get close to the earth was through a woman. I just never could've imagined a culture that different from ours. (2002)

Evaluations of the course always rate Albatross as one of the most significant learning experiences.

Learning about a Specific Country

During the second half of the course, we become culture specific and students prepare a formal research paper on the educational system and its cultural context for one of the countries in which they would like to teach. They read a daily online newspaper from the country, paying special attention to educational issues and news about the United States. At this point, about one-third of the class has received a definite COST placement and the other two-thirds have not.

Because the course is offered only once a year, students sometimes write a paper about a country in which they do not end up teaching. However, the research skills are useful when they do get their assignment overseas. The paper must include material from the country newspaper, journal articles, fiction and nonfiction books and film, guidebooks, and websites. It must also incorporate insights gained by interviewing someone from or with extensive experience in that country. As a conclusion to the paper, students must comment on the challenges they see in adapting to this new cultural milieu. Most years I also require the students to extend the paper by teaching a lesson to the rest of the class.

For several years we had a dearth of Irish students at OU and had to telephone my son's Irish colleague on the International Desk at CNN for an insight into his native land. The interviews are essential to putting a personal face on the country the student is about to visit. Most of my students have had little or no experience out of the United States. The kinds of questions the students ask the cultural consultants are the kinds of questions they can expect once they go abroad. Favorite topics include schooling, dating and marriage practices, child rearing, family life, cultural taboos, and pop culture. They learn that no one ordinary citizen can really be representative of a country. In other words, experience does not equal expertise.

Many students have commented on the worth of the paper in making them feel more at ease about teaching in a different culture. They feel better prepared to ask intelligent questions and seek out the resources they will need.

CONCLUSION

One of the advantages of writing a chapter together is that the authors can learn from each other, which proved true in this case. Our work together on this project has helped each of us think about course-related ideas we might not have otherwise considered. Our collaboration has also allowed us to generate questions that we will ponder as we prepare for another year of teaching candidates preparing to student teach abroad.

- In what ways has it become increasingly important to be sure students know current world events and issues and to help them understand how others see us, as well as to understand themselves?
- How do we balance opportunities for culture-general and culture-specific learning?
- How can we expand our use of technology to more than reading foreign newspapers online and accessing specific country resources on the Web?
- If experience is the best teacher, what further meaningful experiences could we design for our students?
- How can the important concepts we teach be included in course work for all future teachers?

Kwame Anthony Appiah's *Cosmopolitanism: Ethics in a World of Strangers* (2006) raises a final question for us. We wonder: Should we be teaching and should our students be learning about more than "culture" and the "Other"? Appiah's definition of cosmopolitanism includes two intertwining ideals—universal concern and respect for legitimate difference. We work hard on the second, but shortchange the first. Perhaps an Asante proverb can bridge the gap: "It is the human being that counts. We call gold: it does not answer. We call cloth: it does not answer. It is the human being that counts" (Gyekye 1996).

We invite you, our readers, to ponder with us the following questions as you consider requiring your candidates participating in COST courses to complete courses like ours: Can we prepare all teachers to be people who care about strangers, as well as respect them and their differences? Can we prepare all teachers to be able to learn, to converse, to teach, and to act on a universal concern across cultures?

ANNOTATED REFERENCES

These references also include the texts used in our courses.

Texts

Bennett, M. J. ed. 1998. *Basic concepts of intercultural communication, selected readings.* Yarmouth, ME: Intercultural Press. Bennett includes a variety of authors, such as Dean Barnlund, Edward T. Hall, Edward C. Stewart, and Benjamin Lee Whorf. His own introduction to intercultural communication and his chapter entitled "Overcoming the Golden Rule: Sympathy and Empathy" are excellent.

Kohls, L. R. 2001. *Survival kit for overseas living, for Americans planning to live and work abroad.* 4th ed. Yarmouth, ME: Intercultural Press. This trusted guide was first published in 1979 and is a classic. Besides dealing with culture, cultural differences, and culture shock, Kohls has short chapters on "Becoming a Foreigner," "Know Thy Host Country," "Skills That Make a Difference," and "Coming Home."

Storti, C. 1999. *Figuring foreigners out: A practical guide.* Yarmouth, ME: Intercultural Press. A workbook with exercises students do to figure out themselves and people of other cultures. His building blocks of culture are continua of Individualist-Collectivist, Universalist-Particularlist, Monochronic-Polychronic, and Internal-External. The chapters on verbal and nonverbal communication are also helpful. Students do have to be reminded, as Storti points out, that culture is only part of what influences people's behavior.

Trompenaars, F. 2000. *Riding the waves of culture.* London: Nicholas Brealey. Oriented toward business, the book contains a very readable explanation of the building blocks of culture. Also valuable for a number of critical incidents dealing with topics such as expectations of friendship and communication styles. Many cultures are reflected in his examples.

Other Resources

Aboulela, L. 1999. The museum. In *Opening spaces: An anthology of contemporary African women's writing,* ed. Yvonne Vera. Portsmouth, NH: Heinemann. A short story written from the perspective of a woman international student from Sudan attending the university in Edinburgh and her difficult cross-cultural interaction with a well-meaning Scottish student. Useful for students to read as they are interacting with international students on campus.

Appiah, K. A. 2006. *Cosmopolitanism: Ethics in a world of strangers*. New York: W. W. Norton. One of the first books in a new series on Issues in Our Time, edited by Henry Louis Gates, Jr. As a philosopher, Appiah draws on many sources, both classical and his own growing up in Kumasi, Ghana, to make a case for a cosmopolitanism that respects difference but recognizes a global moral community.

Building bridges: A Peace Corps classroom guide to cross-cultural understanding. 2003. Washington, DC: Peace Corps Coverdell World Wise Schools. Simulation "brief encounters" that asks students to adopt the cultures of two unfamiliar groups—one outgoing and casual, the other more reserved and formal—with different social norms. Also lessons on culture in the United States and beyond the United States that are designed for ninth grade and above, but are useful for university students as well.

Christiansen, L. 2001. "Where I'm From: Inviting Students' Lives into the Classroom." In *Rethinking our classrooms: Teaching for equity and justice*. Rethinking Schools.Milwauke, WI.

Culture matters: The Peace Corps cross-cultural workbook. n.d. Washington, DC: U.S. Government Printing Office. Exercises on American culture and diversity and many others.

Cushner, K., Averill McClelland, and Phillip Safford. 1992. *Human diversity in education: An integrative approach*. New York: McGraw Hill. Source for critical incidents in which students choose best explanation of situation. School-based.

Defining America. 2004. *US News and World Report*, special report (June 28–July 5).

Degrees of separation: A survey of America. 2005. *Economist* (July 16).

Devine, T., and P. Logue. 2002. *Being Scottish: Personal reflections on Scottish identity today*. Edinburgh: Polygon.

Gochenour, T. 1993. *Beyond experience*. Yarmouth, ME: Intercultural Press. Experiential approach to cross-cultural education. The section of activities is particularly valuable. Albatross and the Martian anthropology exercise by Donald Batchelder are found here. They both take students out of their comfort zones and help them to question their "normal" perception of reality.

Gyeke, K. 1996. African cultural values: An introduction. Lansing, MI: Sankofa Publishing Company,

Karp, Stan. 2001. Arranged marriages, rearranged ideas. In *Rethinking our classrooms: Teaching for equity and justice*. Rethinking Schools.Milwaukee, WI.

Merryfield, M. M., E. Jarchow, and S. Pickert, eds. 1997. *Preparing teachers to teach global perspectives: A handbook for teacher educators*. Thousand Oaks,

CA: Corwin Press. A handbook for teacher educators that presents a rich collection of case studies. Merryfield's framework chapter contains the Tree of Life Reflection as well as Pa Kanoh's Worldview, which helps students recognize their privileged status within the global system.

Storti, C. 1994. *Cross-cultural dialogues: 74 brief encounters with cultural difference*. Yarmouth, ME: Intercultural Press. Dialogues of Americans and people of a variety of other cultures.

Summerfield, E. 1993. *Crossing cultures through film*. Yarmouth, ME: Intercultural Press. Good ideas about how to use cross-cultural films in courses. We both use films, sometimes excerpts in class, sometimes assigning cross-cultural feature films to be reviewed. One favorite to use in class are excerpts from *The New Americans*, available from PBS, to show cultural differences and cultural adjustment in the United States. by Indians, Mexicans, Nigerians, Dominicans, and Palestinians. Two other films are *Mr. Baseball*, starring Burt Reynolds as a baseball player with an attitude who is traded to a Japanese team against his will and dealing with his slow process of adaptation and the many misunderstandings along the way, and *Close to Eden*, detailing the encounter between a Russian road builder whose truck has broken down and a Mongolian family living in a yurt not far from Ulan Bator; they are curious about each other and open to interaction, and it's a funny, sweet, and visually stunning look at cross-cultural adaptation. Among student favorites to review as feature films are *Anna and the King*, *Bend It with Beckham*, *Whale Rider*, *Rabbit Proof Fence*, and *Where the Green Ants Dream*. The last two deal with the struggle of Aborigines in Australia to maintain their traditional values.

Thiagarajan, S. 1990. *Barnga: A simulation game on cultural clashes*. Yarmouth, ME: Intercultural Press. This short and flexible simulation involves a card game tournament in which each table plays silently and unbeknownst to each other by different rules, leading to an experience of cultural clash.

To See Ourselves as Others See Us

Examples of books that Ohio University students read to understand a foreigner's perspective on the United States and the West.

Bryson, B. 1999. *I'm a stranger here myself*. New York: Broadway Books.

Baruma, I., and A. Margalit. 2004. *Occidentalism: The West in the eyes of its enemies*. New York: Penguin Press.

D'Souza, D. 2002. *What's so great about America?* New York: Penguin Putnam.

Fadiman, A. 1997. *The spirit catches you, you fall down*. New York: Farrar, Strauss & Giroux.

Kim, E. 2001. *The yin and yang of American culture*. Yarmouth, ME: Intercultural Press.

McCourt, Frank. 1999. *'Tis: A memoir*. New York: Scribner.

Voices from the field: Reading and writing about the world, ourselves, and others. n.d. Washington, DC : Peace Corps Coverdell World Wise Schools. Includes many wonderful short stories by returned Peace Corps volunteers. We have used "'Magic' Pablo," "Cross-Cultural Dialogue," and "A Single Lucid Moment."

Zongren, L. 1984. *Two years in the melting pot*. San Francisco: China Books and Periodicals.

Research

Wilson, A. H. 1993a. "Conversation partners: Helping students gain a global perspective through cross-cultural experiences. *Theory into Practice* 32, no. 1 (Winter). Research on the Amigo Experience at University of Kentucky.

Wilson, A. H. 1993b. *The meaning of international experience for schools*. Westport, CT: Praeger. Includes six case studies on teachers with international experience, returned Peace Corps volunteers who teach, an Afghan sixth-grader, a little United Nations elementary school, an international visitors program at a middle school, and an International Studies Academy at a high school. Other chapters explain the context and problems of international experience and schools, the impact of international experience, and ideas for utilizing international experience in schools.

4

THE IMPACT OF OVERSEAS STUDENT TEACHING ON PERSONAL AND PROFESSIONAL DEVELOPMENT

Jennifer Mahon
Kenneth Cushner

In the current edition of the American Educational Research Association (AERA) Report on Research and Teacher Education (Cochran-Smith and Zeichner 2005), there is no mention of international student teaching or internships. In fact, in searching through the entire index, the word *international* is mentioned only twice—referring to international data sets and the International Council on Exceptional Children. Reference is made to the work of Mahan, who has published frequently on overseas student teaching (Mahan and Stachowski 1990; Stachowski and Mahan 1998)—but both studies listed in the AERA volume refer to work the authors completed within the United States—on Native American reservations (1984) and in community-based service learning (1982). Why do studies with an international focus appear to be absent?

We understand that every study on teacher preparation cannot be included in such a volume. However, the editors (Cochran-Smith and Zeichner 2005) state that the review of research was intended to examine what is known about how preservice teachers are prepared to work with diverse students. And we believe there is a viable dimension of professional preparation that supports efforts to improve teachers' abilities to address both domestic and international diversity. Overseas student teaching (OST) offers benefits both on personal and professional levels that strengthen the cultural competency of teacher candidates. It is also becoming increasingly evident that many of the positive outcomes we can document with regard to international teaching experiences are reflected in the literature on culturally responsive teaching and living. A great deal of literature discusses characteristics of culturally competent individuals (Wiseman, Hammer, and Nishida 1989; Hammer 1987; Bhawuk and Triandis 1996), of the effects of general study abroad programs (Kauffmann et al. 1992), of culturally relevant teachers (Ladson-Billings 1994, 1995), and of globally competent teachers (Merryfield, Jarchow, and Pickert 1997). Some commonalities in this literature include enhancing language and communication skills, increasing flexibility or open-mindedness, developing an ability to empathize or understand the position of the other, and a beginning recognition of other value systems and ways of behaving.

The research discussed in this chapter suggests that teacher candidates begin developing these competencies through overseas student teaching, and for that reason, we continue to be strong and critical advocates for this experience. However, the lack of attention to the international dimension in the 2005 AERA report reveals that overseas student teaching is still considered to be on the margins of teacher education. Thus we recognize that we are describing a small sample of the population of student teachers who have traveled overseas, but we believe it should be considered an important element in the teacher-preparation curriculum. Therefore, in addition to updating our ongoing study of our teacher candidates' experiences and discussing suggestions for future research, this chapter also includes a review of the general research on the OST experience. Since both of us have worked extensively with overseas issues and student teaching throughout our careers and have a clear bias for overseas experiences, we acknowledge that negative outcomes may occur. Therefore, we will discuss these limitations accordingly. But first, we turn to the benefits accrued via general study abroad to ground our discussion.

THE BENEFITS OF STUDY ABROAD IN GENERAL

Researchers from the fields of cross-cultural psychology and intercultural training have, for decades, studied the impact that an international or intercultural experience has on people in a variety of settings (Billing-meier and Forman 1975; Landis, Bennett, and Bennett 2004; Cushner and Karim 2004). The role that firsthand experience plays in culture learning has consistently been found to be a critical component to in-tercultural development (Bennett 1993; Cushner and Brislin 1996). The experience abroad, regardless of the level at which it takes place, offers the individual a unique opportunity for intercultural development as it involves both physical and psychological transitions that engage the cog-nitive, affective, and behavioral domains. And this experience occurs twice—once during entry into the host culture and then again upon reentry into the home culture.

One of the goals of study abroad has always been to affect students' knowledge base, and several studies report impact in the cognitive do-main. The majority of students who live and study abroad, for instance, report that their intercultural sojourn challenged their perceptions of themselves as well as of others (see Cushner and Karim [2004] for a comprehensive survey of the research literature on study abroad at the university level). Those who have studied abroad for a semester or longer typically demonstrate an increase in cultural and political knowl-edge (Billingmeier and Forman 1975), and more critical attitudes to-ward the host culture (Yachimowicz 1987). When they return, students who have studied abroad tend to enroll in a greater number of foreign language classes, spend a greater amount of time studying in college, and tend to be higher achieving students than students who do not go abroad (Melchiori 1987).

Intercultural sensitivity, increased autonomy, and openness to cul-tural diversity are also enhanced as a result of study abroad (Pfnister 1972; Zhai 2000). Students who study overseas have a tendency to demonstrate higher levels of cross-cultural interest and cultural cos-mopolitanism than do those who remain at home. In addition, partici-pants also develop more positive, but more critical, attitudes toward their own country than do those who remain at home.

There is evidence of long-term impact as a result of general study abroad as well. Years after an experience, people who have studied and lived abroad continue to have a greater understanding of the intellectual life and traditions of their host country, in addition to an increased awareness of the differences between nations (Billingmeier and Forman 1975). Former study-abroad participants tend to become involved in more international activities upon their return home; have more friends, professional colleagues, and acquaintances in other countries; and read more books and newspapers in foreign languages than do those who remained at home.

Study abroad has an impact on the affective domain as well. Early studies that looked at the impact of study abroad demonstrated that participants report growth, independence, self-reliance, and an increased ability to make decisions on their own (Billingmeier and Forman 1975; Nash 1976). Significant changes in people's tolerance and understanding of other people and their views also occur as a result of study abroad. There is also evidence that an increase in self-confidence, adaptability, flexibility, confidence in speaking to strangers, and gathering information in new and unfamiliar settings occurs.

Evidence also exists that the international experience may generalize to domestic concerns. Those who participate in study-abroad programs tend to demonstrate greater levels of cultural sensitivity and racial consciousness, thus making them more effective at addressing issues related to domestic diversity. Thomas Pettigrew (2001), a prolific researcher in the field of prejudice formation and reduction, reviewed more than 200 studies of ethnic contact, of which one-fourth involved international contact through travel and student exchange. Excluding the relatively restricted encounters that are typical of most tourist experiences, international contact was shown to have greater impact at reducing prejudice than within-nation interethnic contact.

Behavior also changes as a result of an international experience. For many, the overseas experience sets new direction and focus to their career paths (Wallace 1999). Some returnees direct their career toward working with other sojourners and may seek out positions as foreign student advisors or international program coordinators. Some find that the overseas experience has sensitized them to issues and values they never knew they held, and find themselves studying environmental or political issues. And others work to internationalize whatever career they choose, such as becoming global or multicultural educators, international businesspeople, or foreign service officers. Others simply become good cultural mediators in their schools and communities, bringing their overseas experience to the domestic front for the benefit of others.

Further, this research helps guide decisions about programmatic structures that facilitate these outcomes. For students to adequately adjust to a culture, learn the context, and get to know the school program, the number of weeks required should be substantial. This recommendation is grounded in the research that continues to show the value of long-term immersion on improving intercultural interactions (Kauffmann et al. 1992; Koester 1987; Sikkema and Niyekawa 1987). Secondly, the experience should be considered a process, which according to LaBrack (1993), includes predeparture orientation as well as debriefing upon return as crucial elements to a successful and educational experience. Finally, from Weaver (1993), we learn that when individuals cut off all contact from home, it is likely to make adjustment more difficult than less. For example, students need support not only in handling their predeparture requirements but also enabling them to dialogue, reflect, and vent during, as well as after, the intercultural experience.

STUDY ABROAD AND THE FIELD OF EDUCATION

What does the research tell us about the field of education as it relates to study abroad? One area which has been explored is long-term impact on career advancement and personal accomplishment (Martens 1991). Teachers who studied abroad returned with a new sense of authority and a greater desire to share their knowledge and experience with others, had greater academic prestige because of their participation in an overseas program, and were more likely to apply and be selected for additional opportunities for international travel and study.

Other studies examine international course work or field experiences in the overseas context. Bradfeld-Kreider (1999) reports on a cultural immersion experience and its effects on reducing racism via a homestay program in Mexico for preservice teachers. Baker and Giacchino-Baker (2000) discuss a U.S.–Mexico partnership undertaken by three U.S. universities working together. Pike (2000) offers details with regard to establishing a major in international education in a Canadian context, of which overseas student teaching is a component. Landerholm, Gehrie, and Hao (2004) discuss the comprehensive facets included in globalizing an elementary education program, including a component of overseas study. Merryfield, Jarchow, and Pickert (1997) authored an immensely useful work on a variety of aspects of overseas training for teachers. Within this volume are three articles applicable to program administration: Kissock's (1997) overview of overseas student teaching, Case and Werner's (1997) discussion related to building faculty commitment, and Jarchow's (1997) chapter that looks at the dean's role in such efforts. Mc-Fadden, Merryfield, and Barron (1997) discuss both global and multicultural education in a document available from the American Association of Colleges of Teacher Education (AACTE). Partnership issues are considered by Merryfield (1995) in setting up global professional development schools, while Kiely and Nelson (2003) consider a wider number of disciplines in their discussion, and Stachowski and Chlebo (1998) give voice to the overseas partners in discussing host-faculty's suggestions for improving program effectiveness.

In recent years, researchers have begun looking specifically at the nature of the international student-teaching experience and its impact on professional and personal development (Baker 2000; Bryan and Sprague 1997; Calhoon et al. 2003; Cushner 2004; Cushner and Mahon 2002; Mahan and Stachowski 1990; Stachowski, Richardson, and Henderson 2003; Stachowski and Brantmeier 2002; Stachowski and Visconti 1998). Consistent with what the research says about study abroad in general, student teaching overseas has an impact on preservice teachers in both personal and professional ways. In addition to being exposed to new pedagogical approaches and educational philosophies, overseas student teachers gain a significant amount of self-knowledge, and develop personal confidence, professional competence, and a greater understanding of both global and domestic diversity.

ONGOING RESEARCH ON THE IMPACT OF THE COST EXPERIENCE

The existing literature, as well as our own experiences as international travelers, international teachers, and mentors to educators who desire to study abroad, form the background for the curiosities that underpin our research. What is reported here is a continuation of an ongoing study we have reported on earlier (Cushner and Mahon 2002) where we attempt to discover such things as the following:

- Why do students choose to go overseas to student teach? What do they hope to gain from this experience, and do those expectations come true?
- What do students learn about themselves personally as a result of this experience? What elements of the experience facilitate this learning?
- What do students learn about themselves professionally as a result of this experience? What elements of the experience facilitate this learning?
- How does the experience affect the ways students know and understand culture?
- How does the experience translate to the student's life when he or she returns home?
- In what ways has the student's understanding of teaching and learning been enhanced as a result of an international experience?

Our research is continually in progress, as each new set of sojourning students helps us understand the overseas experience in a different way. We believe that investigating these questions will add to the knowledge base about overseas study, increase intercultural competencies, and enable us to improve and broaden the experience.

METHODOLOGY

The findings reported on here come from continuous evaluation of the experiences of participants of the Consortium of Overseas Student Teaching (COST). Each year, COST, a consortium of fifteen universities, sends between sixty and seventy-five U.S. students to complete their student teaching in schools outside the United States. Students can choose to teach in national schools in English-language countries such as England, Scotland, Wales, Ireland, the Bahamas, Canada, Australia, New Zealand, and South Africa. They may also choose to teach in national schools in other countries if the host supervisors determine the student's language proficiency is at fluent or near-fluent levels. Additionally, students may teach in U.S. or International Schools in such countries as Costa Rica, Ecuador, Mexico, Japan, Switzerland, Greece, and Turkey. Depending on the particular requirements of the student, he or she may spend anywhere from six to sixteen weeks overseas— longer if he or she chooses to stay on for travel, study, or work. Student teachers have an in-country supervisor (such as local university faculty or school administrator) in addition to working side-by-side with a co-operating teacher. Approximately two-thirds of the students participate in some form of orientation at their home institution prior to departure.

Returning students responded to an open-ended survey designed to evaluate the nature and value of their time abroad. A sample of questions from the survey includes

- What specific circumstances from your overseas experiences influence you today?
- What have you learned about yourself as a result of your overseas student-teaching experience?
- What did you learn about others as a result of your overseas experience?
- In what ways are you different from those teachers who did not have an overseas experience?
- What aspects of your international experience do you think other teacher-education students could learn from?

The data reported here were compiled from sixty returning students. In addition to the questionnaire designed for the original study, this chapter also utilizes, to a more limited extent, responses from the general program evaluations sent to all COST returnees. As our questionnaire was sent out at the same time, not every student returned both items. For an additional ten students, an in-depth analysis of application essays, predeparture self-reports, and in-country journals was conducted. Finally, four of the students remain in a longitudinal study two years after their experience.

Data were coded and analyzed using constant comparative analysis appropriate to qualitative studies. In general, this is an exploratory study, and the findings that follow are offered as a space to encourage more thought and research into international student teaching.

FINDINGS

Rationale for Student Teaching Abroad: Expectations versus Reality

Why do students choose to go overseas? What do they expect this experience to bring to their lives? Our research reveals a number of similar themes that act as catalysts for overseas study.

Cultural Curiosity   Some students desire to meet new people and to learn more about a different culture. Some have already been exposed to traveling abroad and want to either broaden or deepen their cultural knowledge. Others have a personal cultural curiosity—an ethnicity or affinity with a country or people since childhood. Obviously, many were looking forward to the excitement of just traveling abroad.

Educational Curiosity   Numerous students expressed a desire to expose themselves to different educational systems and to acquire new teaching techniques that they could use at home. In this way they had more ways to broaden what they could bring to their classrooms.

Marketability   Some students hoped to pursue an overseas job upon graduation and they recognized this as a useful experience in the pursuit of that goal. Others hoped to make themselves more marketable in job searches in the United States by having an experience that would help them to stand out from the crowd. For some, developing language skills was seen as a way to be marketable in a competitive marketplace.

Challenge and Adventure   Many students expressed a desire to get out of their comfort zone or to pursue a desire to experience something different from what they had previously known. These challenges were perceived as attainable through experiencing what it is like to live abroad, to live in a non-English-speaking environment, and to travel.

Sense of Impact   Some students seemed to have an intuitive sense that they would be profoundly changed by this experience, even if they could not articulate or pinpoint the exact reasons why. They noted both anticipation as well as anxiety over the realization that they might not be the same when they returned, especially with regards to their relationships with others around them.

As the following shows, many of these expectations came true for students. Of course, there were numerous things that they did not expect and that provided significant learning experiences.

Connections   Students were surprised at things they discovered about relationships—both at home and overseas. These realizations were both positive and negative. Many were surprised to be welcomed so graciously into a family during a homestay. Others were dismayed that they were greeted with anti-American sentiments, or that their host faculty was less hospitable than expected. Some were surprised that they were discouraged from pursuing the overseas experience and that they had to endure resistance, negative comments, and other obstacles from family members. On the other hand, some students commented at how supportive and close they began to feel to their families. And although a few participants anticipated it, most were surprised that their lives and sometimes their close relationships were altered upon their return. One student pursued a spiritual path for the first time in her life due to the way she experienced religion with her host family and culture. And yes, a few students even got married!

Schooling   Students experienced a range of reactions to both the similarities and differences found in schools. In general, predeparture comments detailing expectations about students and teachers abroad were not specific, thus not much can be gleaned as to how they may have felt prior to the experience. Some students were surprised to find they now desired to teach in a completely different grade level, but this could have happened had the student stayed home. Others became fascinated with techniques they never knew or never thought they would use, such as group work or emphasis on the "human touches" in learning. Others seemed to be genuinely surprised at how much they were able to reach students and at how much they could learn about their own professional and personal abilities.

Confronting expectations versus reality, or disconfirmed expectation (Cushner and Brislin 1996), is a strong theme that helps guide our understanding of what is learned through the overseas experience. These categories, combined with the answers to the remaining research questions, demonstrate new understandings of one's own role and culture as well as that of others, and improved abilities to interact and teach in diverse settings. Next we turn to these repositionings of self.

Impact on the Self

As researchers, we were curious about the impact the experience had on students' personal development. Themes that emerged under this category included self-efficacy, being otherwise, and embracing collectivism.

Improved Self-Efficacy   Gibson and Dembo (1984) noted that teachers with high self-efficacy motivate and praise students more, and are better able to guide students in their learning by prompting or offering probing questions. By confronting new and different experiences, perhaps even fearful ones at times, and having to act and make choices, overseas student teachers find they have to rely upon themselves. For many, this may be their first experience at total self-reliance. They may have to find housing, pay bills, and use public transportation in a completely different cultural context and sometimes a different language. As one student stated, "Man, if I can teach fourth grade students four core subjects all in Spanish, in Mexico, in 111 degree weather . . . I can do ANYTHING" [Emphasis in original].

Through facing their personal anxieties and testing their own limitations, students create a space for opportunity and empowerment. In that space, they report the growth of self-confidence and esteem, as well as increased adaptability, confidence, persistence, strength, and risk taking. One student noted, "I am more independent and self-sufficient than I had originally thought. I've learned to take chances in my life—which I really never did before." Another noted, "I've become resourceful in the respect that I am able to deal emotionally in a wide variety of circumstances." Mahan and Stachowski (1990) reported similar findings. Through the combination of being in new and different settings, the opportunity to form new relationships and a greater exposure to different pedagogical philosophies, student teachers can achieve self-assurance and a sense of accomplishment.

One returning student reported an increased ability to take on challenges, saying, "I think that my experience made me more independent, and I feel that I can do anything now. Also, I know that I can make it through anything no matter what it is." This student's comment regarding independence suggests one of the most profound aspects of the overseas experience. Inside the classroom, student teachers appear to have the same support networks as a domestic student teacher. However, when the bell rings and the day is done, students are left to their own devices and must learn to trust and rely on their own capabilities. Such an experience is in many ways similar to the first year of teaching in which teachers must deal with issues such as classroom management, instruction, and communication without the benefit of another teacher in the room.

Being Otherwise   As noted, this increased sense of personal sense and ability may be a new experience for students. For some, a recognition of "being otherwise" came during the experience and directly affected their interaction with others via experimentation with a different way of being. Students who were admitted "loners" learned the value of working with others and striking out to meet new people, while the "social types" began recognizing the value of slowing down, of taking a step back, or simply being alone. One student reflected on the experience of having to engage in conflict where previously it would have been avoided,

> Even if you are a cheerful, generally nice person, sometimes you're going to have those people who get under your skin and who you need to deal with. You can't just walk away. At home, I could just sort of walk away from a person who I did not want to be around. During this experience, I felt I was sort of stuck with that persona and was forced to deal with them—whether that meant telling them how I felt about them or trying to explain myself to them.

Another student acknowledged that it was possible to adapt her behavior and her conception of the self to the situation, "I was really closing off a lot of people from my life. This trip has taught me that not every friendship has to be a soul connection. I can learn a great deal simply from hearing someone's itinerary. Everyone has a story to tell. . . . I have also found that it's totally enriching to know a lot of different people on many different levels."

The following comment by the same student came up in a later entry after the student had met two other teachers while abroad:

> I totally expected this travel experience to be a solo venture, but it looks like I will have company. It's a good thing: I think! Of course I won't get to savor things with the meditative attention I would like, but I will get to experience them through three sets of eyes instead of just one. Also like I mentioned earlier, I am beginning to discover the rich joys of casual meetings and chance friendships. . . . Why not share a part of yourself with as many people as possible? . . . They can teach you new things and highlight aspects of your personality you didn't know existed—both good and bad. It's fascinating. I have learned so much about being a teacher on this trip, but I must admit, that learning to relate to and understand people in totally different ways is the greatest lesson I will take away from my time abroad.

Other students commented on the fact that they learned more deeply about who they are and what they value. One student living in South Africa and experiencing being waited upon by housekeepers for the first time commented, "I found out that a big part of who I am is the little jobs I do around my house and the physical surroundings I help to create around me. Without those, I feel a little lost." Further, this student noted that the experience was a positive one, but realized a previously unacknowledged affinity for home with the comment "I am not sure I would do it for a long period of time in the future again because there are too many things at home that I have found I am too attached to."

Understanding Collectivism   Students comments suggest a beginning move from individuality towards collectivism—in recognizing that the group can alter the quality of one's experience. Throughout students' comments before, during, and after their experiences, the notion of reliance on others came up as a frequent theme. In predeparture writings, when commenting on ideas about support, responses seemed to fall into two categories of expectation—either of hopeful support by their hosts or a fear of stark aloneness. In-country journals also reflected reaction of support. One student expressed her feelings of aloneness this way:

> I wish I had someone to share this experience with me. I have come to the conclusion that for something to be "real" I must verbalize it to someone

who is on a similar wave-length as me. . . . I need those connections for an experience to be complete. This desire to share my life has really clarified the need for a sense of community in my life.

Yet other students recognized just how much support and how many people they had in their lives that they were able to rely upon. Much of this came via the use of e-mail, as one student noted, "Email has made contact with almost everyone from the experience very easy." A number of students reported an increased closeness to their families; for example, "I learned just how wonderful my parents are" and " I will always have support from those at home who care about me. From my professors to my friends to my family, I will never be alone, even when I'm in a different hemisphere."

The value of support networks as a learning tool emerged strongly, especially for the four students who remained in the longitudinal study two years after their experience. Although this group completed pre-departure orientation together, they each traveled to a different location. No expectations were set up for their communication with anyone other than their host and university supervisors. Via e-mail, they formed a support network, which apparently surprised even them, as one noted,

If you would have asked me if I thought I'd still be talking to these women after all of this was over when I first started, I would have said no. I'm not really someone who makes friends quickly, so it was a surprise to me how comfortable I felt with them after just a few meetings. As time went on and we all went our separate ways from COST, I was again surprised at our constant correspondence, and my growing affection for all of us involved. I did not expect to still be talking to these women, to be friends with them, or to count on them as much as I do. . . . I hope to keep in touch with them for the rest of my life, because we all share something so unique, so special, just like we all are.

Another student from the same group noted that the e-mail support network kept her in the placement when things were going badly, admitting, "I have never quit anything in my life, so the decision to leave was huge for me. . . . The girls were supportive and knew what I was going through so that I did not make a decision I would regret today." Another member noted that support came not only from the group but also from others who were perceived as having shared similar experiences.

> There was a lot of stuff to talk about, and definitely a lot of similar experience to be had (even though we were all over the place!). . . . All of these people were people who had similar experiences as to what I was having, and they offered insight on many personal and professional issues. I relied on the fact that I could "vent" to these people, whether it was good or bad, and they would respond quickly and honestly.

Cultural Impacts

Facing Tough "Truths": Challenging Ideas about Self and Other   The aforementioned discussions of self relate to another category of learning that comes from overseas student teaching. In examining what students were learning professionally and culturally, our analysis revealed that students begin to challenge their beliefs about the world and its people, and to develop empathy and trust. "I learned the importance of trying to understand where the other person is coming from," one student reported. Many students' comments clustered around learning to trust others as reflected in comments such as "I learned to be much less suspect of people—most of the time, people are good" or "I learned that people can be much more helpful and kind than I had thought." Another student's empathetic understanding became evident through a lack of language fluency, "I have to get over my fear of sounding stupid, it is the only way I will be able to learn to speak the language. At least now I can relate to others who come to America and have to learn English. It is very difficult when you are older and can be depressing and scary when you can't communicate what you want to be known."

Global Mindedness   Another aspect of increased cultural sensitivity involves learning about one's own culture. Once out of the United States, students are able to reflect back on the country they left, and examine it from a different space. Sometimes this is not a pretty picture. As one student noted, "I learned that other cultures are not as openly racist as in the United States, and that other cultures are more open to African Americans. I felt more welcome as an African American in Europe than

I typically do at home." Hanvey (1982) described this phenomenon as perspective consciousness—an ability to understand that one's own views, beliefs, and experiences are not universally shared—as one student succinctly stated,

> I was put in a position where I had to evaluate my own cultural beliefs. Preceding my trip, I knew no other culture than my own. Why does my country celebrate Halloween—a commemoration of evil spirits? Why do so many people in other countries think that Americans all run around with guns? These were questions I was forced to answer.

Overseas student teachers exhibited a shift in perspective consciousness both in how they viewed their host country and its relation to the United States, as well as their own beliefs about diversity. Explained one student, "I have become more knowledgeable about world events and less ethnocentric. I know that the U.S. is not the center of everyone's thoughts and actions." Still another noted, "Americans know so little about Australians and I think that is sad. Australians know so much about what happens in the U.S."

Further, because of the impact an international experience has on individuals, they begin to question their stereotypes of others and to question aspects of their own culture that had previously gone unexamined. Lambert noted, "Study abroad provides a student with an empathetic appreciation of the variety of perspectives that govern people's behavior throughout the world" (1989, 26). This ability to place oneself in another's shoes encourages the ability to make isomorphic attributions or similar judgments about another's behavior. Such a skill is critical to developing effective cross-cultural understanding and maintaining good communication (Cushner and Brislin 1996). According to Bennett (1998), this ability to shift perspectives is crucial to the development of empathy—an essential component of intercultural effectiveness.

Muddying the Waters: Confounding Stories of Cultural Experience

Our investigation also demonstrates that this learning about other cultures was not always positive. Some students were "appalled" at the things they saw happening in the classroom, as reported by the following student: "I was extremely disheartened to see that the teachers scream, yell, and even hit the kids in this school. The day was completely disorganized and the teacher sat from the back of the room to teach. It broke my heart to see that these students are missing out on a loving, caring, joyful education, but I guess it's up to me to bring it to them."

Negative responses like this bring up questions in two areas, the nature of the attributions students may be making when an experience is negative, and the degree of cultural nuance students are attending to in the experience.

Negative Attributions In terms of attribution, it is not clear whether or not students attributed what they negatively evaluated to aspects of the host culture, to the educational system, or simply to personalities of the educators involved. One student was highly dismayed at differences in supervision, noting,

> My cooperating teacher and other supervisors were largely ignorant of and critical of the U.S. system. They had no idea how to handle a student teacher who had very little classroom experience. . . . My resume had clearly outlined the extent of my experience but this was largely overlooked. . . . My supervisors were more focused on the "failure" of my home university to "properly prepare" me than reevaluation of their own set of criteria. . . . I would like to add that the [name of host university] should not be in the business of supervising U.S. interns.

In another example, a student bemoans the host faculty's lack of knowledge about certain educational principles she had been taught,

> I gathered more of a basal knowledge on exactly how the students are prepared to be teachers. . . . I'm amazed at the differences . . . you'd die if you saw the faces of the future teachers down here when I explained some of the love and logic principles! They just do NOT believe ANYTHING like that could EVER work because kids are all naughty, supposedly. [Emphasis in original]

Further, she describes a conversation with her cooperating teacher to a different pedagogical technique she introduced: "I have explained often the idea of the fiddle toy, but it is NOT taken well down here. 'It is

IMPOSSIBLE for a child to learn if his/her hands aren't in her lap and 100% watching the teacher. Our students can't handle that.' Even though that has been said, I have used a few items with some of my more active children (sneaky me!)."

Nonetheless, this student teacher also demonstrates that she is learning, as reflected upon in a later comment:

> The teacher is really nice outside of the room. However it was today that I began to understand why there are many teachers who are more distant. I made the comment that her students were writing extremely well on an assignment I gave them. I was so excited that they were working so hard!!! And, her reply was, "Well, it amazes me that you say that! You see, we Mexicans are not SO terrible like so many of you think!" Right there I knew what I was up against. They think I am here to be better than them. . . . so I made it my goal to let her know how eager I am to learn, and how we can learn a ton from one another.

Thus it is heartening to see that this student was able to examine the experience from a different perspective, but it is not clear what outcome this had on the student's overall attitude toward the host culture.

Cultural Nuances: Minimizing Cultural Differences?   Responses made by some students also seemed to indicate a lack of ability to detect or discriminate cultural nuances. Many students reported that they had learned that kids were kids the world over. One student commented, "Teenagers are teenagers, I found that my kids, all mostly Polynesian, were very loving and forgiving." According to Bennett (1993), this is a state of minimization of cultural differences, reflecting an ethnocentric understanding of culture. In Bennett's Developmental Model of Intercultural Sensitivity, minimization, along with denial of and defense against cultural differences, is an ethnocentric construal of culture. Minimization is the most advanced ethnocentric stage, directly preceding acceptance, an ethnorelative stage signifying the ability to recognize the validity of different cultures. One student noted, "I will use my experience to study other cultures as well as the Australian culture. Also, to help emphasize that people are the same despite some cultural differences."

In some cases, these nuances were related to the students' assessments of the similarities of the United States versus an international teaching context. Having observed a professional development day that highlighted differences between teachers and administrators, one student noted, "This distance is something I have picked up on in virtually every school I have been a part of in the States. It was fascinating to see the same problem existing in a different country." Another student working in Ecuador noted, "I think my teaching experience was almost equivalent to an experience in the States. What I did learn was how important goals are to the atmosphere and success of a school, which could have been learned anywhere." Another student who traveled to South Africa explained, "Teaching children seems to be the same no matter what continent you are on. Of course there are little differences, but overall, you need to apply the same things to students in Africa as you need to in the U.S. Kids are the same everywhere."

Finally, this lack of nuances also related to students' initial statements in a response that they had not experienced any real differences, even though the remainder of their responses often belied something else. For example, when asked about the possible change in one's philosophy after this experience, a participant responded, "I don't believe it really has other than the fact that I want to make my students more culturally aware through education." Or, in detecting differences between themselves and their U.S. counterparts, one student teacher commented, "I don't necessarily believe I am really different except I have more knowledge about Australia. Someone else may know more about Europe though, so I don't see it as a huge deal." The number of survey responses that indicate the tendency to minimize does bring up questions for individuals working with overseas student teachers, and additional research on the development of intercultural sensitivity could be undertaken.

PROFESSIONAL IMPACT

Translation of Experience to Teaching

We have found that students were able to channel what they learned regarding cultural difference into a view of education and

their classrooms. Their responses showed an increase in cognitive sophistication and flexibility, which Bennett (1993) noted is crucial to
increased cultural sensitivity. Noted one student, "I think a person's
philosophy of teaching is constantly changing and growing. I may not
see the difference in my philosophy of teaching now—it may surface
several years down the road. I am more able to see a balance of
process and content now."

Some students report an increased ability to be flexible and adapt
their teaching to student differences. One student admitted that she
now referred to herself as a facilitator rather than a "knowledge-giver,"
adding, "My time at [host school] taught me to focus on the needs of
children that I was teaching. It was not possible to assume the needs and
the levels of instruction that were appropriate. Because of this experience, I will be more thoughtful in my approach to the children that I
teach."

Another student recounted the experience of helping a student win a
schoolwide speech contest, "I had one student who was a real class
clown—always into mischief for attention. He was one of my ESL students. . . . I learned that even class clowns have talents that need to be
encouraged."

Language and Cultural Differentials

Like the aforementioned example, returnees noted an increased ability to work with second-language learners. In fact, teachers placed in
English-speaking as well as non-English-speaking countries report new
understandings about language teaching. One student placed in an international classroom in Switzerland where English was the language of
instruction reported on how surprised she was that the differences in
native languages would affect her classroom:

> I have learned that I can never take for granted what the students under-
> stand. When asked, 95% of the time the student will tell me that he or she
> understands even when it is clear that he or she does not. Therefore, it has
> become paramount that I encourage questions even when it disrupts the
> immediate lesson. After all, when my students don't understand, what sort
> of lesson is it anyway? Even if generally speaking we are all using the same

language, there are so many subtleties within that language that it has significant implications for how the class learns.

Another student, though not a native Spanish speaker, was placed in a Mexican public school due to her host's impression of her fluency, attested to the impact it had on her skills in the United States:

I now know where many of my students come from. I have many students who come from public schools in Mexico, and because I know the Mexican curriculum, I am able to help students and families with their transitions to the United States. In turn, I help the administration and teaching staff interpret scores and grade levels of students based on their outcome in the Mexican school setting.

One student resonated more with multicultural education after her experience, stating, "The biggest change that happened to me was that I become much more multicultural in my view of the world. I believe that multicultural education happens every day, and that this can become a mindset for the teacher—rather than an occasional effort. I owe this to my overseas teaching experience."

And another student, noting how this influenced teaching techniques, stated,

I have had to alter the work level to fit each student's needs. Many times I have stopped class and discussed the different strategies people have used to solve problems. Looking at everyone's ideas helps others to see that there isn't just one right or wrong answer. Some of the students from different nationalities have used strategies that other students were unaware of.

This observation is consistent with what global educators have proposed. Merryfield suggested that many educators find parallels between the multiple realties that exist in a community or a given country as well as globally.

This recognition is what has led many people concerned with domestic diversity and equity to make connections with global diversity and equity and become interested in how global perspectives can inform multicultural education. For others, the recognition of the interconnectedness of local and global intersections of power, discrimination and identity turned their attention to domestic diversity in order to pursue local ramification so globalization. (2001, 6)

Other students reported on translating their COST experience to new jobs in urban environments. One student, for example, took a position in a large Midwestern urban district.

Professionally, I could have never arrived and thrived in the situation I am currently in without the experience with COST. Six months after my return I was knee deep in [City name] Public Schools, with a class that spoke English, but somehow it was all a different language. I had to utilize all of the tactics from Mexico (not knowing any Spanish) the same way on the West Side of [city]. . . . This wasn't much different than being in Mexico, a whole different culture that I knew little about, be it Mexican or African American. Plucked out of my small town in the UP and put into a new world that I had no experience with, everything was new and different. Personally, being alone in a big city again after living in Mexico City was not as much of a shock as it would have been otherwise. I credit my COST experience with my survival after moving here both personally and professionally. I know I would have never made it through the first year of teaching here in [city] without my COST time, I wouldn't have known how. COST provided me with a safe and supportive environment to test and retest my knowledge and skills. . . . It has made all the difference.

Becoming a Conduit

Numerous students reported on ways in which their presence seemed to have an impact on those with whom they came in contact, both while overseas as well as when they returned home. Some students noted genuine surprise that overseas teachers were interested in U.S. pedagogical techniques or asked questions about things such as research literature. Other host teachers, almost apologetically, commented on the conduct of their students, saying, "U.S. students must be much better behaved than this," which then led to a conversation about student differences.

One student teacher added, "I learned to win the hearts of my students through intercultural exchange. As we put to rest stereotypes, we began to learn and understand each other."

Upon her return, another student noted using her Australian experience to intrigue her students,

> I learned a lot about the natural history of Australia and its ecosystem—and I can apply that to my teaching of biology now. Who doesn't like learning ecology with gum trees and koalas? I use lots of Australian examples in my teaching because a lot of students are interested in Australia, and besides that, I talk to them about going overseas myself to get them interested in going themselves.

This teacher and others were using their experience to encourage others to study abroad. Numerous respondents discussed a desire to speak to current teacher-education students about taking on the experience, saying such things as, "I recommend this experience to anyone who isn't afraid of change. . . . People are also very impressed to hear that I was in NZ. They ask many questions and I enjoy telling them all about it." And in at least one case, an overseas student teacher used the experience to be a conduit into another profession:

> I am definitely still touched and influenced in my daily life and decision making by my experiences abroad. I would have to say that I was consumed with the experience when I first got home, then not much during my bitter "never want to be a teacher phase," and now more than ever since I plan on implementing all that I have learned in a non-classroom sort of way. . . . I was not made to be a traditional classroom teacher, but have found my passion in nonprofit/government administration where I can make a difference in children's lives in a new way.

Finally, this student and many others reported on the continued contact with individuals in their placement. Participants discussed many ways they were still in contact with their experience, including traveling back to the site, pen-pal exchanges in the classroom, having visitors from abroad, sending students or other family members abroad, traveling with hosts or other teachers, and, of course, those few who got married and now travel to see in-laws!

WHAT ELSE WE'VE LEARNED FROM THE DATA

While stronger patterns existed in the aforementioned categories, a few student responses also indicate areas that may prove rich areas for further thought. These include connections between content and context, and negative assessment of support structures.

Context and Content

Few students seemed to make connections between the content they were studying to teach and the place they were teaching—either before or after going abroad. Two secondary English students did make a comment that they had the opportunity to study specific literature, and two others commented on better understanding the whole-language concept after being in New Zealand. However, these students were by far the exception. One student, while commenting on her positive experience, noted that she would never actually teach a unit about Australia; she was an elementary teacher. Merryfield (2000) has frequently discussed the lack of global perspectives in the U.S. teacher-education curriculum.

Negativity

By far, the majority of candidate responses were positive. Having met or exceeded their expectations, students frequently noted that the experience was something that they would carry with them for their lives. In the cases where there were negative responses, these tended to cluster into two areas—accommodations and support. With regard to accommodation, negative responses were most often associated with homestays (and in a few cases, other living arrangements, such as apartments or shared housing). Student concerns indicated extremes—that is, they either felt smothered or abandoned. More research is needed on the nature of homestays; however, again it underscores the need to invest the time and energy into clearly discerning student and host preferences and expectations prior to departure and to determine how this dimension may have an impact on other parts of the experience.

The second area of negative responses comes under the heading of support. This refers to supervision by the host, the home university, or the perceived "friendliness" of the host staff. Some students felt that their in-country supervisors visited infrequently or were too often pulled away by other duties to be effective. Just as difficulties may arise with field supervision in U.S. placements, the overseas context is no different. However, the obvious geographic distance makes swift attention to any problems more challenging for the U.S.-based overseas program coordinator. Conversely, students reported a lack of attention from their home-based faculty. Students who leave with the expectation that they will still have the support of a U.S. supervisor or faculty member are dismayed when they receive less help than expected. Finally, negative responses are found in comments that students perceived their host staff or cooperating teacher either to be unfriendly or simply did not want the student teacher in the room. As one student noted in her journal, "If she didn't want an American student teacher, why did she ever agree to take one in the first place?" This may also be coupled by a perceived anti-American sentiment on the part of the hosts.

FUTURE DIRECTIONS

The data reported in this chapter provide only a snapshot of the overseas student-teaching landscape. More research needs to be conducted in a number of areas to strengthen the understanding of the impact of overseas student teaching, to improve the experience, and to strengthen the database and, in turn, the case for increasing overseas placements for students.

Longitudinal Studies

Cochran-Smith and Zeichner (2005) report that, in general, teacher education is in need of more longitudinal studies. We concur and call for more long-term studies of individuals who have completed overseas student teaching. Studies of this nature could focus on the degree to which personal outcomes such as perceived self-efficacy have endured, the beliefs about diversity, and most especially, if and how teachers might be using their experience to positively affect student outcomes.

Empirical Studies

The majority of studies reviewed were qualitative in nature. Further research could be undertaken that examines attitudes of students predeparture, during the experience, and postreturn—ideally in conjunction with the aforementioned longitudinal studies. Studies of intercultural development utilizing the Intercultural Development Inventory (Hammer and Bennett 1999) or other instruments could also be investigated.

Candidate Characteristics

Studies examining dispositions of the candidates could be measured by instruments such as self-efficacy scales to determine if the reported increase in personal growth in this area is due to programmatic effects or preexisting participant effects. In addition, some students reported events in their lives where they had a previous interest in a culture or country or an experience traveling abroad or meeting international visitors that influenced their decision to pursue international student teaching. Therefore, life-history research into the attributes that define the profile of the international student teacher might yield data that more fully describes the population, helping to differentiate our understanding of recruitment and retention issues.

Structure of the Experience

Reviews of journals by the students as well as e-mail messages show that the students are often not reflecting on aspects of their teacher education unless prompted by an assignment or when a day presents itself as an extreme—either very negative or very positive. Because participants in this study came from a number of different universities, we recommend conducting research that more carefully utilizes the journal to its best ability. Further, we recommend collecting data about the effectiveness of predeparture orientation as a way to evaluate program impact.

CONCLUSION

In conclusion, we believe that research focusing on the benefits of overseas student teaching is rich and ripe. Not only is there ample evidence that past and present candidates reap a great deal from the experience, but evidence also shows that they carry their experiences into their futures. There are numerous research areas we have not explored here and many questions remain. Although we acknowledge that there are strengths and limitation to this research, we have found many ways researchers can continue looking at this topic from multiple perspectives. As research showing the benefits of international experiences for teacher candidates is brought to the attention of those in the education field, we hope that more universities will consider offering overseas options for students preparing to teach.

This review of the literature and our own experience suggest that overseas student teaching adds a rich dimension to the student teacher's cultural competence and the goal of teacher-education programs to prepare culturally responsive teachers. In this way, the field of teacher education can take the lead and broaden its international scope to respond to the needs of children in the twenty-first century and beyond.

REFERENCES

Baker, B. R. 2000. Moving beyond our education community: Student teaching abroad. Paper presented at the annual meeting of the Association for Childhood Education International, Baltimore, MD, April, 17–20.

Baker, F. J., and R. Giacchino-Baker. 2000. *Building an international student teaching program: A California/Mexico experience*. ERDS ERIC Document No. ED449143.

Bennett, M. J. 1993. Towards ethnorelativism: A developmental model of intercultural sensitivity. In *Education for the intercultural experience*, ed. R. M. Paige, 21–71. Yarmouth, ME: Intercultural Press.

———. 1998. Overcoming the golden rule: Sympathy and empathy. In *Basic concepts of intercultural communication: Selected readings*, ed. M. J. Bennett, 191–214. Yarmouth, ME: Intercultural Press.

Bhawuk, D., and H. Triandis. 1996. The role of culture theory in the study of culture and intercultural training. In *Handbook of intercultural training*. 2nd ed., ed. D. Landis and R. Bhaghat, 17–34. Newbury Park, CA: Sage.

Billingmeier, R. T., and D. Forman. 1975. Gottlingen in retrospect. *International Review of Education* 21:215–30.

Bradfeld-Kreider, P. (1999). Mediated cultural immersion and antiracism: An opportunity for monocultural preservice teachers to begin the dialogue. *Multicultural Perspectives* 12:29–32.

Bryan, S. L., and M. M. Sprague. 1997. The effect of overseas internships on early field experiences. *Clearing House* 70, no. 4:199–201.

Calhoon, J., D. Wildcat, C. Annett, R. Pierotti, and W. Griswold. 2003. Creating meaningful study abroad programs for American Indian postsecondary students. *Journal of American Indian Education* 42:46–57.

Case, R., and W. Werner. 1997. Building faculty commitment for global education. In *Preparing teachers to teach global perspectives: A handbook for teacher educators*, ed. M. M. Merryfield, E. Jarchow, and S. Pickert, 189–208. Thousand Oaks, CA: Corwin Press.

Cochran-Smith, M., and K. M. Zeichner, eds. 2005. *Studying teacher education: The report of the AERA panel on research and teacher education*. Mahwah, NJ: Lawrence Erlbaum.

Cushner, K. 2004. *Beyond tourism: A practical guide to meaningful educational travel*. Lanham, MD: Scarecrow Education.

Cushner, K., and R. Brislin. 1996. *Intercultural interactions: A practical guide*. 2nd ed. Thousand Oaks, CA: Sage.

Cushner, K., and A. Karim. 2004. Study abroad at the university level. In *Handbook of intercultural training*. 3rd ed., ed. D. Landis, M. Bennett, and J. Bennett, 290–308. Thousand Oaks, CA: Sage.

Cushner, K., and J. Mahon. 2002. Overseas student teaching: Affecting personal, professional and global competencies in an age of globalization. *Journal of International Studies in Education* 6, no. 2:44–58.

Gibson, S., and M. H. Dembo. 1984. Teacher efficacy: A construct validation. *Journal of Educational Psychology* 76, no. 4:569–82.

Hammer, M. R. 1987. Behavioral dimensions of intercultural effectiveness: A replication and extension. *International Journal of Intercultural Relations* 11:65–88.

Hammer, M. R., and M. J. Bennett. 1999. The Intercultural Development Inventory (IDI) manual. Portland, OR: Intercultural Communication Institute.

Hanvey, R. G. 1982. An attainable global perspective. *Theory into Practice* 21, no. 1:162–67.

Jarchow, E. 1997. The dean's role in infusing global perspectives throughout a
    college of education. In *Preparing teachers to teach global perspectives: A
    handbook for teacher educators*, ed. M. M. Merryfield, E. Jarchow, and S.
    Pickert, 209–25. Thousand Oaks, CA: Corwin Press.

Kauffman, N. L., J. N. Martin, H. D. Weaver, and J. Weaver. 1992. *Students
    abroad, strangers at home: Education for a global society*. Yarmouth, ME:
    Intercultural Press.

Kiely, R., and D. Nelson. 2003. International service learning: The importance
    of partnerships. *Community College Journal* (January): 39–41.

Kissock, C. 1997. Overseas student teaching. In *Preparing teachers to teach
    global perspectives: A handbook for teacher educators*, ed. M. M. Merry-
    field, E. Jarchow, and S. Pickert, 123–42. Thousand Oaks, CA: Corwin
    Press.

Koester, J. 1987. *A profile of the U.S. student abroad—1984 and 1985*. New
    York: Council on International Educational Exchange.

LaBrack, B. 1993. The missing linkage: The process of integrating orientation
    and reentry. In *Education for the intercultural experience*, ed. R. M. Paige,
    241–80. Yarmouth, ME: Intercultural Press.

Ladson-Billings, G. 1994. *Dreamkeepers: Successful teachers of African-Amer-
    ican children*. San Francisco: Jossey-Bass.

———. 1995. But that's just good teaching! The case for culturally relevant ped-
    agogy. *Theory into Practice* 34, no. 3:159–65.

Lambert, R. D. 1989. *International studies and the undergraduate*. Washing-
    ton, DC: American Council on Education.

Landerholm, E., C. Gehrie, and Y. Hao. 2004. Educating early childhood
    teachers for the global world. *Early Child Development and Care* 174, nos.
    7–8:593–606.

Landis, D., M. Bennett, and J. Bennett. 2004. *Handbook of intercultural train-
    ing*. 3rd ed. Thousand Oaks, CA: Sage Publication.

Landis, D., and R. Bhaghat. 1996. A model of intercultural behavior and train-
    ing. In *Handbook of intercultural training*. 2nd ed., ed. D. Landis and R.
    Bhaghat, 1–16. Thousand Oaks, CA: Sage.

Mahan, J. M. 1982. Community involvement components in culturally-oriented
    teacher preparation. *Education* 103, no. 2:163–72.

———. 1984. Major concerns of Anglo student teachers serving in Native Amer-
    ican communities. *Journal of American Indian Education* 23, no. 3:19–24.

Mahan, J. M., and L. L. Stachowski. 1990. New horizons: Student teaching
    abroad to enrich understanding of diversity. *Action in Teacher Education* 12,
    no. 3:13–21.

Martens, M. J. 1991. Analysis of the perception of the participants in the German Marshall Fund of the United States teacher in-service training. PhD diss., Oklahoma State University, Stillwater.

McFadden, J., M. M. Merryfield, and K. Barron. 1997. *Multicultural and global/international education: Guidelines for programs in teacher education*. Washington, DC: American Association of Colleges of Teacher Education.

Melchiori, A. 1987. Relationship between undergraduate academic study abroad and subsequent academic performance. PhD diss., Washington State University, Whitman.

Merryfield, M. M. 1995. Institutionalizing cross-cultural experiences and international expertise in teacher education: The development and potential of a global education PDS network. *Journal of Teacher Education* 46:1–9.

———. 2000. Why aren't teachers being prepared to teach for diversity, equity, and global interconnectedness? A study of lived experiences in the making of multicultural and global educators. *Teaching and Teacher Education* 16:429–43.

———. 2001. Implications of globalization for teacher education in the United States: Towards a framework for globally competent teacher educators. Paper presented at the fifty-third annual meeting of the AACTE, Dallas, TX, March 3.

Merryfield, M. M., E. Jarchow, and S. Pickert, eds. 1997. *Preparing teachers to teach global perspectives: A handbook for teacher educators*. Thousand Oaks, CA: Corwin Press.

Nash, D. 1976. The personal consequences of a year of study abroad. *Journal of Higher Education* 17:191–203.

Pettigrew, T. 2001. Does intergroup contact reduce racial prejudice throughout the world? Paper presented at the second biennial meeting of the International Academy for Intercultural Research, Oxford, MS.

Pfnister, A. O. 1972. *Impact of study abroad on the American college undergraduate*. Denver, CO: University of Denver. ERIC Document Reproduction Service No. ED063882.

Pike, G. 2000. Preparing teachers for global citizenship: The impact of the specialization in international education. *Exceptionality Education Canada* 10, no. 1–2:95–106.

Sikkema, M., and A. Niyekawa. 1987. *Design for cross-cultural learning*. Yarmouth, ME: Intercultural Press.

Stachowski, L. L., and E. J. Brantmeier. 2002. Understanding self through the other: Changes in student teacher perceptions of home culture from immersion in Navajoland and overseas. Paper presented at the annual meeting of the Association of Teacher Educators, Denver, CO, February 2–6.

Stachowski, L. L., and J. A. Chlebo. 1998. Foreign educators provide feedback for the improvement of international student teaching experiences. *Action in Teacher Education* 19, no. 4:119–30.

Stachowski, L. L., and J. M. Mahan. 1998. Cross-cultural field placements: Student teachers learning from schools and communities. *Theory into Practice* 37, no. 2:155–62.

Stachowski, L., W. J. Richardson, and M. Henderson. 2003. Student teachers report on the influence of cultural values on classroom practice and community involvement: Perspectives from the Navajo reservation and abroad. *Teacher Educator* 39, no. 1:52–63.

Stachowski, L. L., and V. A. Visconti. 1998. Service learning in overseas nations: U.S. student teachers give, grow, and gain outside the classroom. *Journal of Teacher Education* 49, no. 3:212–19.

Wallace, D. H. 1999. Academic study abroad: The long-term impact on alumni careers, volunteer activities, world and personal perspective. PhD diss., Claremont Graduate School, Claremont, CA.

Weaver, G. 1993. Understanding and coping with cross cultural adjustment stress. In *Education for the intercultural experience*, ed. R. M. Paige, 137–68.Yarmouth, ME: Intercultural Press.

Wiseman, R., J. Hammer, and H. Nishida. 1989. Predictors of intercultural communication competence. *International Journal of Intercultural Relations* 13:349–70.

Yachimowicz, D. J. 1987. The effects of study abroad during college on international understanding and attitudes toward homeland and other cultures. PhD diss., University of California, Riverside.

Zhai, L. 2000. The influence of study abroad programs on college student development on the College of Food, Agriculture and Environmental Sciences at the Ohio State University. PhD diss., Ohio State University, Columbus.

5

A WORLD OF POSSIBILITIES WITHIN THE UNITED STATES: INTEGRATING MEANINGFUL DOMESTIC INTERCULTURAL TEACHING EXPERIENCES INTO TEACHER EDUCATION

Laura L. Stachowski

There is no question that well-structured international field experiences can result in profoundly meaningful, life-transforming, learning outcomes that have an impact on student teachers in significant ways, both personally and professionally. Kissock, for example, suggested, "It is not possible to describe all the lessons learned by students who student teach in other countries. But we do expect and can observe that these students do develop their teaching abilities, expand their understanding of the role of education in society, and broaden their view of our world" (1997, 135).

Those of us who work with student teachers in overseas schools and communities would undoubtedly assert that *every* prospective teacher should be required to participate in international field experiences, arguing that what these emerging professionals achieve in terms of new knowledge, skills, and insights can seldom be matched by those who remain stateside to student teach, usually in their hometowns or not far from the university campus. However, the reality is that not every teacher candidate can avail himself or herself of the opportunity to participate in field experiences abroad, whether due to financial limitations, family circumstances, fear of flying, parental concern, or other factors that make leaving the country difficult, if not impossible.

Within our own borders, student teachers *can* participate in intercultural experiences that have the potential to result in the same kinds of powerful learning outcomes achieved through international student-teaching placements. As Kissock noted, "Whether in the United States or in another country, by assigning student teachers to communities and schools that introduce them to different cultural groups and economic settings, we can help them expand their worldview" (1997, 126). Merryfield (Knighten n.d.) similarly observed, "Immersion experiences in another culture are incredibly important if teachers are to understand the meaning of culture, reflect on culture learning and teach cross-cultural skills. However, people do not have to live outside the U.S. to have profound cross-cultural experiences." Indeed, well-structured domestic experiences in culturally different settings, characterized by preparation, on-site requirements, and guided reflection, can contribute significantly to preservice teachers' personal and professional growth, to the development of culturally responsive instruction, and to the formation of a broader worldview.

Recent trends reveal an urgent need for future educators, who are increasingly white, to gain the experiences that will enhance their proficiency in crossing cultural boundaries and their effectiveness in our nation's increasingly diverse elementary and secondary classrooms. Howard raised an alarm by asking, "How is it possible, with so much research and information available about multicultural issues today, that prospective educators can complete their entire teacher education and certification program without gaining a deeper grasp of social reality?" (2006, 30). The multicultural education course, today a common ingredient in teacher-training programs and often students' only exposure to diversity themes and issues, has been charged with falling short in preparing future educators to become culturally responsive in the classroom (Reyes, Capella-Santana, and Khisty 1998; Lenski et al. 2005). The problem is compounded in the schools, according to Howard, by the federal No Child Left Behind legislation, which "places little or no emphasis on increasing the cultural competence of teachers to work effectively with children from diverse racial and cultural backgrounds" (2006, 2). Darling-Hammond and Garcia Lopez perhaps sum up the problem most succinctly:

> It is impossible to prepare tomorrow's teachers to succeed with all of the students they will meet without exploring how students' learning experiences

are influenced by their home languages, cultures, and contexts; the realities of race and class privilege in the United States; the ongoing manifestations of institutional racism within the educational system; and the many factors that shape students' opportunities to learn within individual classrooms. (2002, 9)

This, then, brings us back to the development and provision of intercultural field experiences for preservice educators—field experiences located within the United States, giving student teachers the opportunity to immerse themselves in the lives of people who belong to culturally different groups, through school- and community-based placements. In addressing the question, "Why aren't teachers being prepared to teach for diversity, equity, and global interconnectedness?" Merryfield (2000, 429) explored the impact of "lived experiences" on teachers and teacher educators engaging in "significant experiences with people different from themselves" (440). When these lived experiences are combined with critical reflection on the dynamic interplay of identity, culture, and power, people begin to think about issues and events from others' perspectives, thus developing the perspective consciousness that is one of the defining characteristics of a world-minded educator.

The American Indian Reservation Project, offered through the cultural immersion projects at Indiana University-Bloomington, serves as a model of a long-standing, successful, *domestic* intercultural teaching experience whereby student teachers spend a full semester living and working on the Navajo Indian Reservation in Arizona, New Mexico, and Utah. Combining full-time student teaching in elementary and secondary classrooms serving Navajo youth with after-school and weekend involvement in the school's dormitory program and cafeteria, as well as in the local community, the reservation project helps participants "become more culturally sensitive and interculturally competent teachers who are able to adapt themselves and their instruction to be successful in any type of cross-cultural teaching situation" (Zeichner and Melnick 1996, 182). The purpose of this chapter is to describe the rationale, development, structure, and logistics of the cultural immersion projects, focusing specifically on the American Indian Reservation Project; the emphasis on community participation as a cornerstone of the on-site requirements; reported learning outcomes—new knowledge, skills, and insights—that clearly support the reservation project's important role in strengthening the intercultural teaching competence and broadening the worldview of emerging professionals; and recommendations rooted in years of experience for program developers of domestic intercultural teaching experiences.

THE CULTURAL IMMERSION PROJECTS AT INDIANA UNIVERSITY

The American Indian Reservation Project, together with its international counterpart, the overseas project, constitute the cultural immersion projects offered as optional alternatives to conventional student teaching through the Indiana University School of Education. Following an in-depth preparatory phase spanning two to three semesters, reservation project participants are placed for seventeen weeks in schools on the Navajo Indian Reservation, while overseas project participants complete a minimum of ten weeks of in-state student teaching, followed by eight-plus additional weeks of classroom teaching experience in primary and secondary schools of Australia, China, Costa Rica, England, India, Ireland, Kenya, New Zealand, Russia, Scotland, Spain, Turkey, and Wales. Characterized by a significant academic component and on-site cultural and community involvement, the cultural immersion projects have provided more than 3,000 preservice educators with professional experience in reservation and overseas schools while broadening their perspectives on others' ways of thinking, doing, and living.

Theoretical Framework of the Cultural Immersion Projects

Indiana University has a long history of involvement in both domestic and international projects and activities, largely through the early efforts of the late Chancellor Herman B. Wells, whose vision and commitment to scholarship and research resulted in the development of a vast network of national and international programs and connections that contribute to its world-class reputation today. Within the School of Education, the cultural immersion projects extend professional preparation through cross-cultural field experience featuring a sharply focused study of a particular cultural group by means of working and living within the host school and community. Recent years have witnessed a reconceptualization of teacher education at Indiana University, resulting in the emergence of six principles designed to undergird effective teacher-preparation programs. Applied to the cultural projects, these principles provide guidance and definition as the projects continue to evolve, ensuring that participants' needs are met and School of Education integrity is maintained. Thus, the reservation and overseas projects seek to

1. foster a sense of community among all parties involved, including participants, project staff, reservation and host-nation schools, and the local citizenry served by these schools;
2. encourage critical reflection on the multiple contexts in which schools function and on diverse perspectives on social and educational issues;
3. promote lifelong intellectual, personal, and professional growth and appreciation of learning;
4. include meaningful experiences in placement schools and communities;
5. promote well-grounded content knowledge and multiple forms of understanding what pupils bring to the classroom setting; and
6. provide personalized learning allowing participants' interests and values to shape major aspects of their reservation project or overseas project experiences.

Motivation, History, and Evolution of the Cultural Immersion Projects

The American Indian Reservation Project, with graduate-level preparatory and on-site requirements, was first implemented at Indiana University in the 1973–1974 academic year by Dr. James M. Mahan. Attending a "Triple T" (Trainers of Teacher Trainers) meeting in the early 1970s in Cleveland, Mahan was greatly inspired by three presenters—John Aragon, president of Highlands University in Las Vegas, New Mexico; Eugene Sekaquaptewa, chief administrator for the Hopi Reservation schools; and Barbara Sizemore, a prominent black educator from Chicago—who, together, called for greater minority involvement in teacher education. Already recognizing then the concerns that are widely cited today, Aragon, Sekaquaptewa, and Sizemore challenged teacher educators to move beyond the white, middle-class model dominating teacher preparation to include classrooms and communities outside of the mainstream, thus extending the experiences and sensitivities of preservice educators to include cultural groups different from those with whom the student teachers had grown up and been educated. Mahan responded to this challenge, eager to decrease some of this "more of the same" approach to teacher education these presenters saw taking place across the country, and ready to share the responsibility with school personnel and community members in preparing new teachers for the nation's changing demographics. With contacts on American Indian reservations in the Southwest, the reservation project emerged in the first semester of 1973–1974 as an integrated, academic, and field cultural option for student teachers, combining classroom experience with community and cultural participation. The overseas project followed a year later, through Mahan's professional connections with Dr. Ross Korsgaard, director of the Wisconsin-based Foundation for International Education. Mahan added the overseas project to bring an international dimension to cross-cultural field experiences with placements made in England, Wales, Scotland, Ireland, Australia, and New Zealand. Thus, the cultural immersion projects were born.

I (Laura Stachowski) am the current director of the cultural projects. I participated as a student teacher in the overseas project in 1979 and returned in the early 1980s to work with Mahan as a graduate student and eventually full-time assistant until his retirement in 1995, when I then assumed directorship of the cultural projects. Early in my graduate school experience, I was influenced by Robert Hanvey's *An Attainable Global Perspective* (Merryfield 1997), appreciating even today its timeless applicability to both the overseas and reservation projects in promoting perspective consciousness, "state of the planet" awareness, cross-cultural awareness, knowledge of global dynamics, and awareness of human choices. In 1996, I began to expand the host-nation options offered through the overseas project by developing placement sites in India. These efforts were then extended to Kenya, Costa Rica, Spain, Russia, China, and most recently, Turkey. Concurrently, connections were forged with new schools on the Navajo Indian Reservation. I have

also continued the close collaboration started by Mahan with the Foundation for International Education, working with Korsgaard on program
development efforts, publications, and conferences. Noteworthy, too, is
the recognition the overseas project received in 2005 as a co-recipient
of the Excellence in International Education prize awarded by the
Goldman Sachs Foundation and Asia Society, and in 2001 as the sole re-
cipient of the Best Practice Award for Global and International Teacher
Education awarded by the American Association of Colleges for
Teacher Education.

Thus, these cultural projects began more than thirty years ago
through the inspired vision and dedication of their founder, Jim Mahan, and over the years have developed into sought after and respected student-teaching options preparing and placing more than
150 participants in reservation and overseas schools and communities
annually. Their continued success is deeply entrenched in the close,
collaborative efforts of people across the globe who carry joint responsibility for the ongoing development, implementation, and evaluation of the reservation and overseas projects. New initiatives are continually being explored, and it is expected that the cultural projects
will continue to thrive, due in large part to the support they receive
from the Indiana University Teacher Education Program and School
of Education administrators.

AMERICAN INDIAN RESERVATION PROJECT

With the framework and history of the cultural immersion projects serving as a backdrop, we turn now to a closer examination of the American
Indian Reservation Project, including its goals, implementation, and logistics, as well as its emphasis on participants' cultural and community
participation in conjunction with full-time student teaching. Focused
academic study undergirds both the preparatory and on-site phases of
the reservation project, requiring that participants explore beyond the
surface of the "cultural iceberg" (Brown and Kysilka 2002, 69) to acquire new learning and related professional and cultural insights that
can be applied in any classroom setting.

Goals of the American Indian Reservation Project

Five major goals serve to guide the experiences of participants in the reservation project:

1. provide opportunities for student teachers to live and work in a culturally different setting and to utilize culturally appropriate and pluralistic learning activities and materials in the classroom;
2. enhance the teaching performance of elementary and secondary student teachers with an emphasis on their ability to function as effective and understanding educators of American Indian youth;
3. increase student teacher understanding of the history, culture, values, and aspirations of American Indians;
4. augment the instructional resources of school systems serving American Indian pupils through the annual provision of highly motivated, well-prepared, and dedicated student teachers; and
5. make a small contribution toward the development and acceptance of "cultural pluralism" in our national life.

With the unofficial motto of "learning through experience," the reservation project seeks to develop and hone the professional skills, knowledge, and dispositions of preservice educators through sustained classroom experience, while contributing to their understanding of issues surrounding race, culture, language, and socioeconomic concerns through active, required community participation.

Implementation and Logistics of the Reservation Project

Program applicants enter the American Indian Reservation Project early in the academic year preceding student teaching, typically their junior year, to undergo extensive preparation for the educational practices and cultural values, beliefs, conditions, and lifestyles of the reservation schools and communities in which they will be placed. Preparatory activities include class sessions, interviews, readings, abstracts and papers, a two-day workshop, and sessions with both former project participants and Navajo consultants. The preparatory assignments are

completed *in addition to* the students' regular course requirements in
their teacher-education programs. One such assignment, for example,
engages each project participant in a structured interview over
Fedullo's (1992) *Light of the Feather*. With a reservation project coordinator, the student examines Fedullo's journey into "contemporary
Indian America" through a discussion of issues surrounding culture
shock, stereotypes, verbal and nonverbal communication patterns, assimilation and acculturation, education practices, and American Indian values. A second required text, *American Indians: Answers to Today's Questions* (Utter 2001), combined with a series of articles
available on electronic reserves, requires that participants explore and
write about such themes as American Indian education and culture,
Navajo identity, Navajo education, culturally relevant classrooms, and
contemporary issues facing American Indians. Taken together, these
requirements not only familiarize the student teachers with the
schools and culture in which they will be expected to operate, but they
also serve as an effective self-screening device in that applicants whose
primary motivation may be to "see the Southwest" are discouraged by
the intensive preparatory work. The preparatory phase receives ongoing review and evaluation by the project director and staff, and feedback from project participants, as well as from collaborators in the
reservation schools, is utilized in revising assignments to better fit the
students' preparatory needs.

During the student-teaching semester, participants in the reservation
project are placed for sixteen to seventeen weeks in Bureau of Indian
Affairs, contract/grant, and public schools across the Navajo Nation, in
a range of elementary, secondary, and K–8 settings. Placement requests
are sent directly from the cultural projects office to the collaborating
reservation schools, who are pleased to accept the recommended student teachers and provide the necessary support in terms of supervision,
guidance, and evaluation. Students are generally placed in pairs, with
consideration given to relative location (some of the reservation sites are
extremely isolated, whereas others border sizeable towns such as Gallup
and Farmington), transportation (efforts are made to ensure that at least
one student in each pair intends to take a vehicle to the reservation site),
and gender (school housing usually is shared in the school dormitory).
Placement in pairs encourages peer support and helps ease safety con-

cerns, especially on weekends when most of the dormitories close (boarders are bussed home), although the student teachers are permitted to remain.

While at their reservation sites, project participants are placed with supervising classroom teachers and expected to engage fully in all teacher-related functions of the school, including classroom instruction, pupil supervision, committee participation, meeting attendance, and extracurricular involvement. Participants live in isolation rooms or apartments in the placement school's dormitory and provide academic tutoring, companionship, role modeling, and "life enhancement" activities for the young Navajo dorm residents. They also assist in the preparation and serving of breakfast and dinner in the adjacent cafeteria. Further, they visit social service agencies and the local chapter house, attend public meetings, shop at local businesses, and take part in local and reservation-wide fairs and festivals. Such dormitory, cafeteria, and community experiences enable the student teachers to interact closely with people at the grassroots level in a wide range of activities—from the ordinary tasks of daily life to special events and traditional ceremonies— and thus learn firsthand about the people and communities from which their school pupils emerge. Often the student teacher for the first time is a "minority of one," adapting to, and fitting into, a world that is far different from "back home."

Ongoing reflection and academic reporting are critical components of the on-site experience, with structured biweekly reports and two major projects required of each participant. The seven biweekly reports are designed to document the student teacher's involvement in the school, dorm, cafeteria, and community; to provide a mechanism for highlighting new experiences and related insights across each reporting period; and to explore in depth a range of topics pertinent to reservation schooling, conditions, and community life through structured essays. For example, student teachers are required to identify specific cultural values they have observed operating in their placement communities, and to describe the ways in which an understanding of these values has an impact on their involvement in school and community contexts. They study important institutions in their placement communities and the extent to which these institutions serve the local residents. They identify current issues affecting the Navajo people, seeking to understand the various

sides of the issues they have selected and the solutions people are offering to resolve these issues. They write essays on such topics as pupil
achievement, dormitory life, the impact of No Child Left Behind, and
gender roles in Navajo society. They also look inward to write about, and
understand, the prior assumptions they held that have been challenged,
and the ways in which their perceptions of their "home" culture may
have shifted. Each biweekly report concludes with an "unstructured
personal expression" through which the student teachers share additional new insights and information that may not easily fit into other
parts of the structured reports, often using poems or sketches as their
means of expression.

In addition to the biweekly reports, reservation project participants
are required to complete a service learning project in the placement
community and a final "graduate" project. One option for the final project is a second service learning project, although most student teachers
choose the inquiry project, which may take the form of a position paper,
a research project, a set of curriculum materials, or a PowerPoint presentation. Specific guidelines and criteria are provided for each option to
maintain the structure and academic integrity of the students' on-site
work. As a whole, the on-site assignments require that student teachers
examine what Heuberger calls the "characteristics and systems of culture" (2004, 98), helping them grasp the complexity of culture by de-
constructing complicated ideas, dynamics, and relationships, and thus
seeing the similarities and differences more easily.

Contact is maintained with the cultural projects office throughout the
on-site experience by telephone and correspondence. Staff members
write detailed feedback letters to participants upon receiving their assignments and reports, and calls are placed when concerns arise or
points require clarification. The project director visits each participant
at the beginning of the semester to ensure that the student teachers are
off to a strong start, to resolve any early concerns, and to connect with
the classroom teachers, administrators, and dorm supervisors who will
be working with the student teachers over the subsequent weeks. Mid-
way through the semester, a staff member returns to conduct formal
classroom observations, to "troubleshoot" with those student teachers
who need the extra support, and to conduct a daylong seminar for the
entire group at a centrally located school. Reservation school personnel,

usually administrators or department heads, are designated as external supervisors who observe, provide feedback, and serve as resources should questions or problems arise at any time in the semester. Further, all reservation project participants know that the cultural projects office is a phone call away, and with few exceptions, e-mail enables the student teachers to maintain contact with project staff as often as needed and re-ceive feedback on their academic assignments within a few days of sub-mitting them electronically.

In addition to earning their student-teaching credit through the cul-tural projects, participants also earn a minimum of nine credits at the 500-level (master's) for the academic work completed during the preparatory phase and while on site, and for the cultural immersion ex-periences achieved through reservation school, dormitory, cafeteria, and community involvement. Although a few students apply their graduate credits toward the completion of their undergraduate degrees, most choose to "bank" those credits to use as electives later on in a master's program and/or to apply toward incremental salary increases once they have begun in-service teaching.

Thus, the American Indian Reservation Project is designed in such a way that emphasis is placed on *both* classroom teaching and community involvement experiences. Project participants cannot "just student teach"; rather, they must immerse themselves into the lives and cultures of the people with whom they live and work. Consequently, members of the placement community, along with the children, educators, and su-pervisors in the placement school, become vital contributors to student-teaching learning on many levels.

Cultural and Community Participation as a Cornerstone of the Reservation Project

Since its early beginnings more than thirty years ago, required cul-tural and community involvement has been a cornerstone of the Amer-ican Indian Reservation Project and remains an integral component of the project today. It is based on the premise that community members can and should have an active role in preparing student teachers for their work in local schools, and that knowledge of the community and an understanding of how to incorporate this knowledge into classroom practice can contribute significantly to the development of their inter-cultural teaching competence. Banks and co-workers asserted,

> The challenge of teaching diverse learners starts the moment teachers be-gin planning ways to connect their students with the subject matters they intend to teach. For this connection to occur, teachers must know their students—who they are, what they care about, what languages they speak, what customs and traditions are valued in their homes. This suggests that teacher education needs to include a variety of opportunities for teachers to learn about their students and the communities from which they come. (2005, 264)

The involvement of teachers in the communities served by their schools becomes even more significant in situations where the school and community may have different agendas and value systems, as Rhodes (1994) suggested is the case on some American Indian reserva-tions. Similarly, Gilliland voiced concern that "teachers are often not aware of the seriousness of the problems children have in being Indian in the non-Indian world of the school, problems rooted in the difference in cultures" (1995, 17). Gilliland advised teachers to "visit with people in the community at every opportunity. Let them see that you respect them and their culture, that you will be honest with them, that you are . . . interested in other things in the community besides the school" (22). Cleary and Peacock perhaps best summed up the need for teachers to connect with the communities which their schools serve:

> All told, the most important endeavor for teachers in Indian schools and in schools where Indian children are served is to see themselves as learn-ers, learners who are open to understanding the reasons the children and communities are the way they are, learners who are willing to discover and consider the differences between the cultures of the school and the home of the child, and learners who are willing to change their ways of teaching so that the children have a better chance in school and a better chance to have purpose and hope in their lives thereafter. (1998, 6)

Only then can prospective teachers gain new insights and perspectives on their placement communities and better understand and appreciate the circumstances of their pupils' lives.

Indeed, student teachers in the reservation project *live* in the same communities as their pupils, and through the semester-long placement, they complete specific requirements that necessitate their direct engagement with local community people. Contributing to the residential life program in the dormitory, assisting in the cafeteria, completing the service learning project, and even addressing the questions on the biweekly reports all require that the student teachers are talking with people, seeking their perspectives, working alongside them in a multitude of tasks, visiting them in their homes and community centers, and learning about their lives and traditions, thus tapping into the invaluable "funds of knowledge" (Moll et al. 1992) that informs their classroom practice and efficacy (Mahan and Stachowski 1993–1994).

Because of its emphasis on community involvement as a means of helping prospective teachers create bridges between their pupils' homes, the community, and the school, Zeichner and Melnick (1996) closely examined the American Indian Reservation Project as part of a five-year study funded by the U.S. Department of Education, the Office of Educational Research and Improvement, and the National Center for Research on Teacher Learning at Michigan State University. The reservation project was then featured by these authors in a chapter on community field experiences in their coedited book, *Currents of Reform in Preservice Teacher Education*. Zeichner and Melnick reported that through the preparatory and on-site phases of the reservation project, "there is a continual emphasis on the importance of adapting one's teaching to reflect, utilize, and build on cultural values and learning patterns," and that in their interviews with program participants and graduates, they found "much evidence of student teachers' making efforts to connect their classrooms to community people, practices, and values, even when cooperating teachers did not support these practices" (1996, 185).

Zeichner and Melnick (1996) further cited limited evidence that the outcomes reported by participants may continue to have an impact on their professional lives beyond the student-teaching experience. Deciding to teach in schools serving other ethnic minorities, advocating for an examination of curriculum materials from various cultural vantage points, and developing instructional units with American Indian themes are among the examples the authors offered. Zeichner and Melnick also described a "fundamental personal transformation" that appears to take place in project participants, often as the result of being a minority in a culturally different setting: "Most of the program graduates that we interviewed spoke to us with enthusiasm about how [the reservation project] had changed their lives and made them better people—more patient, less selfish, more understanding and open-minded and more aware of their privileged position in the world" (189).

Finally, Zeichner and Melnick (1996) observed that the extent to which the student teachers embraced the opportunities to become involved in his or her placement communities and forged friendships with local people seemed to be "a critical factor in determining the degree to which adaptations are made in the classroom based on cultural insights about one's pupils and their lives outside of school." In spite of the design of reservation project requirements to immerse participants in the community, some student teachers seemed to "minimize their contacts outside of school to superficial relationships" (191), remaining on the periphery and consequently not gaining the knowledge, insights, and support network necessary to have an impact on their instructional practice.

In concluding their examination of the American Indian Reservation Project, Zeichner and Melnick (1996) summarized that "the carefully structured community experiences in [the reservation project] serve to promote greater self-understanding and cultural learning on the part of most students," adding that "when community participation is great, student teachers are more likely to engage in culturally relevant teaching" (192). They recommended that teacher educators must find ways to include community field experiences in teacher-preparation programs, adding that the increasingly popular partnerships between universities and schools must also extend to the local communities if the development of teachers' intercultural competence is to be realized.

OUTCOMES REPORTED BY STUDENT TEACHERS IN THE AMERICAN INDIAN RESERVATION PROJECT

Much smaller in enrollment than its international counterpart (the overseas project), the American Indian Reservation Project serves approximately thirty to forty student teachers annually, placing them in schools and communities scattered across the vast, 27,000-square-mile Navajo

Indian Reservation. The experiences participants have on the Navajo Reservation are just as challenging, equally important, and as capable of being life-transforming as any student-teaching placement abroad. Student teachers in reservation schools struggle to understand children and teens who are straddling two worlds, caught between their Indian identity and the world of the majority culture, with the school context often a major disconnect between the two. Some of these children are angry and aggressive, not understanding why. The student teachers seek to provide meaningful instruction for children whose ability levels, in any given classroom, may vary from nonreaders to those who are well advanced for their age. In the school, dormitory, and community, the student teachers experience—often for the first time in their lives—what it means to be a minority in terms of race, language, and culture, wanting desperately to be liked and to gain acceptance but uncertain as to how to go about it in a society with its own set of social cues, mores, and unspoken rules for relationships and communication. The student teachers are usually geographically isolated, in communities that may be hours away from the nearest off-reservation town where they can shop and enjoy the kinds of activities that usually appeal to the twenty-something age group. In short, the reservation project is not an easy alternative to conventional student-teaching placements, and applicants are informed of this from the start. Instead of focusing only on school, participants must integrate the classroom experience with required community involvement, cultural study, ongoing reflections, and academic reporting.

Over the years, data have been amassed documenting the multiple outcomes of participation in the American Indian Reservation Project. Data collected by means of student teachers' on-site reports, during supervisory visits, and through ongoing correspondence with project participants and graduates have provided support that considerable new learning results from teaching and living on the Navajo Reservation, and that the connections fostered with Navajo educators, youth, and community members yield new experiences and insights that go far beyond the scope of student teaching alone. In the past eight years, a number of reports have emerged from these data, resulting in published articles describing the outcomes documented by participants. With topics ranging from service learning to the influence of cultural values, the message sent is that intercultural field experiences, combined with assignments that require community participation and critical reflection, result in new learning and related insights that move well beyond the classroom sphere, although have significant implications for classroom practice. Synopses of some of these reports follow.

Service Learning in Reservation Communities

As mentioned earlier, participants in the reservation project are required to plan, perform, and report on at least one service learning project that takes place in the local community, with the support of community citizens and/or agencies. In selecting their service learning projects, the student teachers must adhere to the "3 Rs" in that their projects should be *realistic, reflective,* and *reciprocal.* Stachowski and Frey (2005) analyzed the written reflections of thirty-nine student teachers who completed a total of fifty-three service learning projects in recent semesters. Projects were both family based (e.g., helping with the care of livestock, including herding sheep, goats, and cattle; repairing a hogan; helping with harvesting, hauling hay and water, and chopping wood; and assisting with preparations for traditional ceremonies) and community based (e.g., assisting with community fund-raisers; preparing and serving food at community Thanksgiving dinners; helping prepare and serve food at a funeral reception; and organizing a community cleanup for Earth Day with the dorm pupils).

In reflecting on their service learning projects, the student teachers reported overwhelmingly that these were eye-opening experiences, resulting in important new learning and insights they would never have gained otherwise. Five themes emerged from their written accounts of their service learning experiences. First, many of the student teachers appreciated that they were recipients of the gift of new knowledge about culture and society, given by the Navajo people with whom they lived, worked, and served. For example, Leana reflected on all she had learned through her assistance and participation in a "Blessingway," a traditional ceremony performed for a person's general well-being. The ceremony was for one of the dormitory staff, with whose family she had forged a close bond. "Learning about a people, their culture, and traditions firsthand has been the experience of a lifetime," she wrote. "It cannot be read in a book or taught in a classroom" (Stachowski and Frey 2005, 111).

A second theme that emerged in the student teachers' reflections was the development of a deeper appreciation for the circumstances in other people's lives, including a better understanding of the pupils in their classrooms and colleagues in the school. Annie and Beth, for example, had looked forward to herding sheep once they were on the reservation, and when the opportunity arose to help the family of one of Annie's pupils, Nate, they realized they had underestimated the amount of skill and patience that were necessary to herd sheep effectively. Twelve-year-old Nate and his elderly grandmother became the teachers, showing Annie and Beth how it should be done. Annie's subsequent reflections revealed her new appreciation for her fifth-grader:

> When Beth and I went to Emma's and I got the chance to see Nate in his environment, doing all his chores, I felt like I respected him more, cared about him more, understood him more. I realized he didn't go home every day and lounge in front of the TV, like I did when I was his age. Instead, he chopped wood or herded sheep, or he did another job that needed to be accomplished. That is far more than I can say when I was 12. I remember being selfish and lazy, to be quite honest, when I was that age. But watching Nate with his mother, grandma, and brother, I realized his responsibilities were those of a man. Knowing his life is probably not always easy, I feel as if I'm more understanding when he comes to school tired or even in a grumpy mood. He has added responsibilities to his homework load, and I can't imagine how a growing 12-year-old handles this type of load. (Stachowski and Frey 2005, 112)

A third theme involved the student teachers' belief that their service learning efforts resulted in greater acceptance in their placement communities, as community members recognized their willingness to work and learn, regardless of the tasks at hand. Rachel and Maggie, for example, had contributed in multiple ways to the funeral reception for their school's beloved bus driver, who had died unexpectedly. With the reception held in the school cafeteria, the student teachers helped prepare food, served, and cleaned up afterwards. They felt this had been a turning point in their acceptance into the community. Rachel reflected:

> Through all of my experiences on the reservation and this one in particular, it has become increasingly evident that it really does take a while to be

let into people's lives. I learned that in order to be let in at all, you have to make a conscious effort to show people who you are and why you are there through active involvement in the community. You must demonstrate your intentions through direct action. (Stachowski and Frey 2005, 115)

Fourth, some student teachers believed that their service learning projects resulted in important personal insights as they were challenged by new experiences, often well outside their comfort zones. Kathleen, for example, had offered to help out at a Hawaiian-themed birthday party that one of the cafeteria workers was throwing for family members. She described the personal impact of the experience as "profound," reporting that "it put me in the situation of being the racial minority. I had not been in this position before." Initially self-conscious, she wrote, "I was really sensitive to how people looked at me, whether or not they were talking about me, and whether or not I was going to do something stupid" (Stachowski and Frey 2005, 116).

For Rachel, it was grappling with her own "whiteness" that provided the greatest personal insight as she assisted at the funeral reception for Mr. Charley, the bus driver.

Almost all of the guests, in particular family members, said thank you to each server individually as they went through the line. Mrs. Charley even gave each of us a hug to show her gratitude for our efforts. Except for her, whose thank you was so sincere that I almost cried, those interactions made me somewhat uncomfortable, although I am not sure exactly why. I have theories, one of which is that it is not common for mainstream American culture to go out of your way to thank cafeteria workers or other people in menial positions. My other theory is that as the guest looked into my comparatively light brown eyes and saw my white skin, I felt that they should not have to thank me. While this experience had no resemblance to any major historical event, I felt like it was a confrontation with history. Here I was, one of two Anglos among a completely Navajo crowd, attempting to create a sense of amity between the Anglo and Navajo communities, a goal that has been consistently attempted and easily forgotten throughout history. And my ultimately insignificant presence as a volunteer at this community event could not possibly achieve such a lofty goal. (Stachowski and Frey 2005, 117)

Finally, a number of student teachers reported that their service learning activities helped them clarify their role on the Navajo Reservation.

Yes, they were there to teach, but it was more than that. For some, the service learning project was a segue into further service and social activities with people in the placement community. Leana valued the freedom to assume multiple roles in her community, whether tutoring children in the dorm or serving meals in the cafeteria, chaperoning dances and other school and dormitory events, or merely "playing" with the children after school. "While this leads to feeling stretched regarding our personal time," she reflected, "the rewards are countless. We are able to know the students inside and outside of the school. It offers us a perspective most teachers cannot have. What a gift" (Stachowski and Frey 2005, 118).

Influence of Cultural Values on Student Teachers' Classroom Practice and Community Involvement

Following the recommendations of Merryfield (1997), Sleeter and Grant (1999), and McLaughlin (2000) regarding the need for educators to study the diverse cultural values, patterns, and attributes of their pupils, Stachowski, Richardson, and Henderson (2003) examined the written reflections of student teachers in reservation and overseas communities, pertaining to the influence of cultural values, beliefs, and traditions on their classroom practice and community involvement. A total of twenty-eight participants in the reservation project generated 183 values, which were then grouped according to the following themes: traditional lifestyle, clan/family, community/group harmony, superstition/taboos, perception of time, elders, humor, Navajo language, sharing/reciprocity, modesty, and education. Further, the student teachers described their application of the values they identified in a range of professional, social, and personal ways.

For example, student teachers on the reservation usually learn early in their placements that clan affiliation is an important personal identifier, when Navajo teachers and dorm staff introduce themselves in terms of their clan membership. They discover, too, that the complex concept of "family" extends to clan members and distant relatives as well. Kate observed,

The Navajo people show the bond a family can have. Navajos are linked to their relatives by a strong rope that creates a web, interlocking them and allowing the exchange of duties and responsibilities. The young help the old by gathering crops, piñon nuts, and firewood for the winter. The elderly aid the youth by raising them and teaching them the ways of life. (Stachowski, Richardson, and Henderson 2003, 58)

In responding to the importance placed on the Navajo family and clan system, a number of student teachers planned activities in which their pupils outlined their clan trees rather than family trees. Several student teachers suggested that pupils could interview their grandparents and other family members to learn more about their childhoods and to strengthen the links between the youth and their elders. Others sought to encourage the participation of family members in classroom and dormitory activities.

In terms of "traditional lifestyle," many of the student teachers described the Navajos' strong oral tradition and love of storytelling, recognizing it as a way for people to pass on their values, traditions, and history, as well as a means for laughing, teasing, and showing appreciation for others. Student teachers' applications of this value included inviting elders to the classroom for traditional storytelling sessions with the pupils, having the class volunteer to spend time at a local senior center, and planning lessons on coyote tales and other aspects of Navajo folklore. Sensitive to the value placed on "group harmony," Debra sought to promote group harmony and a sense of community by planning dormitory projects and activities for multiage groups of girls, with the girls helping and teaching one another. She reflected, "This will encourage them to take responsibility for each other" (Stachowski, Richardson, and Henderson 2003, 60). Overall, the student teachers on the Navajo Reservation demonstrated sensitivity to the people in their placement schools and communities based on an emerging understanding of the values by which they sought to live their lives. By identifying and clarifying these values, and by exploring appropriate applications in a variety of classroom and community settings, the student teachers have shown that the insights gained can help them to gauge and modify their own behavior in school and community life.

Student Teachers' Reflections on Professional and Cultural Learning

Zeichner suggested that most preservice field experiences, including student teaching, narrowly focus on the classroom setting, lacking at-

tention to larger contexts, and consequently, they "often fail to prepare
student teachers for the full scope of the teacher's role" (1996, 216). In
the reservation project, participants are required to explore both classroom and community dynamics, issues, and trends, resulting in professional and cultural learning of a broader scope than that which Zeichner
described. Stachowski and Frey (2003) examined on-site report questions that served to direct the student teachers' identification of specific,
major professional and cultural learning outcomes. In terms of the "professional lessons" the student teachers learned through their semester-
long placement in reservation schools, they described insights related to
the art of teaching, classroom discipline, personal-professional characteristics, school pupils, curriculum, relationship building, and school
culture. Not surprising, many of the specific examples they cited represent the kinds of learning outcomes that also result in conventional
student-teaching assignments, such as developing daily and long-term
lesson plans, incorporating variety into lessons and activities, and differ-
entiating instruction. However, others were reflective of the student
teachers' placements in Navajo Reservation schools. For example, a significant professional insight for Helen was the realization that although
many of her elementary pupils were bilingual, they were proficient in
neither English nor Navajo. Thus, they experienced difficulty in following written and oral directions. Eventually, she discovered that the children "understood much better how to do things when it was explained
to them in Navajo, even if they could not speak it" (Stachowski and Frey
2003, 40) and consequently she teamed with her Navajo supervising
teacher and classroom assistant to present directions and explanations in
both languages.

On the other hand, the "cultural lessons" that the student teachers described supported the credence that when community participation and
cultural study are required components of field experiences, student-
teacher learning moves well beyond the sphere of the classroom and
school alone. Through their interactions with people in the dormitory and
cafeteria, and through their involvement with community organizations
and local families, the student teachers described insights related to the
relationship between traditional and modernity, contemporary Navajo society, cross-cultural communication, cultural competence, challenges in
Navajo education, pupils' living conditions, and historical understanding.

Although space prohibits a close examination of all of these topics, the implications for enhanced cultural sensitivity and intercultural teaching competence are clear.

For example, one of the primary reasons for incorporating community participation in the reservation project is to enable the student teachers to better understand their pupils' home circumstances, thus serving them more effectively in the classroom. For many non-Indian teachers, the cultural differences, material poverty, and unique social expectations for Navajo children are difficult to accept or even understand. Further, for many Navajo youth, family responsibilities occasionally are in conflict with the school's expectations. Pupil absenteeism is high in reservation schools, in part because many youth and their families are forced to choose between school attendance and participation in important, sometimes lengthy, cultural events and activities. One of the student teachers, Aaron, recalled attending the first night of a five-day Blessingway, observing that family members came and went throughout the night. Although many pupils will attend such ceremonies after school, others may be absent from school for a week or more to fully participate. Just as regular attendance is critical for pupils' school success, regular participation in the ceremonies is vital for Navajos to learn about their culture.

Changes in Student Teachers' Perceptions of Home Culture

In a somewhat different vein, Stachowski and Brantmeier (2002) asked sixty student teachers, thirty each on the reservation and overseas, to reflect upon their on-site experiences as a way of illuminating their changing perceptions of their "home" culture, which for most of them is "mainstream" U.S. culture. For many of these student teachers, this may have been the first time they were required to examine the factors that contribute to who and what they are, and the forces of family, ethnicity, community, and nation that shape the ways in which they perceive themselves and those around them. The thirty reservation project participants reported 111 different changes in their perceptions of "home" as a result of their intercultural experiences on the Navajo Reservation. These were categorized as having either a positive or negative slant and then further organized into themes. For participants in the reservation project, several themes emerged where the student teachers looked favorably upon new insights they had gained about their home culture: the education system, better communication, desire to learn more about home culture, convenience (including access to material goods), increased appreciation of family and interpersonal relationships, greater focus on environmental issues (including recycling policies), and better pet care and treatment.

On the other hand, far more changes in the student teachers' perceptions of the home culture were cast in a negative light. It seemed that student teaching in a culturally different setting—even within our nation's borders—led participants to analyze and question many of the aspects of their lives they had always assumed were a given, perhaps believing that their values and practices were universally shared. Among the themes in this category were the pace of life, an awareness of assimilation practices toward the Navajo, less importance placed on family and interpersonal relationships, a lack of community support, a lack of a sense of tradition/heritage, materialism, and wastefulness of energy and resources. For example, several participants believed that mainstream culture is overly materialistic based on their experience of relative poverty in the Navajo Nation. Wrote one student teacher, "Living out here has made me realize you don't need a million conveniences at your fingertips to be happy" (Stachowski and Brantmeier 2002, 17). One of the most significant changes in perception with a negative slant was a lack of a sense of tradition in the student teachers' home culture. One student reflected on the bonds of community felt and seen at a powwow he attended: "I cannot think of one thing in our culture that brings us together like that" (17). Another student seemed to feel cheated by her perceived sense that she "lacked" culture: "I don't feel the same sense of culture, tradition, and unity that I sense and observe among the Navajos. In my first week on the Rez, I came to the rude realization that I didn't think I had a culture, minus video games and shopping for 'stuff'" (17).

Just as Adler (1975) had suggested that although a cross-cultural experience may begin as a journey into another culture, it ultimately becomes a journey of enhanced awareness and understanding of oneself and one's home culture, which was indeed the case for the student teachers. In essence, they were given the opportunity to "see the self through the other," and in doing so, more fully understood themselves and others through living, teaching, and participating in Navajo schools and communities.

Student Teachers' Efforts to Promote Self-Esteem in Their Navajo Pupils

A final report to be examined here focuses on the efforts documented by forty-three student teachers on the reservation to promote, increase, and enhance the self-esteem of the Navajo youth in their elementary and secondary classrooms (Stachowski 1998). A total of 304 strategies and techniques, projects and activities, and specific books and materials were described by the student teachers, which were then organized into the following themes: using culturally relevant teaching units, materials, and resources; providing experiences that ensure pupil success, using positive reinforcement and other incentives, empowering pupils, encouraging the exploration of pupils' lives and identity; using alternative modes of teaching/learning/evaluation; promoting a sense of classroom community; individualizing efforts to meet the needs of specific pupils; and presenting to other classrooms and displaying pupils' work.

Overwhelmingly, the student teachers sought to make culturally relevant instruction a part of their classroom practice, responding to Gilliland's challenge, "How can Indian children believe that you really respect them, that you respect their culture, their ideas, and their people, unless you include the culture throughout their activities?" (1995, 94). They identified seventy-eight different approaches they had used in incorporating culturally relevant units and resources into a range of curricular areas including literature, science, math, art, music, and social studies. For example, one student teacher reported, "My students gave presentations on stories by a Navajo woman named Luci Tapahonso. By using the stories in class, they are legitimized in the eyes of the students as material worthy of study. Navajo stories are not big in mainstream literature, so it is important for students to know that good work from their culture exists" (Stachowski 1998, 342).

An especially creative student teacher developed a game of "Navajo Jeopardy" for her class. She described the activity as "The questions ranged from clan representation, value systems, community leaders, and mythology, to [slang] words in Navajo. This was a FABULOUS period because kids were speaking their first language, reeling off their clans with PRIDE, and are now devising their *own* questions for use in Navajo Jeopardy II!" (Stachowski 1998).

Her commitment to providing a culturally relevant education for her pupils was evident in her final reflections: "Students realize that my classroom is structured with an environment that rewards their cultural and filial knowledge, therefore raising both self and class esteem" (Stachowski 1998, 344). Overall, the student teachers heeded Gilliland's recommendation that "the Indian culture should become an integral part of basic instruction" (1995, 11), and in doing so, they also became learners in the process, often with their Navajo pupils leading the way.

Unstructured Personal Expressions and Additional Evidence of the Reservation Project's Success

Beyond the published reports summarized in the previous sections, an abundance of data exists, lending additional support that the American Indian Reservation Project has indeed been successful in providing the kinds of intercultural experiences that lead to enhanced cultural sensitivity, culturally competent instruction, and a broader worldview. The "unstructured personal expression" mentioned earlier on student teachers' biweekly reports, project evaluations completed at the conclusion of the experience, reflections on the annual "employment survey" mailed out a year later, and personal correspondence with current and former participants—often years after they graduated—provide evidence that the reservation project's life-transforming, mind-broadening experiences shape participants in profoundly important ways, professionally and personally.

Sandra, for example, cherished the opportunity to become so intimately involved with the Navajo people in her community, while experiencing what it is like to be in the minority:

There are so many advantages associated with being in the reservation project. There is no greater way to completely immerse yourself in someone's culture. We are living with the Navajo people, eating with them, working with them, and taking care of their children. We have been able to get to know our students on a level different from any other student teacher. It was important to feel what it is like to be the minority. I never really felt like this at school, but more so when we would go to outside cultural events, such as fairs. One of the biggest advantages for me was to get out of my comfort zone.

Similarly, Bill reported that "making friends with people of a different culture has explosive benefits," among which he listed:

- a more complete understanding of the Navajo culture
- an overall better understanding of the world and the United States
- a better understanding of what I believe in as an educator
- learned about a different lifestyle and outlook on life
- saw with my own eyes the problems that still exist in the United States

Bill was not the only student teacher who suggested that his reservation project experiences broadened his knowledge and understanding of the world; Tammy, too, offered the following observation:

I have noticed some changes in myself that I never expected or even thought about before living on the Navajo Reservation. I used to feel removed when I would hear about the news and politics; however, recently the events in our country and in the world seem more personal to me. I think of it all on a smaller scale. It is ironic that I am physically very far removed from the society that I consider my culture, yet the events in the world seem closer to me than in the past.

Nelson, too, reported that his experience on the Navajo Reservation had contributed significantly to his global perspective. His placement was in a community that was built around the intersection of two northern Arizona highways; heading north, Monument Valley is just across the Arizona/Utah border, and heading west, the Grand Canyon is perhaps a few hours' drive away. Because of its location, and unlike most of the communities across the reservation, the town boasts three hotel chains, gas stations, a Bashas' supermarket, *both* McDonald's and Burger King, and an old trading post that also now houses a Radio Shack. In recent communication, Nelson reported that because of these factors, the "number of visitors from other countries is staggering." He wrote,

Often when people think about the Rez, their minds are filled with images so far away from the reality. The truth is that [this town] is a global community filled with people who speak many different languages, to communicate with the tourists from all over the world. This fact alone makes the perspective of this town much more broad, as they have an awareness of so many large scale issues that affect millions of people. For instance, since 9/11 the tourism industry here has suffered because of fewer travelers from international locations. The impact of these international travelers cannot be ignored as certain shops and businesses in town are constantly catering services to people from other nations.

Nelson concluded by considering the ramifications of the meeting of cultures in his placement community—the Western Europeans who come to enjoy the breathtaking natural beauty of American Indian land: "This occasionally creates an aura of connectivity and culmination between the old, respected Western cultures and an even older but less respected Native culture of the Western Hemisphere."

For Jayson, discovering himself—as a person and a teacher—was a profoundly important outcome of his experience on the reservation. He wrote, "Being immersed in a new and different culture was a great way for me to find myself and my teaching style. New faces, new ideas, new surroundings, and new people all led me to really know myself and who I am as a teacher." Later, as an "unstructured personal expression," he offered the following poem, which he called, "Reflection of Self on a Reservation Shelf":

A mirror on a shelf seizes my mind . . .
Out here, living on the Rez,
I will sometimes catch myself in the most wonderful place and time,
and smile, real large, trying not to show my teeth.
Out here, teaching on the Rez,
I will sit back in my teacher's chair, see my students achieving on their own,
and cry, real soft, trying not to show my tears.
Out here, learning on the Rez,
I will feel like I am ten-years-old while listening to elderly Navajo speak their
        wisdom,
and breathe, real quiet, trying not to show my white skin.
Out here on the Rez,
I see myself through the respecting eyes of my neighbors,

I see myself through the idolizing eyes of my students,
I see myself through the unflinching eyes of a mirror on a shelf,
And I laugh at who I have become, someone I always wanted to be.

Interestingly, many of the student teachers whose stories and words have been included in this chapter chose to remain on the Navajo Reservation for their first teaching position, either in the schools where they student taught or on other parts of the reservation. A study is currently underway to explore factors that contributed to these young college graduates' decisions to remain in geographically isolated communities to embark on their careers, to understand the challenges and rewards of teaching and living in reservation communities, and to determine the extent to which cultural and community participation continues to be an integral part of their reservation lives. The early findings are thus far fascinating and suggest that these former reservation project participants, now licensed teachers, have indeed internalized many of the professional and cultural lessons they learned as student teachers, as they continue to grow and develop in their roles as elementary and secondary educators.

RECOMMENDATIONS FOR PROGRAM DEVELOPERS OF DOMESTIC INTERCULTURAL TEACHING EXPERIENCES

The American Indian Reservation Project represents a realistic model for domestic intercultural teaching experiences that can be replicated in teacher-education programs on other university and college campuses. In existence for more than thirty years, the project has survived in part because of the support of the School of Education's administration and financial backing through inclusion in the annual budget of the school. However, salient features of the project, first implemented in its infancy, are in place yet today, and these are the factors that have contributed to its long-term success. Based on these features, six key recommendations are offered to guide the development and structure of new programs as they emerge.

First, student teachers must be prepared for the intercultural school settings and communities in which they will be expected to function.

They need to have a working knowledge of educational issues, challenges, priorities, mandates, and practices in the schools where they will be placed. They also need to possess at least basic information about the political, historical, social, economic, and cultural forces operating in the placement communities, as well as an understanding of current issues that affect community life. We are doing our student teachers *and* their school and community hosts a disservice if even a basic preparation is not provided prior to their departure.

A second suggestion is to require that participants live in the communities in which they are teaching during the course of their student-teaching assignment. The reservation project is successful because the student teachers are living *on the reservation*—not in the border towns of Gallup, Flagstaff, or Farmington. To maximize the extent to which cultural immersion can happen, participants in intercultural field experiences cannot "escape" their pupils' world at the end of the day to return to their own comfortable and familiar surroundings. As one student teacher noted earlier, participants need to "live, eat, and work" with members of the host cultural group; they need to shop where the local people shop, visit in their homes, and participate in community activities and events. If participants leave their inner-city school at the end of the day, for example, to return to their home in the suburbs, vital cultural learning—the kind of learning that takes place through sustained community involvement—is impossible to achieve.

Hand-in-hand with the need for participants to live in their placement communities is the third recommendation, that community involvement must be an integral component in intercultural field experiences. Assignments that require student teachers to move beyond the walls of their classrooms, school buildings, and living spaces to interact closely with local people of all ages and from all walks of life are critical for the cultural learning to occur that can then translate back into classroom practice. Student teachers can be required to engage in service learning projects, to interview people to gain local perspectives, and to prepare essays that can only be completed with the knowledge they have gained through their community-based interactions. The outcomes of community involvement are priceless, and as the reservation project has shown, can have an impact on student teachers in powerful and profound ways.

Fourth, the intercultural experience needs structure and focus. Student teachers should go with specific expectations and responsibilities, as well as requirements for written reflection and processing of new learning. Otherwise, we run the risk that deep meaning and important insights will be lost to superficial exposure to significant events, trends, values, and interactions in both school and community settings. The deliberate, professional, and cultural learning that is woven into the reservation school and community activities, for example, can and does follow the student teacher to subsequent situations, where an awareness of and sensitivity to cultural differences, where instruction geared to meet the learners' needs based on these differences, and where thoughtful reflection on school and community participation will contribute to our students' long-term success. Indeed, the next step for our participants is graduation from the university, a teaching license in hand, and their own elementary and secondary classrooms. The intercultural placement requires that the student teachers accept personal responsibility in its multiple forms and to operate as the emerging professionals they are. Unless they are required to do this, they will not be able to effectively assume responsibility for other people's children in their own classrooms.

Fifth, program developers should foster relationships with placement site personnel—school administrators, teachers, community agencies, and others who are likely to assume an active role in the student teachers' on-site experiences. These personnel need to understand program goals and requirements, and they should have the opportunity to make recommendations for appropriate learning activities and readings to include in the preparatory phase. They need to be perceived and treated as close collaborators in the teacher-education process to maximize their commitment to placing and supervising program participants semester after semester. They need assurance that the college or university program developers are there, too, when problems arise—that the student teachers are not forgotten about once they have left our campuses for their distant cultural sites. Taking on student teachers means extra work for school and agency personnel; however, well-prepared student teachers who are successful in their intercultural placements can also be candidates for teaching positions in the very schools that accepted them for student-teaching assignments in the first place.

Finally, rather than attempting to reinvent the wheel, program developers should tap into existing programs as much as possible. For example, the American Indian Reservation Project is open to students from other universities, and every year, participants from a number of other institutions, in Indiana and beyond, join their Indiana University counterparts for student teaching and community involvement experiences on the Navajo Reservation. By working together, each of us can do more than we could individually, and the sharing of resources, ideas, procedures, and connections is priceless.

CONCLUSION

This chapter has explored a number of dimensions of one intercultural teaching experience—the American Indian Reservation Project—as a viable alternative in cases where students are not interested or able to go overseas. In the best-case scenario, domestic intercultural placements would be offered alongside international opportunities, giving students a choice in the kind of field experience they pursue. The student teachers who participate in the reservation project conclude their experiences having learned important lessons—lessons about education, about schooling, about culture, about community, and about life in our diverse world—that we hope will remain with them and continue to shape the kinds of educators, and people, they are today. Many of these lessons are undoubtedly learned through trial and error, oftentimes with tears and frustration. However, the insights they gain as a result can be far-reaching, going well beyond the borders of the Navajo Reservation to influence and inform the student teachers' lives, as well as those with whom they work and live.

I believe the reservation project is successful because of its marriage of professional practice with cultural and community involvement, requiring that participants integrate community service into their student teaching and record their learning in structured assignments. The assignments provide a means for the student teachers to process the multitude of new experiences, to develop and organize emerging new ideas, and to reflect on and make sense of the institutional, social, and cultural setting of their placement schools. By combining action in the community with reflection in structured assignments, the student teachers are better prepared to be the culturally sensitive and interculturally competent educators we need in our schools today.

Matthew's words perhaps best sum up the kinds of insights that can be gained through intercultural teaching experiences and provide the impetus for those of us who are teacher educators to continue making intercultural opportunities an option for our student teachers: "I have learned that two completely different cultures can have the same values, morals, ideas, and similarities. Two different cultures can unite to make something special that, with hard work and determination, can benefit everyone."

REFERENCES

Adler, P. S. 1975. The transitional experiences: An alternative view of culture shock. *Journal of Humanistic Psychology* 15, no. 4:13–23.

Banks, J., M. Cochran-Smith, L. Moll, A. Richert, K. Zeichner, P. LePage, et al. 2005. Teaching diverse learners. In *Preparing teachers for a changing world: What teachers should learn and be able to do*, ed. L. Darling-Hammond and J. Bransford, 232–74. San Francisco: Jossey-Bass.

Brown, S. C., and M. L. Kysilka. 2002. *Applying multicultural and global concepts in the classroom and beyond*. Boston: Allyn & Bacon.

Cleary, L. M., and T. D. Peacock. 1998. *Collected wisdom: American Indian education*. Boston: Allyn & Bacon.

Darling-Hammond, L. D., and S. P. Garcia-Lopez. 2002. What is diversity? In *Learning to teach for social justice*, ed. L. Darling-Hammond, J. French, and S. P. Garcia-Lopez, 9–12. New York: Teachers College Press.

Fedullo, M. 1992. *Light of the feather: Pathways through contemporary Indian America*. New York: Morrow.

Gilliland, H. 1995. *Teaching the Native American*. 3rd ed. Dubuque, IA: Kendall/Hunt.

Heuberger, B. 2004. *Cultural diversity: Building skills for awareness, understanding and application*. 3rd ed. Dubuque, IA: Kendall/Hunt.

Howard, G. R. 2006. *We can't teach what we don't know: White teachers, multiracial schools*. 2nd ed. New York: Teachers College Press.

Kissock, C. 1997. Student teaching overseas. In *Preparing teachers to teach global perspectives: A handbook for teacher educators*, ed. M. M. Merryfield, E. Jarchow, and S. Pickert, 123–42. Thousand Oaks, CA: Corwin Press.

Knighten, B. n.d. The importance of a global education: Interview with Dr. Merry Merryfield. At www.outreachworld.org/article_print.asp?articleid=77 (accessed February 26, 2006).

Lenski, S. D., K. Crawford, T. Crumpler, and C. Stallworth. 2005. Preparing preservice teachers in a diverse world. *Action in Teacher Education* 27, no. 3:3–12.

Mahan, J. M., and L. L. Stachowski. 1993–1994. Diverse, previously uncited sources of professional learning. *National Forum of Teacher Education Journal* 3, no. 1:21–28.

McLaughlin, T. H. 2000. Values in education. In *Key issues in secondary education*, ed. J. Beck and M. Earl, 109–17. London: Cassell.

Merryfield, M. M. 1997. A framework for teacher education in global perspectives. In *Preparing teachers to teach global perspectives: A handbook for teacher educators*, ed. M. M. Merryfield, E. Jarchow, and S. Pickert, 1–24. Thousand Oaks, CA: Corwin Press.

———. 2000. Why aren't teachers being prepared to teach for diversity, equity, and global interconnectedness? A study of lived experiences in the making of multicultural and global educators. *Teaching and Teacher Education* 16, no. 4:429–43.

Moll, L. C., C. Amanti, D. Neff, and N. Gonzalez. 1992. Funds of knowledge for teaching: Using a qualitative approach to connect homes and classrooms. *Theory into Practice* 31, no. 2:132–41.

Reyes, S. A., N. Capella-Santana, and L. L. Khisty. 1998. Prospective teachers constructing their own knowledge in multicultural education. In *Being responsive to cultural differences: How teachers learn*, ed. M. E. Dilworth, 110–25. Thousand Oaks, CA: Corwin Press.

Rhodes, R. W. 1994. *Nurturing learning in Native American students*. Hotevilla, AZ: Sonwai Books.

Sleeter, C. E., and C. A. Grant. 1999. *Making choices for multicultural education: Five approaches to race, class, and gender*. 3rd ed. New York: John Wiley & Sons.

Stachowski, L. L. 1998. Student teachers' efforts to promote self-esteem in Navajo pupils. *Educational Forum* 62, no. 4:341–46.

Stachowski, L. L., and E. J. Brantmeier. 2002. Understanding self through other: Changes in student teacher perceptions of home culture through immersion in Navajoland and overseas. *International Education* 32, no. 1:5–18.

Stachowski, L. L. and C. J. Frey. 2003. Lessons learned in Navajoland: Student teachers reflect on professional and cultural learning in reservation schools and communities. *Action in Teacher Education* 25 no. 3: 38–47.

Stachowski, L. L., and C. J. Frey. 2005. Student teachers' reflections on service
    and learning in Navajo Reservation communities: Contextualizing the class-
    room experience. *School Community Journal* 15, no. 2:101–20.
Stachowski, L. L., J. W. Richardson, and M. Henderson. 2003. Student teach-
    ers report on the influence of cultural values on their classroom practice and
    community involvement: Perspectives from the Navajo Reservation and
    abroad. *Teacher Educator* 39, no. 1:52–63.
Utter, J. 2001. *American Indians: Answers to today's questions.* 2nd ed. Nor-
    man: University of Oklahoma Press.
Zeichner, K. 1996. Designing educative practicum experiences for prospective
    teachers. In *Currents of reform in preservice teacher education,* ed. K. Ze-
    ichner, S. Melnick, and M. L. Gomez, 215–34. New York: Teachers College
    Press.
Zeichner, K., and S. Melnick. 1996. The role of community field experiences in
    preparing teachers for cultural diversity. In *Currents of reform in preservice
    teacher education,* ed. K. Zeichner, S. Melnick, and M. L. Gomez, 176–96.
    New York: Teachers College Press.

6

DEVELOPING BILITERACY TEACHERS: MOVING TOWARD CULTURE AND LINGUISTIC GLOBAL COMPETENCE IN TEACHER EDUCATION

Reyes L. Quezada
Cristina Alfaro

My entire experience in the International B/CLAD Teacher Education Program has taught me to critically think "like a teacher across borders." It taught me the interconnectedness between language, culture, society, and educational politics from a global perspective.

—American biliteracy student teacher in Querétaro, Mexico

Demographic shifts are bringing increasing numbers of international students from diverse racial, ethnic, religious, class, and linguistic backgrounds into the public schools. The goal of this chapter is not to debate whether it is important to address diversity in the public schools. We see diversity as an inescapable reality in public education (Quezada and Osajima 2005). Instead, the goal is to help teacher educators think about diversity globally in a broad and integrative manner by providing what we find to be important and valuable perspectives in internationalizing teacher education. We begin with a discussion of cultural proficiency and argue that an important first step is to think reflectively about one's own position and the school of education's position in relation to cultural and linguistic proficiency as a global perspective. Cultivating a willingness, openness, and commitment to meet the challenge of diversity through a global perspective is a vital foundation for the development of effective biliteracy teachers in global teacher-education programs.

This chapter is organized to provide an overview of key areas: demographics, cultural and linguistic proficiency in teacher education, approaches to internationalizing teacher education, biliteracy teacher education abroad as a model for a transformative teacher-education program, the international teacher-education program profile, program evaluation, key aspects of program development, constraining and challenging factors, and program successes. We also include a summary, guiding questions, and selected readings in the area of global student teaching. In each section, we discuss the important theoretical and research work that informs approaches to biliteracy international teacher-education programs and practices. We argue that it is important to take a comprehensive approach to diversity, one that sees relations among classroom learning, school environments, and home/community influences (Quezada and Osajima 2005). Because home/community influences begin in the home country of origin of the pupils, we think it best to prepare our future biliteracy teachers in the home country of our immigrant children where they learn and experience the home culture, the home language, the nation's cultural and educational norms, and education system through an extended living experience in the host country. There are many global student-teaching abroad programs for English-speaking teacher candidates and none were found that grant bilingual certification with a Spanish emphasis. Only one program leading to bilingual certification exists, offered through the California State University System-International Teacher Education Program (CSU-ITEP), which includes a specific curriculum approved by the California Commission on Teacher Credentialing to help ease the gap of highly qualified teachers to meet the needs of culturally and linguistically diverse students (Kuhlman et al. 2003).

THE DEMOGRAPHY WITHIN OUR BORDERS— SETTING THE STAGE

The national demographics of public schooling present twenty-first-century educators with a critical challenge. On the one hand, the population is becoming increasingly diverse, along racial, ethnic, cultural, and linguistic lines. Between 1990 and 2000, for example, the Latino and

Asian populations grew by 61 percent and 69 percent, respectively (Zhou 2003). It is predicted that by 2025, nearly half of all students will be students of color (McFalls and Cobb-Roberts 2001, 164). Already, in major metropolitan areas, the public school population is majority "minority." California reported an enrollment of 6,322,083 and over 65 percent of the K–12 student population were ethnic minority students in the 2004–2005 academic year. Hispanics comprise 46.8 percent of the total student population (CDOE 2006). In the Los Angeles Unified School District, 70 percent of the 700,000 students are Hispanic. About half of these are from poor families, and more than a third are English-language learners (Zhou 2003, 216). In Miami, nearly 80 percent of the under-eighteen child population is Hispanic or black (216). In New York, 70 percent of the under-eighteen population is Hispanic, black, or Asian (216). On the other hand, the demographic profile of teachers and administrators contrasts sharply with the student population. Hodgkinson (2002) reports that nationally 86 percent of teachers and 84 percent of principals are white. The enrollment of English-language learners (ELLs) in U.S. schools has surged in recent years. The 2003–2004 language census reported that ELLs make up 9.19 percent of the total K–12 student enrollment, totaling 5,013,539 (OELA 2006). In California alone, the ELL enrollment for 2004–2005 was reported at 1,591,525 million, representing 25.2 percent of the total student enrollment, with various language groups other than Spanish included (CDOE 2006).

CROSSING BORDERS THROUGH A CULTURAL PROFICIENCY MODEL

In moving toward a discussion of global teacher-education programs, it is important to think first about how to cultivate schools and colleges of education that would support and encourage the development of international teacher-education programs at their sites. There are various models that promote multicultural and language-acquisition education theory and that support teacher educators in their endeavors on how to best prepare biliteracy teacher candidates to meet the diverse needs of English-language learners. Conducting a culturally proficient biliteracy international teacher-education program is one more step to create culturally and linguistically competent teachers to support and teach immigrant children in our U.S. schools.

The cultural proficiency model presented by Lindsey, Robins, and Terrell (1999) can be utilized as a conceptual framework in the development of international teacher-education programs. The model provides theoretical frameworks that will help faculty in teacher-education programs to think about and interact in culturally and linguistically diverse international environments. An emphasis of the model is on an "inside-out" approach to assessing teacher-education programs and their faculties' abilities to work with diversity. The inside-out approach can encourage colleges and schools of education and teacher educators to assess where the educators and their institutions are situated with respect to dealing with cultural and linguistic differences regarding international teacher-education programs and practices (Quezada and Osajima 2005). The cultural proficiency model provides a useful framework to guide that reflective assessment. The cultural proficiency continuum represented in the diagram below identifies six factors to consider in planning international teacher-education programs to better prepare culturally proficient global teachers.

Cultural Destructiveness

Lindsey, Robins, and Terrell (1999) describe the lowest, most negative point in the continuum as *cultural destructiveness*, referring to attitudes, policies, and practices destructive to cultures and individuals within a culture. Examples of cultural destructiveness are English-only policies and the elimination of bilingual education programs, essentially prohibiting students from using their native language at school. Such policies enacted at a statewide level can reverberate at the school level and fuel resistance to working flexibly with non-English-proficient students (Quezada and Osajima 2005). In a teacher-education program, cultural destructiveness can be seen when programs that certify bilin-

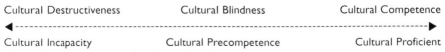

Cultural Destructiveness	Cultural Blindness	Cultural Competence
Cultural Incapacity	Cultural Precompetence	Cultural Proficient

Figure 6.1. Cultural Proficiency Continuum

gual teachers are eliminated. We believe the initiatives that have passed are not based on what is best for educating culturally and linguistically diverse student populations, but often based on "those who can vote" and who are usually the ones least affected by the laws. Cultural destructiveness is also evident when institutions do not allow teacher candidates to student teach abroad because such teaching does not appear to meet state certification mandates.

Cultural Incapacity

Cultural incapacity describes "an organization or individuals that show extreme bias, believe in the superiority of the dominant group, and assume a paternal posture to so-called lesser groups" (Lindsey, Robins, and Terrell 1999, 34). Organizations or individuals at this stage often hold rigid stereotypes and fears, which severely limits opportunities for change. In teacher-education programs, these stereotypes can be reflected in conversations or through program planning where the beliefs that only teacher preparation received in the United States is valuable, while other countries' teacher certification is inferior and therefore cannot have reciprocity with state programs.

Cultural Blindness

The third point, *cultural blindness*, as described by Lindsey, Robins, and Terrell "is the belief that color and culture make no difference and that all people are the same" (1999, 35). This is similar to the level of minimization in Bennett's (1993) model of intercultural development referred to in other chapters of this volume. Lindsey, Robins, and Terrell further note that this is the most vexing point on the continuum, for culturally blind educators' well-intentioned beliefs make it difficult to recognize the persistence of problems linked to cultural and racial differences. When cultural blindness operates, the results can have an opposite view by faculty or teacher candidates participating in international teacher-education programs. An example of cultural blindness is stating that teaching culturally and linguistically diverse children in schools abroad is the same as working with culturally and linguistic diverse children in the United States without taking into consideration socioeconomic factors, community influences, families, or structural in-equities in the education practices and programs of each nation.

Cultural Precompetence

Fourth, *cultural precompetence* "is an awareness of limitations in cross-cultural communication and outreach (Lindsey, Robins, and Ter-rell 1999, 36). People usually want to provide fair treatment but are of-ten unaware of the range of options available to them. In an interna-tional teacher-education context, candidates would be allowed to student teach abroad; however, they would also be required to repeat the entire student-teaching component in the United States in order to be fair to those who cannot student teach abroad or because of existing beliefs that U.S. teacher candidates do not receive quality supervision by a cooperating teacher and university supervisor.

Cultural Competence

The fifth point on the continuum, *cultural competence*, is evident when colleges and schools of education "accept and respect differences, carefully attend to the dynamics of difference, continually assess their own cultural knowledge and beliefs, continuously expand their cultural knowledge and resources, and make various adaptations of their own belief systems, policies and practices" (Lindsey, Robins, and Terrell 1999, 37). In such a context, teacher candidates would be allowed to participate in student teaching abroad, and faculty would accept and re-spect the experiences of candidates' overseas teaching and would value the learning and knowledge brought back to the United States.

Cultural Proficiency

The final point of the continuum is *cultural proficiency*. Culturally proficient colleges and schools of education and their faculty would sup-port culturally proficient practices in all phases of the learning and teaching process. Faculty and teacher candidates function effectively in different cultural contexts and, when presented with new groups and situations, know how to gather research and resources to help in learning about cultures. Culturally proficient educators seek to institutional-ize cultural knowledge and attendant practices into the fabric of their in-stitutions. They take proactive steps to involve a wide variety of people in educational decisions (Quezada and Osajima 2005). In an interna-tional teacher-education context, faculty would support student teach-ing when strong formal partnerships have been created with other col-leges of education from abroad. Teacher candidates would student teach and/or have extended practicum field experiences in both nations and would be involved in community service projects at their international site. In addition, faculty from both nations would be involved in the teaching and supervision through faculty academic exchange programs in order to be at the highest point of the cultural proficiency continuum.

The cultural proficiency continuum is a critical tool that educators can use to assess the readiness and willingness of faculty and institutions of higher education to move toward culturally proficient practices in an in-ternational teacher-education context. We believe that when teacher ed-ucators have a genuine interest in assessing all of the levels of cultural pro-ficiency in institutions of higher education, then engaging in activities that increase knowledge and open dialogue will result in support of a strong educational environment. As a consequence, this environment will pro-vide an effective education by creating a diverse teacher-education force that will be prepared to teach with a global perspective (Quezada and Os-ajima 2005). As student teachers move toward cultural proficiency, their willingness and commitment to work with students from linguistic and culturally diverse backgrounds increases, as does their ability to learn more about students and about the range of global (cultural and language) educational theory and practices available.

APPROACHES TO INTERNATIONALIZING TEACHER EDUCATION

In moving teacher-education programs to prepare teachers with a qual-ity global teaching experience, institutions must set the mechanisms of support both in financial resources and program models. Teacher educa-tors need to look at teacher-education models that have proved to be ef-fective in preparing biliteracy teachers to work effectively with children who are culturally, racially, and linguistically different from native English-speaking Americans. Educational institutions typically follow a traditional curriculum and, thus, the teacher-certification process is based on the completion of a certain number of courses that usually stress the attitudes and values held by the dominant society and have as common principles the reproduction of a set of canons that are monolithic and noninclusive (Bell and Munn 1999–2000). By perpetuating the values and social stratification existent in American society, teacher education becomes a tool that promotes the reproduction and legitimization of the worldview of the dominant majority, thus ignoring the perspectives held by people of color (Delpit 1995; Darder 1992; Smith and Zantiotis 1989). Freire (1997) promotes the notion that biliteracy/multiliteracy teacher-preparation programs should provide situational learning experiences and dialogical interactions. These experiences should also expose and allow teacher candidates to view their world through multiple realities and cross-cultural lenses. Only through these multiple lenses will they begin to struggle to construct their own ideological and political clarity.

In a review of the literature, Quezada (2005) identified two program models for student teaching abroad. The first model may be defined as "faculty-initiated, university-sponsored," whereby school of education faculty have created or developed bilingual student-teaching programs by themselves and then partnered with global education opportunities or programs that already exist. The second model, defined as an "affiliated program," is one that includes schools of education that are part of a consortium made up of various universities in the United States and partnered with host-country universities. In the latter type of program, students complete their student teaching in four possible types of school settings: (1) Department of Defense K–12 schools, (2) United States Department of State American-sponsored overseas schools, (3) Independent International/American schools, and (4) host-country public and private schools.

The Department of Defense K–12 schools serve children of military families stationed abroad. The language of instruction is English, and curriculum is American. Such schools can be found in Europe, Asia, Guam, Puerto Rico, Panama, and Cuba.

United States Department of State-sponsored overseas schools are private schools open to all children on a tuition basis. The schools are supported by the Department of State and serve as models for American education overseas. Some are housed in U.S. embassies, with most being located in areas with large numbers of American expatriates. Often children from diplomatic families attend these schools. The language of instruction is usually in English, but sometimes instruction is in two languages, English and the host language.

The third type of schools is private schools having a U.S. or British, Canadian, or an international curriculum not sponsored by the U.S. State Department. The language of instruction is English; however, these schools usually offer two languages, English and the host language. A growing number of schools that are American-sponsored as well as those called Independent International/American offer the International Baccalaureate (IB) programs.

The fourth type is host-country schools, which are public schools attended by the local children whose language of instruction is the country's primary language. In order to offer international student-teaching opportunities, some universities participate in international consortiums with U.S. universities and universities abroad. Other universities base their international student-teaching programs in schools of education when they have developed international partnerships with specific elementary or secondary schools or universities abroad. Keeping in mind the necessity of providing strong situated learning experiences abroad for teacher-education candidates, we will now present the development of an existing teacher-education model that prepares biliteracy teachers who will be culturally and linguistically proficient to work with a diverse student population in the United States.

INTERNATIONAL TEACHER EDUCATION PROGRAM (ITEP): A MODEL FOR A GLOBAL TEACHER-EDUCATION PROGRAM

In the state of California, specifically, teacher-education programs professionally prepare teacher candidates with a repertoire of best teaching strategies. These strategies are aligned to the California Standards for the Teaching Profession (CSTP), or in the case of wanting to ascertain the highest level of an accomplished teacher, another set of standards, those outlined by the National Board for Professional Teaching Standards (NBPTS), is followed. Interestingly enough, neither the CSTP nor NBPTS addresses the importance or necessity for teachers to develop cultural and linguistic global competence. It is within this greatly diverse linguistic, cultural, and socioeconomic population that a teacher's knowledge and experience of biliteracy and bicultural development has the most profound impact. With this in mind, we need to prepare qualified teachers to work effectively with the large Spanish-speaking and other diverse language-speaking population in our communities.

The International Teacher Education Program (ITEP) is a California State University (CSU) systemwide bilingual (Spanish/English) credential program for elementary multiple-subject teacher candidates. The program, administered through the CSU International Programs Office, was approved in 1994 by the California Commission on Teacher Credentialing (CCTC) and authorized to credential teacher candidates seeking a multiple-subject credential with a Spanish/English authorization. The program was first originated in Mexico City, and then moved in 1998 to the state and city of Querétaro, Mexico. Besides San Diego State University, where the program was initiated, nine other CSU campuses participate: San José, Fresno, Hayward (now East Bay Campus), Long Beach, San Bernardino, Sacramento, Sonoma, Bakersfield, and Fullerton.

The goals of ITEP are aligned with the work done by Hollins, King, and Hayman (1994). Their work on preparing teachers to be effective with diverse populations focuses on developing teachers where culture and sociopolitical issues are central, and includes the following: culturally and linguistically sensitive teaching, instructional strategies for exceptionalities, the centrality of culture in human experience and ways that culture and cultural difference influence learning and teaching, and community-based and culturally diverse field experiences for teacher candidates. The program's immediate mission not only encourages teacher-education students to embrace the philosophies behind bilingualism and biculturalism but also to learn how to engage in a process "wherein individuals learn to function in two distinct sociocultural environments: their primary culture, and that of the dominant mainstream culture of the society in which they live" (Darder 1992, 48). Several scholars have called the process *biculturalism* because of the interaction between two cultural systems, the individual's ensuing state of mind, and response to this process (Darder 1992; Ramirez and Castaneda 1974).

The International Teacher Education Program (ITEP) asks individuals undertaking the profession of teaching to go beyond reading the additional cultural chapter or bringing in a guest speaker, which merely offers a basic understanding of the changing ethnolinguistic context in which they will be working. Rather, prospective teachers in this program engage in situated learning experiences that position them in contexts that allow them to negotiate their *own* sociocultural and political position in a global context. It asks each individual who takes the opportunity to understand not only the students they will soon educate but also themselves in the role of both teacher and social being with an identity represented by history, culture, and personal realities.

The program, in its current form, brings CSU students from throughout the state to San Diego State University (SDSU) for one partial spring and two partial summer "bookend" sessions of course work and student teaching. The other part of the summer, fall, and spring academic year is spent in Mexico. Participants attend course work and student teach for a total of nine months in Mexico and three months in the San Diego, California, area. During their stay in Mexico, candidates have access to private, indigenous, and public schools.

Candidates who complete the credential program receive a multiple-subject elementary Bilingual Cross-Cultural and Language Academic Development (B/CLAD) credential from the California Commission on Teacher Credentialing (CCTC) (CSUS n.d.). This represents the only international credential program in California approved by CCTC. The program was initially designed for teacher candidates who have minimal oral fluency in Spanish, although Spanish was their mother-tongue language. In the past five years, a large number of fluent Spanish speakers have participated to further professionalize their vocabulary and develop deeper cultural and linguistic knowledge. The appendix depicts the series of courses B/CLAD teacher candidates have taken, both in the United States and Mexico.

The current program has developed a partnership with the Secretaria de Educacíon Publica (Querétaro State Department of Education) that allows U.S. biliteracy teacher candidates to student teach in Querétaro, Mexico, a colonial city of approximately 1,000,000 residents located about 125 miles north of Mexico City. After a program orientation at SDSU, biliteracy teacher candidates spend nine months studying at the Escuela Normal del Estado de Querétaro (Normal State Teachers College of

Querétaro) and conduct their student teaching in all three settings: private, public, and indigenous schools. Their indigenous experiences have included schools throughout Mexico, from Oaxaca to Atlacomulco in the State of Mexico. Biliteracy teacher candidates participate for eight weeks in public schools, two weeks in private schools, and three weeks in indigenous schools during their student-teaching practicum, as well as take education methods courses taught by Mexican professors and university supervisors. Upon their return to the United States, biliteracy teacher candidates complete their teacher credentialing program methods courses at SDSU and engage in ten additional weeks of student teaching in a dual-language setting with cooperating teachers who already hold a B/CLAD credential (Alfaro 2003).

During their nine-month stay in Mexico, biliteracy teacher candidates live with host families, or sometimes with families of program faculty, and interact with other Mexican national teacher-education candidates in educational, cultural, and language workshops. Thus, teacher candidates learn both the California state standards as well as Mexican education standards and enrich their experiences having various situated learning and teaching opportunities. While in Mexico, teacher candidates are taught methods, language, and cultural courses by Mexican faculty. The opportunity to teach in different sociocultural contexts with culturally heterogeneous student populations forces teacher candidates to experience cultural, pedagogical, and ideological dissonance, a sensation that promotes increased ideological clarity (Alfaro 2003). The pedagogical experiences are structured in such a manner that they propel teacher candidates to juxtapose their personal belief systems with those of the dominant society in both the visiting country (Mexico) and the United States. As a result, teachers are compelled to critically examine the political and ideological dimensions of minority education on both sides of the U.S./Mexico border. The experience plays a large part in cultural learning (Cushner and Brislin 1996).

IMPACT OF THE PROGRAM

From 1994–2006, approximately 200 teacher candidates participated and graduated from the ITEP program, with 80 percent currently teaching in biliteracy settings and 20 percent in sheltered English classrooms in the United States. Of course, this is not to imply that every candidate has automatically been transformed through these experiences. Candidates' reflective journal entries, program evaluations, anecdotal notes, and questionnaires indicate that those who initially enter the program with the predisposition (80 percent) to critically analyze issues related to teaching, and who have the willingness to acquire multiple perspectives on both sides of the border, typically develop deeper ideological and pedagogical clarity (Alfaro 2003).

Quezada and Alfaro (2007) conducted a research study that investigated the heuristic process of four teachers from the CSU-International Teacher Education Program (ITEP) and their experiences with respect to the ideological dissonance they faced as they negotiated their cultural positioning in becoming biliteracy teachers in a global context. The study analyzed the biliteracy teachers' "self-reflection" accounts of their experience in a global student-teaching setting with respect to teaching elementary students from diverse cultural, linguistic, and socioeconomic backgrounds. The study examined the underpinnings of their instructional ideological orientation, significant practical experiences, and key dimensions that propelled biliteracy teachers to develop ideological clarity and a teaching ideology with a global perspective.

Four themes emerged from the investigation: (1) perceived inequities, (2) teachers as change agents, (3) student intimacy, and (4) internal versus external relationships. These four phenomena were explored in relation to the proposed learning outcomes of the participation in the ITEP program in Mexico. Accounts of the tensions perceived between the professional responsibilities as biliteracy teachers versus personal beliefs about educating English-language learners were a central part of the interviews conducted for this study. Biliteracy teachers recalled experiences that marked their decisions to teach or impart their own personal beliefs through their own "hidden" curriculum.

Perceived inequities, the first theme in the study, relates to biliteracy teachers' abilities to reflect on inequities that affect children on both sides of the border due to language, national origin, skin color, or socioeconomic status. Two Latino participants realized that what they brought to "the table" could affect children and, therefore, they needed to be conscious of not perpetuating the same perceived inequities.

The *change agents* theme refers both to challenges encountered and to the notion that biliteracy teachers have the power to be change agents in their own classrooms through their personal commitments. Biliteracy teachers felt that the ITEP program was aligned with the pedagogical needs of their students in their present classrooms. The perception is a result of the philosophical underpinnings and instruction provided by the Mexican professors. Biliteracy teachers spoke to the issue of "transfer" and how what biliteracy teachers learned from their experiences student teaching abroad has easily transferred and how they have applied their skills in new situations, both professional and personal.

The theme of *student intimacy and significance* refers to the impact the children and their community had on the biliteracy teachers and how the strong relationships and connections forged between them has been significant in their lives as professionals and assisted them in developing ideological clarity.

The fourth theme, *external versus internal pressures*, refers to the pressure felt by biliteracy teachers in their current teaching positions as a result of a standards-based curriculum that is a mismatch for their English-language learners. The biliteracy teachers believed that the current system perpetuates a deficit model and that it does not take into account their children's socioeconomic, cultural, and language conditions. Therefore, in developing a clear teaching ideology, the tensions between what the school district expects and what biliteracy teachers believe is right for children supports biliteracy teachers' activist role in defining their teaching ideology.

We also collected the voices of past students as they demonstrate their reflections as they come to their own ideological clarity as a means for teaching with courage, passion, solidarity, and ethics because of their experiences in this program. Their accounts show that what they learned through this program is intimately connected to what they already knew and to their development as accomplished biliteracy teachers. All of the following statements are from American biliteracy student teachers in Querétaro, Mexico.

> My participation in this program has allowed me to view life through multiple perspectives, I came into this program with a couple of windows to my house. I now have multiple windows.

This program has allowed me to come to know teaching as a relational activity by becoming a caring, empathetic teacher, which includes care for self, students, their language, culture, parents, and their communities.

My experiences in the private, public, and indigenous schools, both in and out of class, have helped me to realize that teaching in all its grandeur, is plainly about making personal connections with students and their communities.

The entire process taught me to "think like a teacher" in two worlds, Mexico and California. It taught me the interconnectedness of the intellectual, spiritual, emotional, social, and moral dimensions involved in teaching.

I remember this program in a bitter-sweet manner, when things got tough, in a country that I was unfamiliar with, and trying to improve my language skills, I got to know who I really was first as a human being, then a professional. It's in moments of discomfort that you come to know who you really are. I was transformed!

I learned so much about teaching and learning. This experience opened my eyes to "critical pedagogy." I continue to question what is happening in the area of bilingual education. Because of this I continue to develop political clarity and have proceeded to a leadership position in bilingual education.

The other very significant experience was working with the indigenous community in Oaxaca in a bilingual school. Here, I don't even know where to begin. . . . Um, "pues" well, O.K. . . . because this event carried over to my classroom in California.

I learned to live in very humble conditions; this is not to say that I come from a materially privileged background. I realized after living and working in Mexico that what I considered to be humble conditions were nothing compared to how I lived when working with the indigenous Masahua community. I am ashamed to confess that I was starting to become very materialistic and somewhat assimilated to the values of the dominant culture, but after living and working in this community I was able to rekindle my appreciation for aspects of life that don't carry a "$" sign.

The personal meaning that I attached to my cultural experience in the indigenous community allowed me to recognize and appreciate cultural differences in terms of values. I began to develop a frame of reference shift when communicating with my students and their community.

The personal meaning that I attached to my cultural experience in the indigenous community allowed me to turn the corner . . . umm . . . you know a transformation. I was beginning to internalize my own culture—the different culture I was living and working with. This was a powerful feeling to know that I could comfortably move in and out of this community with total ease and joy! I learned how to be humble, I was timid before and that is very different from being humble.

My student teaching situations both in Mexico and California were exclusively with Latino children. Nothing wrong with that, but in my present teaching situation, I have other children of color that come from different ethnic backgrounds. So my new lens includes a multicultural perspective, a stretch from my bicultural view.

The voices above depict how this program has allowed new teachers to develop beyond what traditional teacher-education programs can provide in California. Through this program, teachers have gone through the process of learning about Mexico and California teaching standards. Most significantly, teacher candidates have become reflective practitioners by developing not only in the areas of teaching strategies for second-language learners, content-area standards, and classroom management but also in the area of "self-knowledge." To attain self-knowledge required their participation in a shared cultural metaphor and the continuity of knowledge, perception, wisdom, and experience afforded to them through this program. Teachers become empowered through the realization that they are part of a greater human story of being and becoming. They learn to expand their vision of themselves and their teaching, and their contributions to education reach beyond the *California Standards for the Teaching Profession.* They come to the place that educators talk about (Alfaro 2003).

INTERNATIONAL TEACHER EDUCATION PROGRAM: A HISTORICAL PERSPECTIVE

The CSU-ITEP teacher-preparation program was developed for the purpose of increasing the number and improving the quality of bilingual teachers with a global perspective. The focus has always been to prepare teachers globally to teach better locally. Approximately twelve years ago, Dr. Richard Sutter, then director of the International Programs (IP) Office of California State University (CSU), along with a few interested faculty, began investigating the possibility of sending CSU bilingual teacher candidates to Mexico for all or part of their credential preparation in an effort to enhance their language and cultural experiences. This would help meet the needs of those teacher candidates interested in becoming bilingual teachers but who are not sufficiently language proficient or who have acquired Spanish through academic means but have little oral fluency. Another group of potential candidates includes those whose home language is Spanish but whose academic skills in Spanish have not been developed. A third group includes those who are native speakers of Spanish who have either had substantial experience attending schools in Mexico and/or had the benefit of well-developed bilingual programs in the United States. The latter group, it should be noted, tend to be fully bilingual and biliterate. The first group usually has not had any extensive experience with the culture of the language group, while the second group may have had such an experience in the home, but not necessarily in the country from which the majority of our California Latino students come. The third group has not had the opportunity to study the Mexican system of teacher preparation (Kuhlman et al. 2003).

The process for creating the Mexico Bilingual Cross-Cultural, Language and Academic Development (B/CLAD) credential program was met with many challenges. First, a cadre of faculty in the CSU system came together to discuss the possible curriculum of such a program. They formed the International Teacher Education Council (ITEC) in order to collaborate in a formal way. The ITEC decided that the Mexico model should follow the B/CLAD competencies; however, the courses students would take would not match exactly with those at any one of the original four campuses included in the project (San Diego [SDSU], Long Beach [CSULB], Fresno [CSUF] and Sacramento [CSUS]). Also, some of the course work would be taken in California while the remainder would be completed in Mexico. During this process is when the program initially encountered the cultural precompetence point in the continuum described by Lindsey, Robins, and Terrell (1999), as a keen awareness that issues of cultural competence had different value among the participating campuses. Creating the curriculum itself was a challenge from the beginning, but as this was a creative and dialogical process, campus representatives eventually reached consensus. The content-area courses advocate personal discovery with a curriculum that is student centered and constructivist in nature.

After the details of curriculum were decided upon in California, the next step was to begin the process of obtaining permission for the program in Mexico. It was initially decided to use the Universidad Iberoamericana in Mexico City, since the CSU International Program already was in place there for undergraduates. Negotiations were held over several months with various levels of the Mexican Ministry of Education and the Iberoamericana, and agreements were eventually reached. A proposal was written and submitted to the California Commission on Teacher Credentialing (CCTC) for the Mexico B/CLAD credential, which was approved in 1994. The approved document could be appended to any one university's CCTC approved B/CLAD credential program. In essence, summer sessions (or "bookends") are held in California (at San Diego State University), while the academic year would be in Mexico. Student teaching would take place in both locations, with the primary language experience to be in both public and private schools in Mexico, while the required Cross-cultural, Language and Academic Development (CLAD) student-teaching experience would occur during the second summer in San Diego. Course content that was generic (e.g., math basics and psychological foundations of education) would be taught in Mexico, while California specific methodologies, standards, and frameworks would be handled at SDSU (Kuhlman et al. 2003).

A DECADE OF TRANSFORMATION

The International Teacher Education Program has been continually revised and updated since its inception eleven years ago. The following sections contain a summary of the program since its inception, with the focus given to the program's challenges, successes, and modification as we have learned and adapted throughout the process. It is important to discuss specific areas of development (faculty, curriculum, language proficiency), areas in which bilingualism developed (formal, informal, *intercambios* [exchanges]), field experiences that include working and knowing the communities with the type of students that come to California classrooms, and finally with the voice of graduates regarding the overall experience.

Once the program's international infrastructure was in place in the CSU system, the journey began. In June 1994, the first cohort arrived in Mexico City, where they were suddenly confronted with the intensity and complexity of the program. Some of the problems encountered by the participants included experiencing homesickness and difficulty adjusting to living with a family in Mexico. In addition, taking all course work in Mexico in Spanish, needing to understand and participate in classroom discussions in the host language, plus having to read texts and write papers in Spanish created a major challenge for the students. During this process, students reflected upon and related their own experiences on how it felt to be in a different country and be challenged to engage the curriculum in Spanish as their second language.

In January 1995, the students began eight weeks of student teaching in Mexican public schools teaching in Spanish to Spanish speakers. While they expected many curriculum differences between the schools in Mexico and those in California, the Mexican faculty and the supervisors of the student teachers also had adjustments to make due to the differences in the California student teachers and Mexican teacher candidates in terms of curricular expectations. The first group of nine ITEP candidates returned to California in May and completed the California specific methods courses needed for the Bilingual Cross-cultural, Language and Academic Development (B/CLAD) credential. They also performed another eight weeks of student teaching, this time in bilingual classrooms with Cross-cultural, Language and Academic Development (CLAD) English-only cooperating teachers and/or B/CLAD cooperating teachers. With minimal modifications, this was the model used for the first five years of the program (Kuhlman, et al. 2003).

INSTITUTIONAL CHANGES ON BOTH SIDES OF THE BORDER

After the first-year program evaluation was undertaken on both sides of the border by faculty, students, and the consortium, it was determined by ITEC that changes had to be implemented. The second-year cohort was moved to the Universidad Pedagógica National (UPN) in Mexico City, which had more of a focus on pedagogical issues, rather than the Universidad Iberoamericana, which only had a graduate program in education and was not prepared to meet the needs of preservice teachers. The program remained at the UPN from 1996 until it was moved from Mexico City in 2000 to Querétaro.

During the second year, ITEC expanded to include CSU Hayward (now East Bay Campus) and San Bernardino. In addition, the program added three weeks of student-teaching experience in one of two indigenous schools located in the states of Puebla and Oaxaca. All students considered the indigenous experience to be the most significant and transformative experience of the year. Teacher candidates lived at rural boarding schools or in nearby villages, and students often completed projects in the communities in which they were student teaching (e.g., painting murals, organizing libraries). In this way, a true *intercambio* (exchange) of experiences took place, which became a stalwart of the program.

In years three and four, the program remained at the Universidad Pedagógica National, with the program, faculty, and curriculum modifications made both in California and Mexico. By the end of the fifth year (June 1999), approximately fifty-five candidates had completed the program. However, during the 1998–1999 year, ITEC began discussing and investigating the possibility of moving the program, and eventually decided to move the program to Querétaro in 2000–2001 due to health and safety issues encountered in Mexico City. Querétaro, a colonial city of approximately 1,000,000 (as opposed to the 22 million in Mexico City) located about 125 miles north of Mexico City, is very clean, virtually smog-free, and much quieter than the frenzy of the Federal District just three hours away.

The CSU resident director for the program worked diligently during the year to make a smooth transition, identifying faculty in Querétaro's schools who could be used for student teaching, and negotiating with the Office of the Secretaria de Educación de Querétaro (Office of the Secretary of Education in Querétaro) for approval to have the students study at the Escuela Normal and continue their student teaching in public and indigenous schools.

The program did not operate during 1999–2000 to allow for negotiations with the Office of the Secretaría de Educación de Querétaro to be completed and to make the physical move from Mexico City. This also allowed ITEC to take the time to reflect on the first five years of the program and to determine aspects that should be retained or modified. To further support this year of reflection, ITEC received a five-year Title VII Professional Development grant from the U.S. Office of Education, Office for Bilingual Education and Minority Affairs (OBEMLA), now Title III, Office of English Language Acquisition (OELA), for approximately $1.5 million. These monies were primarily used to support the teacher candidates in the program.

The 1999–2000 year ended with a symposium and *convenio* in April 2000, at which time the official agreement between CSU and the Secretaría de Educación de Querétaro was signed. The symposium was attended by dignitaries from the United Sates and Mexico, including the director of education for the Estado de Querétaro, the directors of the Escuela Normal and the Instituto Tecnológico de Monterrey-Campus Querétaro (ITESM), where Spanish classes are held, the director of the International Programs Office for CSU, and deans and faculty from CSU. Presentations and workshops were held on a variety of topics and issues related to the program, and on the future of education in both countries. The symposium provided opportunities for faculty and classroom teachers on both sides of the border to exchange ideas and methodologies and discuss critical issues faced by students in both countries.

The Seventh Year: Curriculum Changes and Year One in Querétaro

Several things changed as the program resumed in summer 2000. ITEC decided to move the students directly to Querétaro after a brief one-week orientation at SDSU, rather than holding the six-week summer session in San Diego, as had been done with previous cohorts. This would ease the financial obligation for those who did not live in San Diego (dormitories were relatively inexpensive for the one week in Querétaro), and students could quickly begin their Mexican living experience. Another change was that CSU faculty would go to the Querétaro

site and teach some of the initial classes that had previously been offered at SDSU. CSU faculty were able to meet and interact with their
Mexican counterparts, as well as ease the students into the Mexican curriculum. The students would remain in Mexico from July until the end
of March each year, when they would return to San Diego for an extended period (approximately ten weeks) to complete California-based
course work and student teaching.

In the curriculum, courses were added to the California credential
program to ensure that recently approved state standards of certification
under the provisions of Senate Bill 2042 were being addressed by
B/CLAD teacher candidates. An additional unit of English-Language
Development and Specially Designed Academic Instruction in English
(ELD/SDAIE) methods was added in the Mexico portion of the program, as many of the student teachers had been asked to teach small
groups of children the basics of English. They were to act as role models for English in the classroom and to tutor Escuela Normal students in
English while the Escuela Normal students reciprocated by helping the
California students improve their Spanish. These opportunities allowed
for a true exchange between the California teacher candidates and their
counterparts in Mexico, and proved quite useful.

The Mexico B/CLAD program began July 2000 in its new environment with nineteen teacher candidates. A new location was found for
the indigenous (*internado*) experience in Atlacomulco, approximately
two hours from Querétaro in the Estado de Mexico. Since the students
would need more time at the end in San Diego, the program began at
the end of June and the students returned to San Diego at the end of
March. During the first summer, they took intensive Spanish-
language classes at the ITESM, where the undergraduate program
was housed, and their B/CLAD methods courses at the Escuela Normal, primarily from Escuela Normal faculty. Teacher candidates were
integrated with the Normal teacher candidates in a variety of ways.
Another change was that the applicants for the program tended to
have a higher proficiency in Spanish than their Mexico City predeces-
sor cohorts. Regardless, the level of Spanish and knowledge of the
community and culture all were obviously enhanced by the experience
in Querétaro.

The Eighth Year: Year Two in Querétaro

More changes were made during the 2001 academic school year. All of the public school teaching experiences were moved to the *Centro* (downtown) part of the city, where many rural students are brought to receive their education. A formal rural experience was added at the end of the fall semester, allowing the B/CLAD students to live and work with Normal teacher candidates in Jalpan, a city in the Sierra Gorda, approximately four hours from Querétaro. Teacher candidates again deemed this as a highlight of the year, as had been the experience in Atlacomulco. Also, in order to intermix the B/CLAD and the Normal teacher candidates, an attempt was made to have them share the math methods course. This was not overly successful due to conflicts in both groups' schedules, and the program had to investigate other avenues for exchanges. Graduates of the program, however, were again in high demand in the schools in California and were fully prepared to meet the needs of U.S. bilingual/bicultural classrooms. One of the graduates from that year remained in Querétaro and obtained a teaching position in one of the private schools (Kuhlman et al. 2003).

The Ninth Year: Year Three in Querétaro

The particular group of teacher candidates in 2003, who named themselves "Con Ganas" (with desire), benefited from the experiences gained in past years, yet they still encountered some critical challenges. After analyzing the responses and reflective journal entries of the previous groups, directors noted that one of the recurring themes and key program components that needed to be seriously addressed was candidate reentry to California, which was strongly identified by all groups as a missing link in the program. They needed to have the space to process, in a very deep manner, the wealth of experiences, both good and bad, from their journey in Mexico. Given this feedback, and with the guidance of an expert on community learning circles (Diné or Navajo) in the United Sates with Native American languages, program directors scheduled two sessions. Using an organic process of inquiry and reflection, the group was able to address personal and professional tensions, questions, concerns, and beliefs. It became a time for students to deconstruct, construct, and reconstruct their pedagogical and ideological orientations (Alfaro 2003). Additionally, teacher candidates were able to provide important program feedback and offer suggestions to improve the program for the next cohort.

Another program component that was strategically incorporated was a mentoring session between the graduating cohort and the entering cohort. This session proved to be very productive and informative, but more importantly, it provided a certain level of professional and personal kinship with the new cohort.

The Tenth and Eleventh Years: Years Four and Five in Querétaro

From 2004 to 2006, two cohorts totaling thirty-five (seventeen and eighteen, respectively) students from throughout California began their journey in each academic year. Their program orientation was focused on critical inquiry, reflection, examination, and interrogation about their ideological orientations. The orientation took place with the guidance of the same community learning circles facilitator. Teacher candidates developed trust and community-building activities to use periodically under the goals of community and trust building and maintenance. Since the teacher candidates chose to focus on community and trust amongst themselves, they were able to imagine surviving and coping with their upcoming experiences. The facilitator encouraged the teacher candidates to create a nonjudgmental, safe place to process deep-seated biases and/or dialectical situations, or "go deep" with their stories and tensions.

A DECADE OF PROGRAM SUCCESS

The ten-year mark was critical for the program in that it was time to revisit the vision and mission to prepare biliteracy teachers with a global perspective. Program feedback was used to critically analyze what had been done well and what needed improvement. Candidates kept daily journals, reacted to personal adjustments and professional experiences, and completed course evaluations. Candidates had two language assessments, one performed at the beginning of the academic year and one at the end of the experiences. Faculty competencies were both evaluated at the end of each first summer session and were repeated after each segment. Informal and formal group discussions took place and proved to be valuable in making adjustments to the overall program. A summative evaluation occurred at the end of each year. At the end of Year One, all nine candidates received their B/CLAD credentials. Four of them have now served as master teachers for student teachers for the new cohorts. Three have now completed their MA degrees at SDSU and are teaching in biliteracy programs. Several others have become principals and curriculum directors in school districts throughout California.

During the eleven years of the program, approximately 200 teacher candidates have completed their credentials, and many teach in California schools. If each teacher had only twenty-five pupils per year, then these teachers are having an impact on hundreds of children each year. Given its eleven years, it is estimated that the program has affected over 5,500 pupils. While the enrollment numbers each year were low, the quality of the teachers was exceptionally high, and the cultural experiences of these students were unlimited. The stories they tell are incredible. These teachers have completed a transforming experience unlike any other. They have become culturally and linguistically proficient global teachers and leaders who can better teach locally because they were prepared to teach and think globally (Alfaro 2003).

PROGRAM'S CHALLENGES, TENSIONS, AND NEGOTIATIONS

A major challenge for the program has always been to work around the politics of both countries faculty and academic exchanges. The following sections explain some of the challenges the program faced.

Faculty

Working with faculty colleagues has presented cross-cultural challenges to both nations. The Mexican faculty, talented individuals and academicians, have strong background knowledge in constructivist pedagogy. They did need to understand the California requirements for the teaching profession. This was initially solved by working with teacher educators at the Universidad Pedagógica Nacional in Mexico City, and later by working with professors at the Escuela Normal del Estado de Querétaro and others involved in teacher development. Nonetheless, without imposing a "California system," resident directors of ITEP had to reconcile the credentialing needs of U.S. institutions, which often are different from those used in Mexico, with the standards, teaching style, and strengths of teacher preparation in Mexico. In addition, much planning and discussion was required to develop the roles of cooperating teachers at school sites and the university supervisors for the varied student-teaching experiences in Mexico. After six years of the program in Querétaro, such issues continue to be a challenge due to the constant change in leadership, both in the government and in the Secretaria de Educación Publica in Mexico (Office of the Education Secretariat). However, our counterparts are always willing to work with us and believe in our program's ideology. California faculty have provided faculty and supervisors in Querétaro with workshops on supervision, and several Mexican faculty have had the opportunity to join their counterparts in California, visiting schools and teacher-preparation classrooms, and exchanging ideas with their peers. The tension that exists here is one of symmetry. California has benefited greatly by having our teacher candidates study in Mexico. The future challenge is how we can provide a similar experience for the Mexican teacher candidates.

Intercambios (Exchanges)

An underlying agenda for the Mexico B/CLAD program is to provide avenues for exchanges between the student teachers as well as the teachers/professors in both countries. In addition, the intention is to "give back" to Mexico, as a way of thanking the Estado de Querétaro for providing this unique opportunity for our teacher candidates.

This has occurred in a variety of ways. Mexican faculty are hosted by their counterparts in California, and they participate in cultural, language, and curricular workshops and field experiences. American teacher-education candidates had many opportunities to mix with Mexican teacher-education candidates through the *talleres* (workshops) that are offered at both the Instituto Tecnológico y Estudios Superiores de Monterrey (ITESM) campus, and at the Escuela Normal. At the ITESM, these *talleres* are usually either in the sports (e.g., soccer, basketball) or in the arts (e.g., Ballet Folklórico, guitar). At the Escuela Normal, the *talleres* cover a broad range of areas but are specifically applied to the field of education. These may include using the arts, using games in the classroom, or discussing issues of human sexuality. One workshop provides instruction in the Otomí language, which is native to the Querétaro area.

The SDSU teacher candidates themselves also "left their mark" in a variety of ways, from sharing music of both countries to helping to make school campuses more environmentally conscious. Many of the California students have shared housing with their Mexican peers, and a few have married Mexican nationals whom they met in Mexico. During their indigenous experiences, now in Jalpan and Atlacomulco, teacher candidates live with the families of Escuela Normal teacher-education candidates or with teachers and they have exciting exchanges of life experiences. They also complete community projects together at their school sites, which is also a major purpose of the program.

The major purpose of the Mexico B/CLAD program is to position teacher candidates in environments that require them to learn from a wide array of experiences and sources, including their own past experiences and preconceived notions. Through this process, teacher candidates come to understand the importance of the whole person in the act of learning, unlearning, relearning, and knowing (Alfaro 2003).

Experiences in Mexico have prompted teacher candidates' probing beneath the surface of their intellect and emotions to pose the following kinds of questions: What kind of teacher do I want to be? What are the origins of what I know? What are the political, social, cultural, linguistic, gendered, and emotional circumstances in which I have learned? What kind of changes do I need to make to my teaching that will enhance students' learning? And what are my blind spots?

The *intercambios* (exchanges) engage teachers in professional learning that is different from other forms of learning in California universities. They involve far more than the traditional teacher-preparation program where most of the emphasis is on meeting the standards, reading an additional chapter in a book, taking a field trip, or listening to a guest speaker.

PROGRAM COMPONENTS LEADING TO A BILITERATE AND BICULTURAL TEACHING FORCE

Formal Instruction

In the year-long program, teacher candidates begin their time in Mexico with an intensive three-week summer session of Spanish-language instruction conducted at the Instituto Tecnológico y Estudios Superiores de Monterrey (ITESM). This is followed in the fall semester by an additional course in Spanish and one in Latin American culture, taught in Spanish. In addition, those who test "advanced" on the ITESM examination are able to take additional advanced courses (e.g., Spanish literature and drama). Finally, in the short winter semester, students take a course in children's literature, again taught in Spanish. This course generally includes discussion of the key influences on education in Mexico, including the history of curricular changes with respect to literature. In addition, virtually all of the methods classes taught at the Escuela Normal del Estado de Querétaro (ENEQ) in the fall semester are taught entirely in Spanish, while some of the texts may be in English.

Field Experiences

In the fall semester, CSU B/CLAD student teachers spend one day per week in a Mexican private school, observing the teacher, helping with small-group work, and perhaps giving some instruction in the English language. They are able to listen to both the teacher and the children as they interact in Spanish, which provides another opportunity to enhance their own Spanish-language skills. In the spring semester, teacher candidates begin their formal student teaching in public schools in Querétaro. In the fourth and fifth weeks, if they are ready, they take full responsibility for teaching in the classroom. This work includes preparing their lessons, and evaluating and instructing the students—all in Spanish. This encourages the teacher candidates to higher levels of Spanish-language usage. This experience is followed by three additional weeks living and teaching in the indigenous community in Atlacomulco, Mexico. Living with the families of pupils or teachers, they again have ample opportunity to practice using Spanish, and to teach and learn in an indigenous community on a daily basis.

Informal Experiences

CSU teacher candidates are encouraged to get to know their Mexican counterparts in a profound manner. They begin this experience with a one-month homestay with a Mexican family. In this more informal environment, teacher candidates are encouraged to learn to use everyday Spanish and to get to know the ways and culture of the Mexican family. They are then encouraged either to stay with their "families" for the remainder of their time in Querétaro, or to find independent housing with ITESM or Escuela Normal teacher candidates, because when CSU students share apartments together their tendency is to fall back into using English. Since the students are typically social and young, they often attend fiestas and go to the local discos where they have the opportunity to meet Queretareños (locals), not necessarily in the field of education. These are great opportunities to expand their language and to make new friends (Kuhlman et al. 2003).

Formal Evaluation of Spanish Language Development

The California students, as mentioned at the beginning, come with various levels of knowledge of Spanish. Some are fluently bilingual/biliterates; others (about one third) are competent in oral language but lack competency in literacy skills, while a small number are challenged at all language levels. Teacher candidates have a variety of ways in which to enhance their Spanish-language skills, regardless of their present level. Teacher candidate growth in Spanish-language competence can be clearly seen in this program, based on the assessment of participants' oral language exit interviews.

PROGRAM IMPROVEMENT FACTORS

Since the program's inception, a number of issues have been addressed, including finances, money, recruitment, cross-cultural adjustment, the curriculum, and reciprocity to the host country.

Prior to the Title VII grant, recruitment was a major concern. While it is very attractive to spend a year in Mexico, it is also costly and requires leaving family and friends. The cost of the year, including all tuition, books, and room and board, is around $14,000, about what it would cost if teacher candidates lived away from home for a year. Candidates are eligible for all financial aid that they would receive if attending their home campus; however, they cannot work in Mexico. The addition of the Title VII grant monies was instrumental in helping reduce the cost by providing each student with approximately $5,000 in support during the year. Unfortunately, now that grant funds have been depleted and the 2005–2006 cohort participated without the benefit of the scholarship, fewer students participated in the last cohort.

We have also become more sophisticated in the ways in which we recruit. Placing ads in school newspapers and having regular orientation meetings that are widely publicized have all helped. Our number one recruitment device, however, is word of mouth created by the returning graduates. As the years go by, we have more and more applicants saying "I heard it from . . . who is now teaching at the school where I'm a teacher's aide." One teacher candidate came because the woman she was tutoring in Spanish found out about the program and they both joined the cohort.

Creating curriculum itself was a challenge from the beginning. Initially, four CSU campus representatives, along with a representative from CCTC and the ITEP director, came together to attempt to develop one common program, borrowing elements from all the participating campuses. This was a long and creative process, but consensus was reached after numerous meetings. Course numbers were chosen from SDSU (the California site) and the regular IP program (for the intensive language courses among others). The syllabi have continually changed, and have been updated to match changing requirements in California. However, other aspects of the program were worth reexamining.

First, the decision was made to move the students directly to Querétaro after a brief one-week orientation at SDSU, rather than holding the six-week summer session in San Diego as with previous cohorts. Another change was that CSU faculty would go to the Querétaro site and teach some of the initial classes that had previously been offered at SDSU.

In the curriculum itself, the ITEP faculty and director decided that a three-unit Standards/Frameworks course would be added to the California portion of the program to ensure that recently approved standards were seriously addressed by the B/CLAD teacher candidates. Also, a Reading Instruction Competency Assessment review course (reading methods test required of all those applying for elementary credentials in California) was embedded into the student-teaching seminar. A one-unit English-Language Development and a Specially Designed Academic Instruction in English (ELD/SDAIE) methods course had already been added in the third year, but this course would also now include the California-approved ELD Standards.

Recruitment of faculty from the CSU was not a major problem. As most of the teaching is during the summer, for those not at SDSU, it required relocating for a short time. The faculty are able to manage the spring courses, even though most campuses are still in session in April and May. The biggest challenge for these individuals was to adapt their campus syllabi to meet the special needs of the Mexico B/CLAD teacher candidates.

Integrating the Mexican faculty into the program created a special challenge. The faculty are talented teachers, but the program curriculum was aligned with California requirements, which often were quite different from those used in Mexico. In addition, much planning and discussion was required to implement the concept of master teacher and university supervisor for the student-teaching segments in Mexico. Finding new faculty, clearly stating expectations, and providing orientation to the new faculty and student-teaching supervisors were all discussed during the 2005 school year. The new faculty and supervisors in Querétaro have benefited from these previous experiences and have already attended several workshops on clinical supervision. The student-teacher handbook also provided a helpful tool for all those participating in the program.

SUMMARY

We know that there is an increase in efforts to internationalize our institutions of higher education, which necessitates the need to infuse, integrate, and implement international student-teaching programs. If we are to develop global citizens that support efforts of language, cultural, and global diversity, what role will colleges and schools of education play in the preparation of culturally and linguistically competent, global, proficient teachers? Will our graduates be equipped with the knowledge, skills, and dispositions required of twenty-first-century citizens? Will they have the required skills and be sensitive and have respect for human dignity and be able to improve current and future conditions? These are the fundamental questions that we as educators face as we prepare future teachers (Kirkwood 2001).

The chapter was organized to help educators in teacher-preparation programs think about language and cultural diversity in a global and integrative perspective. To prepare teachers, leaders, and other school personnel to meet the challenge of language and cultural diversity, a first and critically important step is to think reflectively about where one's institution, its school or college of education, and its teacher-preparation programs are situated in relation to the cultural proficiency model. The discussion of cultural proficiency was intended to help teacher educators locate themselves, their peers, and their teacher preparation on the continuum, via an inside-out reflective assessment, in hopes of moving teacher educators and their teacher-preparation programs toward cultural and linguistic global competence.

Supported with an interest and commitment to cultural and linguistic global competence, the remainder of the chapter provided teacher educators with an overview of the California State University-International Teacher Education Program (ITEP). The overview included demographics, the ITEP as a transformative model as a biliteracy teacher-education program, ITEP'S profile, program development, and evaluation. It also emphasized the need to develop collaborative partnerships with host-country government and educational institutions. Further, a discussion on the constraining and challenging factors and program successes was featured in order to allow strategies to consider in the planning and development of future global biliteracy teacher-education programs. We hope the discussion serves as an introduction to key issues in the areas of international/global teacher-preparation program development, and provides a base from which further understanding and actions can be developed in order to prepare culturally, linguistically, and globally proficient teachers. Providing global student-teaching experiences is the key ingredient if we want our future teachers to be linguistically, culturally, and globally literate in meeting the challenges that confront them in our U.S. classrooms.

SOME QUESTIONS TO CONSIDER

The following guiding questions will assist teacher educators, program directors, faculty, and others in the development and planning of global teaching-abroad programs. It will ensure that a culturally and linguistically global, proficient teaching force is ready and able to meet the needs of our global citizens.

- Where on the cultural and language proficiency continuum would you locate yourself? Where would you locate your peers, the teacher-education program, or school of education you work in?
- What attitudes, circumstances, and/or conditions help or hinder your movement (and the movement of your peers, the teacher-education program, or the school of education) toward global cultural and language proficiency?
- In thinking of the teacher-education population in your school of education, what are the global curricular approaches embedded in teacher-education courses? What opportunities or support would you need in order to bring those approaches into your work?
- In what ways can you better support biliteracy teacher candidates to address the needs of English-language learners? What additional information, resources, and support would you need on global teacher education to better serve your biliteracy teacher candidates?
- In what ways can you further support your biliteracy teachers through global teaching experiences that will enhance the relationship between the school, the home, the community, and their countries of origin?
- What learning outcomes do you believe are the most critical for biliteracy teachers as a result of participating in a global teaching experience through a teacher-education program?

REFERENCES

Alfaro, C. 2003. Transforming teacher education: Developing ideological clarity as a means for teaching with courage, solidarity and ethics. PhD diss., Claremont Graduate University and San Diego State University.

Bell, E. D., and G. C. Munn. 1999–2000. Can we create dreamkeepers for diverse classrooms? *National FORUM of Teacher Education Journal* (online journal), 11E: 3. At www.nationalforum.com/BELLte8e3.html (accessed May 24, 2003).

Bennett, M. J. 1993. Towards ethnorelativism: A developmental model of intercultural sensitivity. In *Education for the intercultural experience*, ed. R. M. Paige, 21–71. Yarmouth, ME: Intercultural Press.

California State University System (CSUS) B/CLAD Certificate Program, Mexico. n.d. *International Teacher Education Consortium Brochure* (online). At www.gateway.calstate.edu/csuinet/B/CLAD (accessed May 15, 2004).

California Department of Education (CDOE). 2006. *DataQuest: Educational demographics unit*. At www.data1.cde.ca.gov/Dataquest/ (accessed May 25, 2006).

Cushner, K., and R. Brislin. 1996. *Intercultural interactions: A practical guide*. 2nd ed. Thousand Oaks, CA: Sage.

Darder, A. 1992. Review of the book "Pedagogy of the Oppressed." *Nation* 255:301–2.

Delpit, L. 1995. *Other people's children: Cultural conflict in the classroom*. New York: New Press.

Freire, P. 1997. Letters to North American teachers. In *Freire for the classroom*, ed. I. Shor, 211–14. Portsmouth, NJ: Boynton/Cook.

Hodgkinson, H. L. 2002. The demographics of diversity. *Principal* 82:14–18.

Hollins, E. R., J. E. King, and W. C. Hayman, eds. 1994. *Teaching diverse populations: Formulating a knowledge base*. Albany: SUNY Press.

Kirkwood, F. T. 2001. Preparing teachers to teach from a global perspective. *Delta Kappa Gamma Bulletin* 67, no. 2:5–12.

Kuhlman, N., C. Alfaro, J. Attinasi, M. Driesbach, and R. Merino. 2003. Transforming California teachers: A biliteracy program in Mexico. *Mextesol* 26, nos. 3–4 (Winter/Spring).

Lindsey, R. B., K. N. Robins, and R. D. Terrell. 1999. *Cultural proficiency: A manual for school leaders*. Thousand Oaks, CA: Corwin Press

McFalls, E. L., and D. Cobb-Roberts. 2001. Reducing resistance to diversity through cognitive dissonance instruction: Implications for teacher education. *Journal of Teacher Education* 52:164–72.

Office of English Language Acquisition (OLEA). 2006. The growing number of limited English students, 1993/94–2003/04. At http://ncela.gwu.edu/stats/2_nation.htm (accessed August 6, 2006).

Quezada, L. R. (2005). "Beyond educational tourism:" Lessons learned while student teaching abroad. *International Education Journal* 5, no. 4:458–65.

Quezada, L. R., and C. Alfaro. 2007. Biliteracy teachers' self reflections of their accounts while student teaching abroad: speaking from "the other side." *Teacher Education Quarterly* 34(1) 95–113.

Quezada, L. R., and K. Osajima. 2005. The challenges of diversity: Moving toward cultural proficiency. In *Current issues in school leadership*, Ed. L. W. Hughes, 163–82. Mahwah, NJ: Lawrence Erlbaum.

Ramirez, M., and A. Castaneda. 1974. *Cultural democracy, bicognitive development, and education*. New York: Academic Press.

Smith, R., and A. Zantiotis. 1989. Practical teacher education and the avant-garde. In *Critical pedagogy, the state, and the cultural struggle*, ed. H. A. Giroux and P. McLaren, 105–24. Albany: State University of New York Press.

Zhou, M. 2003. Urban education: Challenges in educating culturally diverse children. *Teachers College Record* 105:208–25.

APPENDIX

Mexico Bilingual Crosscultural, Language and Academic Development Credential
(BCLAD) AY 2005–2006

Start Date: June 20, 2005, End Date: June 23, 2006

Summer 2005: Querétaro, Mexico

Course Number	Course Title	Number of Units
SP 315	Intermediate/Advance Spanish	3.0
PLC 911	Teaching Social Studies to Bilingual Elementary Students	2.0
PLC 932	Skills in Teaching Reading to Bilingual Elementary Students/ELD SDAIE (Three Weeks)	3.0
PLC 901	Introduction to Teaching Portfolio	2.0

Total Summer Units: 10

Fall 2005: Querétaro, Mexico

Course Number	Course Title	Number of Units
PLC 923	Psychological Foundation of Education & Bilingual Students	3.0
PLC 910	Teaching Mathematics to Bilingual Elementary Students	2.0
SP 351	Development of Spanish Communication Skills	3.0
HS 316	Mexican & Latin American Civilization and Culture	3.0

(continued)

Fall 2005: Querétaro, Mexico (continued)

Course Number	Course Title	Number of Units
LI 430	Children's Literature in Spanish	2.0
PLC 960	Student-Teaching Seminar for Bilingual Students	2.0
PLC 961	Student-Teaching Seminar for Bilingual Students	3.0

Total Fall Units: 18.0

Spring 2006: San Diego State University

Course Number	Course Title	Number of Units
PLC 686	Student Teaching for Bilingual Elementary Students	3.0
PLC 963	Student Teaching for Bilingual Elementary Students	4.0

Total Units: 7

Summer 2006:

Course Number	Course Title	Number of Units
PLC 931	Skills in Teaching Language Arts to Elementary Students	3.0
PLC 962	Student Teaching (Field Experience)	8.0
PLC 960	Student-Teaching Seminar for Bilingual Elementary Students	3.0
PLC 915	Teaching & Learning in the Content Area: English Language Development/SDAIE	3.0
PLC 912	Teaching Science to Bilingual Elementary Students	3.0
PLC 902	Professional Portfolio /RICA	1.0

Total Units: 21

Prerequisite Courses (Granting Credentials)	Number of Units
Class Adaptation for Special Populations	2.0
Health for Educators	1.0
Technologies for Education	3.0

Total Prerequisite Units: 6.0

	Number of Units
Summer 2005	10.0
Fall 2005	18.0
Spring 2006	7.0
Summer 2006	21.0
Prerequisites	6.0
Total IP BCLAD Credential Program Units	**62.0**

7

PROMOTING REFLECTION DURING OVERSEAS STUDENT-TEACHING EXPERIENCES: ONE UNIVERSITY'S STORY

Sharon Brennan
Julie Cleary

The University of Kentucky (UK) has a firm and long-standing commitment to international education, which is one of the essential ingredients in building sustainable international programs identified by Mahon and Espinetti in chapter 2 of this book. The overseas student-teaching program, established more than thirty years ago by UK and several other universities, represents one of many examples of institutional commitment to this important aspect of the educational process.

As noted in chapter 1, the University of Kentucky's program was created under the auspices of the Consortium for Overseas Student Teaching (COST) to provide intercultural experiences for students preparing to teach. The organization was formed out of concern that teacher candidates at participating institutions had very limited experiences working with culturally diverse groups. One source of concern noted by UK officials was the high percentage of candidates from rural, homogeneous, and sometimes insular communities who were entering the teacher-education program. A major goal in establishing the program was to broaden the cultural perspective of these candidates to include a global view. Program founders wanted candidates to develop what some scholars today regard as culturally responsive practices (Gay 2002; Hollins and Guzman 2005; Ladson-Billings 1999), and to become what

Lindsey, Robins, and Terrell (1999) describe as culturally proficient teachers.

Since its inception, program faculty involved in shaping the overseas student-teaching experience for UK candidates have worked to carry out the goal of improving candidates' level of cultural proficiency. Early on, developers established high standards and program requirements to ensure quality. Over the years, the requirements have been periodically reviewed and revised in order to maximize the benefits of the experience and to monitor program quality. This *re-vision* process has kept the program vibrant.

Our purpose in writing this chapter is to explain how UK's overseas program developed. In the chapter, we discuss changes made to help participants deepen their understanding of other cultures in ways that translate into practice. We focus much of the discussion on describing a structure recently built to enhance reflection about cultural and pedagogical issues and sharing what we have learned through the process. We present this as a story that is still unfolding. We hope our account will be useful to colleagues at other universities who wish to create international programs for their teacher candidates or revise existing programs.

PROGRAM PARTICIPATION, STANDARDS, AND REQUIREMENTS

Although we do not have official records regarding participation in UK's program dating back to when it formally began in 1973, it appears the pattern of participation has been consistently strong. The program has served candidates with varying interests, needs, and experiences. For the past decade, fifteen to twenty candidates have participated each year and student-teaching placements have been made in many parts of the world. University of Kentucky candidates have learned to teach in Central and South America, Europe, Australia, New Zealand, and South Africa. Most subject areas and grade levels have been represented over the years, ranging from preschool to high school, and from music to physical education. Candidates preparing to teach special education and art have completed their culminating field experience in other nations

us to ask how we might help our overseas participants think critically about their experiences.

BUILDING A STRUCTURE FOR REFLECTION

The introduction of electronic mail (e-mail) several years ago paved the way for improving the reflective process. Once student teachers gained access to e-mail, they began corresponding informally with their supervisors about their experiences. However, the electronic connection did not address the issue of superficial reflection immediately. It seemed that supervisors received more pictures and stories of travels than substantive analytical reflections. At that point, we knew we needed to structure the reflection process differently.

Capitalizing on the electronic communication system to solicit deeper reflections, we made three significant changes in the process. We moved from a paper medium for recording reflections to an electronic one to facilitate interaction; we created a schedule to prompt reflection at pivotal times during the placement; and we created questions to help candidates focus on specific aspects of the experience. We used questions developed by Cushner and Mahon (2002) as a springboard for creating questions that fit our situation. We organized the questions into four sets roughly corresponding to the phases of student teaching (i.e., orientation, observation, instruction, and transition) and sent them to participants at regular intervals, roughly every three weeks. We retained the surveys and debriefing sessions. However, we replaced the individual sessions with focus group meetings to increase interactive opportunities so several supervisors and student teachers could debrief together. We also added a celebratory, welcoming touch by providing lunch for the meeting.

The purpose of the first set of questions is to help participants reflect on initial impressions regarding the host culture (school and community) in relation to their expectations prior to arrival. We want our candidates to think about cultural issues in terms of comparing the school where they are placed and schools where they completed earlier field placements. The intent of the second question set is to help participants reflect about what they are learning about "being American" and what they are learning from their cooperating teacher. The third set focuses on how student teachers are helping their pupils become acquainted with their (the student teacher's) home culture. In the fourth set, we want candidates to think about what they have learned about themselves personally and professionally (e.g., how they have confronted challenges, what they have gained from the experience, changes in their global awareness) and how they will apply what they learned in the international setting to their teaching practice. The survey, which is completed shortly before candidates leave the host country, focuses on issues related to quality of preparation, support and guidance provided during the placement, and the value of the experience as a whole. The purpose of debriefing is to help returnees think about reentry issues, how they will highlight the value of the experience in job interviews, and to comment on the value of a structured reflection process. We also use the debriefing session as an opportunity to follow up on any unclear responses to prompts made during the placement. Although questions vary somewhat depending on the situation, they always relate to the purpose of the set. We have included a list of representative questions in appendix A. To ensure that candidates are fully apprised of the procedure, we distribute and review questions during the orientation session held shortly before they depart for the host country.

SUMMARIZING PARTICIPANTS' RESPONSES

Last year (2005–2006), we launched the structured reflection process. Since we retained the end-of-placement surveys and debriefing sessions as part of the procedure, we now have six distinct data points for examining the level of reflection and for tracking growth. However, we have not yet conducted a fine-grained analysis of the data since we are still refining the questions. What we report here is a summary of responses to provide a sense of participants' reflections about cultural and pedagogical issues as they progress through the overseas experience.

To augment this general discussion, we have included one discussion of perceptions in the appendix written by a COST graduate. Rachael Humbert (see appendix B) completed her student-teaching placement in West Sussex, England, in elementary education during the spring 2004 semester. Her article, entitled "Learning by Leaving: What I Learned from Student Teaching in England," was published in the fall 2004 issue of the newsletter we distribute to partners in our field network.

Fifteen candidates used the new reflection process in the 2005–2006 academic year, seven during the fall semester and eight in the spring. All seven who participated in the fall were enrolled in the elementary education program; four were placed in England, two in Australia, and one in Ireland. Of the eight student teachers who participated in the spring, four were preparing to teach at the secondary level, three at elementary level, and one at the middle-school level. During that semester, the middle- and secondary-school candidates all taught in Cape Town, South Africa. The elementary education students were in Australia, Ireland, and New Zealand.

Comparing School Settings

In comparing school settings, the difference most often mentioned was the frequency of breaks in the school day. Comments about break periods were also made in responses in the third question set and during debriefing sessions. The frequency of break-related comments and degree of enthusiasm with which they were delivered suggest this practice made a deep impression on our candidates. Several noted that breaking up the day seemed to renew pupils and teachers, especially due to morning and afternoon tea, which several pointed out does not exist in U.S. schools. A response by a candidate teaching in an elementary school illustrates this point. She described small breaks in the school day, when teachers would direct students to stop working and touch something in the room with a specified characteristic (e.g., something colored blue). Some respondents mentioned that longer lunch breaks, which were largely unsupervised, provided unstructured time for pupils to play and teachers to meet.

Respondents also described curricular differences between the host school and schools in Kentucky. For example, candidates who taught social studies mentioned that they were required to teach about weather, which was not part of their preparation program in social studies since weather is part of the science curriculum in U.S. schools. Other respondents noted lags in technology in the classroom, principals teaching classes, an emphasis on strict discipline that sometimes involved public humiliation, respect for adults, enthusiasm for learning, and terminology (e.g., "jumper for sweater") as differences. The comment about language usage is congruent with Andersen's discussion in chapter 8 about language differences noted by pupils and cooperating teachers in New Zealand who worked with our student teachers. Respondents said that while they saw differences in customs, they also noticed numerous similarities. Several mentioned that the "pop culture" prevalent in America was evident everywhere. Some respondents made the point that children around the world are very similar. One comment sums up the sentiment well: "Kids are kids everywhere with the same hopes and dreams."

"Being American" and Learning from the Cooperating Teacher

The question of perceptions about "being American" elicited a variety of negative comments. Five respondents expressed dismay about the negative image of America in the world. Several expressed concern about the lack of courteousness on the part of Americans they encountered and their narrow view of the world. One respondent lamented being immediately recognized as American and another noticed a tendency to stereotype Americans. On a more positive note, one candidate placed in New Zealand commented that her pupils seemed eager to learn about America, which is in concert with comments made by pupils in Andersen's study. Reflections about mentoring by the cooperating teacher in this question set were quite positive. Most respondents cited benefits in the area of classroom management gained through observations and conferences. Respondents also mentioned specific skills such as "energizers" during transition times when intense periods of academic work were intermingled with short periods of physical activity (e.g., stretching, running) and more general skills, such as time management.

Teaching about Home and Host Cultural Issues

All respondents discussed ways they helped pupils become acquainted with their home (U.S.) culture. Several discussed lessons in which they had pupils compare traditions in the United States with traditions in the host country. Other strategies mentioned include teaching about holidays and other customs in the home and host countries, introducing artifacts from home (e.g., handcrafted instruments), telling stories, playing games (e.g., Jeopardy, focusing on home and host country), and corresponding with pupils in classrooms of colleagues in the United States. One student created a digital portrait of her life, including childhood pictures, as a way to introduce herself to her pupils. She enlisted their help revising the portrait to include information about her work with them during the semester. She also helped them build their own digital portraits, copies of which she brought home. Two of the secondary teachers discussed lessons they taught about historical and geographical aspects of the host country, which they described as both challenging and rewarding. Two others wrote about how their involvement in the school's extracurricular activities helped them learn about the culture and strengthen relationships with pupils as well as faculty.

Challenges, Growth, and Application to Teaching

Responses to the fourth question set, regarding challenges encountered, growth, and application to teaching, suggest that candidates achieved the program goal of promoting cultural learning. Respondents mentioned various challenges, including overcoming homesickness, adapting to the culture, adjusting to different expectations and resources, dealing with discipline and classroom management issues, and becoming more flexible. Several candidates commented that overcoming challenges served as a catalyst for growth. Respondents used a variety of key terms to describe their growth and some terms were used by many participants. These included independence, cultural sensitivity, open-mindedness, success adapting to different customs, gaining confidence, realizing that different doesn't mean "better or worse," and developing a "can do" attitude. Participants' responses suggest that all experienced a broadening in their global awareness. Responses included seeing more similarities in people around the world than before participation, increased awareness of the country, and a new respect for other cultures. Regarding how they will apply what they learned when they begin practicing, student teachers' comments included helping pupils

"look outside America for answers," emphasizing global education, examining complexities of cultural practices, and making connections with
other parts of the world. Respondents also indicated they plan to teach
about other cultures using resources acquired during the experience,
such as artifacts, books, and maps. Some indicated they would teach
about climate, share stories, and examine different perspectives as well
as different uses of the English language. Several said they will "lobby
for morning tea."

Value of Experience, Preparation, Guidance, and Support

Responses to survey questions indicate that all found value in the program. Several indicated that they learned as much or more from their
pupils as they taught. (See Rachael Humbert's article in appendix B for
a vivid example illustrating this point.) All indicated they would recommend participation to others; many punctuated their statements with
exclamation points. Respondents indicated that they felt well prepared
to teach overseas and well supported during the experience by supervisors in the host school and at home. All noted the preparatory course described in chapter 3 helped them learn to deal with stages of culture
shock and examine cultural practices. Several said they found the assignment to work with amigo partners particularly helpful as it provided
opportunities to hone their communication skills. Respondents cited
constructive feedback from cooperating teachers and their modeling of
effective practices as helpful forms of guidance.

Reentry Perceptions, Preparing for Interviews, and Structured Reflections

All returnees noticed differences in their fellow Americans when they
returned home. One returnee commented that Americans seemed loud,
another said people seemed demanding, and another mentioned that
food here seemed strange. Several commented on the large number of
overweight people they noticed when they returned home compared to
those they saw in the country where they taught. Returnees indicated
they felt well prepared to highlight the value of the experience during
interviews for teaching positions, frequently using examples of what

they had learned about the host culture during interviews. Examples described in the articles included in the appendices are representative of activities discussed during the debriefing sessions. Several said they thought that confidence gained living and teaching abroad would help during interviews. Returnees generally liked the structured reflection process. Some said it helped them focus, and others indicated they needed structure to stimulate the reflective process. However, several mentioned that responding sometimes proved challenging, such as when they had power outages or when they felt pressed by teaching demands. Participants said the questions targeted important points and found the feedback helpful.

FINDING CONSISTENCIES AND MAKING CONNECTIONS

Clearly, we cannot draw definitive conclusions about the effectiveness of the structure in terms of deepening reflection at this point. The data are limited and we have not conducted a formal, systematic analysis of the responses. However, the consistencies in responses, especially in areas related to cultural learning, are encouraging. There appears to be strong agreement in perceptions about cultural differences and similarities, overcoming challenges, and applications to practice. Interestingly, the areas of cultural growth described by these participants are the same areas identified by participants in past years. Even though reflections were not documented in previous years, summary reports suggest broad agreement.

What we find particularly interesting about the responses is the compatibility of the perceptions of our participants with those of cooperating (associate) teachers and pupils in New Zealand who participated in Andersen's study, as discussed in chapter 8. Teachers in his study who worked with COST participants noticed student teachers battling homesickness when they arrived and sensed their reluctance to leave when the placement was over. Regarding overall value, our participants commented positively throughout the reflective process about gains in understanding both the host culture and their own way of life resulting from their overseas experience. Comments from teachers and pupils on the receiving side in New Zealand suggest similar benefits to hosts. According to Andersen's report, COST participants helped hosts examine their own assumptions and become better informed about New Zealand as well as about the United States. "Similarity of language" was one faulty assumption noted by Andersen's respondents as well as ours.

It appears that student teachers in the surveyed group attained a high degree of cultural proficiency during the overseas experience. Their responses showed awareness of nuances in the host culture, which earns a top rating on Hanvey's cultural awareness scale (1975). Their involvement in the host school and community places them in the cultural proficiency category using Lindsey, Robins, and Terrell's taxonomy (1999). Responses also indicate that participants meet Gay's criteria for culturally responsive practice (2002), which include recognizing and respecting values, traditions, communication patterns, and learning styles of different cultural groups.

REFINING THE PROCESS

The richness of participant responses inspires us to move forward with the task of refining the process. When revising questions, we will reconsider how pieces of the structure fit together (i.e., points addressed in the preparation course, reflective prompts, and survey and debriefing questions). In chapter 3, Wilson and Flournoy underscore the importance of thorough preparation, and in chapter 2, Mahon and Espinetti emphasize the value of follow-up during the reentry stage to help candidates think through their perceptions and fully utilize their experiences as they begin their careers.

Now that we have a more comprehensive process in place to help candidates reflect while they are overseas, we will work to better connect the parts. For example, we would like to include in the data set information collected prior to departure. This includes documentation of participants' goals, expectations, and perceptions as well as demographic information. Through e-mail dialogue that occurs during the placement, we can probe more to foster deeper reflection. At the same time, we don't want to be overbearing and realize we need to proceed thoughtfully. Like other supporters on the home front, we must take care not to disrupt the growth process while candidates are abroad. This is especially important during the initial phase of cultural adjustment when participants tend to struggle with homesickness. We want to help them examine their discoveries, and at the same time, give them room to overcome challenges on their own so they will assimilate into the culture and gain independence.

One way we might give candidates some breathing room is to reshape the reflection structure slightly. We are contemplating the idea of combining the survey with the fourth set of questions to achieve that goal. Since some items in the survey overlap with questions posed in the last set, we should be able to consolidate them without difficulty. We might actually achieve better results through this consolidation. Since candidates will respond via the interactive electronic system to all questions posed while they are abroad, probes can be used for clarification and expansion of ideas.

RESEARCH POSSIBILITIES AND FUTURE DIRECTION

The creation of a database system opens many opportunities for research for us and for others. For example, we can now conduct formal studies using data generated through the process, and our first project will be to carefully examine the data we have collected. To do that, we will need to use a formal data analysis system. We are considering Hatton and Smith's (1995), since their categories fit with the kind of reflection we want to promote.

We can use what we learn from data analyses to strengthen the overseas program and to strengthen our teacher-education program as a whole. Student teachers who do not travel overseas to complete their placements could use the reflection structure in local schools. Interestingly, the candidates in Whipp's (2003) study taught in domestic settings and improved their reflections through electronic dialogue with supervisors during their student-teaching placement. Whipp found, as did we, that candidates needed frequent prompting to examine their assumptions and deeply reflect about their practice. Our teacher-preparation program is grounded in a theoretical model of reflection with a strong commitment to promoting culturally responsive practice. Therefore, questions like those we are revising might help all our candidates, wherever they teach, reflect deeply about cultural issues as they work with pupils.

Of course, there are various other possibilities for studies beyond looking at what we have in hand or might use for our own program improvement. One is to look at the whole continuum of teacher growth from the time candidates apply to student teach overseas through at least the initial phase of their teaching careers. We would like to understand more about how COST graduates maintain culturally rich classrooms over time and how their efforts to foster global thinking actually influence learning. We would also like to know whether and how COST graduates become involved in international initiatives within the local community. We know that several of our graduates are actively involved in such initiatives in the Lexington area, but we don't know much about those who are teaching in other communities.

Taking a slightly different direction, we would like to know more about the relationships that develop between our participants and the hosts at receiving sites. Andersen's report piqued our curiosity and helped us realize that we know very little about how our participants contribute to the communities where they are placed. We were intrigued by the similarity of perceptions of the COST participants compared with the cooperating teachers and pupils with whom they worked in New Zealand. The parallel reports about misperceptions and comments alluding to universal traits that cut across cultures were particularly intriguing. We would like to explore the degree to which learning together enhances feelings of connectedness and how those feelings translate into future actions. Comments such as "kids are kids everywhere," made by one respondent in our pool, helped us see the many possibilities for research in this area, especially in light of what we know about minimization.

We feel pleased with the progress we have achieved over the past two years, building a structure that better stimulates reflection. One clear benefit is that we now have a systematic way to monitor the cultural development of our participants. What we have attempted to do in this chapter is tell the story of the changes made to encourage deeper reflection. Telling the story has helped us think about what has been accomplished and it has given us a clearer sense of direction. We will use questions like those that prompted us to build the current structure as a basis for moving forward. We agree with Mahon and Espinetti when they said in chapter 2 that the key to program sustainability is constant questioning. Program leaders at our university have always used questioning as a way to guide revisions that may explain the program's longevity.

REFERENCES

Dewey, J. 1933. *How we think*. New York: Heath.

Cushner, K., and J. Mahon. 2002. Overseas student teaching: Affecting personal, professional and global competencies in an age of globalization. *Journal of International Studies in Education* 6, no. 2:44–58.

Gay, G. 2002. Preparing for culturally responsive teaching. *Journal of Teacher Education* 53, no. 2:106–16.

Hanvey, R. 1975. *An attainable global perspective*. New York: Center for War/Peace Studies.

Hatton, N., and D. Smith. 1995. Reflection in teacher education: Towards definition and implementation. *Teaching and Teacher Education* 11, no. 1:33–49.

Hollins, E., and M. Guzman. 2005. Research on preparing teachers for diverse populations. In *Studying teacher education: The report of the AERA panel on research in teacher education*, ed. M. Cochran-Smith and K. Zeichner, 477–548. Mahwah, NJ: Lawrence Erlbaum.

Humbert, R. 2004. Learning by leaving: What I learned from student teaching in England. *Field Notes about Teaching and Teacher Education* (Fall).

Ladson-Billings, G. 1999. Preparing teachers for diverse student populations. *Review of Research in Education* 24:211–48.

Lindsey, R. B., K. N. Robins, and R. D. Terrell. 1999. *Cultural proficiency: A manual for school leaders*. Thousand Oaks, CA: Corwin Press.

Loughran, J. 2002. Effective reflective practice. In search of meaning in learning about teaching. *Journal of Teacher Education* 53, no. 1:33–43.

Whipp, J. 2003. Scaffolding critical reflection in online discussions: Helping prospective teachers think deeply about field experiences in urban schools. *Journal of Teacher Education* 54, no. 4:321–33.

Yost, D. S., S. M. Sentner, and A. Forlenza-Bailey. 2000. An examination of the construct of critical reflection: Implications for teacher education programming in the 21st century. *Journal of Teacher Education* 51:39–49.

APPENDIX A

Sample COST Participant Structured Reflection Questions

Notations regarding timelines for question prompts are approximate and are tailored to fit individual circumstances.

Set 1: (Week 3)   What have you learned about your host culture?

How does this relate to your expectations about the culture before your arrival?

In what ways is the school different from schools where you completed your field placements at home? In what ways is it similar?

Set 2: (Week 6)   What are you learning from your cooperating teacher that is helping you grow professionally?

What are you learning about "being American" as you view it from another vantage point?

Set 3: (Week 9)   What have you done (or are doing) to introduce your pupils and others to your "home culture"?

Are you teaching any content that relates specifically to the host culture? If so, what?

Set 4: (Week 12)   What aspects of teaching in the host culture are proving to be most challenging? How are you addressing the challenges?

How have you grown personally and professionally from completing this experience?

Has the experience broadened your global awareness? If so, how?

How are you going to apply what you have learned from teaching in another culture in your practice?

Survey: (Week 14)   What aspect(s) of your preparation were most helpful in preparing you for this intercultural student-teaching experience?

What were the most beneficial aspects of the preparation course (EDC 554) that helped you with the intercultural experience?

Did you find the support and guidance you received during the experience helpful? In what ways?

Did you find the experience valuable? Would you recommend the program to other teacher candidates? Explain.

Debriefing: (Shortly after returning home)   Does anything about the United States or your community seem different than before you left in terms of your perceptions?

What unique strengths do you bring to teaching as a result of this experience?

What would you say to a principal or interview committee about the experience in terms of how it has prepared you to be an effective teacher?

Did you find the structure used to promote reflection helpful?

Were the questions helpful?

Do you have suggestions for changing the structure and/or questions?

APPENDIX B

Learning by Leaving: What I Learned from Student Teaching in England

Rachael Humbert

The day I left for England was unforgettable. My mother's last words to me were, "Don't forget to pluck your eyebrows," and my Dad told me that England was "not that far away." I hugged them both and chuckled inside. Then, I found my window seat and wrestled with the "happy to go but sad to leave" emotions welling up inside of me. For seven hours I stared at the light at the end of the airplane wing and thought, "What am I getting myself into?" I had joined the University of Kentucky's Consortium for Overseas Student Teaching (COST) Program and was on my way to complete my student teaching in another country. As it turned out, I learned much more than I taught—and I taught a lot.

I realized as soon as I stepped off the plane at Heathrow Airport that I had made the right choice. I was scared, nervous, alone and I loved it. To me there's nothing better than wandering outside of my comfort zone just to find out how big it really is. I learned a lot at the airport—mainly I learned to KEEP LEFT! Driving on the other side of the road means walking on the other side of the hallways and going through the other double door—not as easy as I thought but simple enough to remember. Crossing the street—now that's a bit more difficult!

After the first day ensconced in my new home in West Sussex, England, I learned to walk behind the British people when crossing the street; I could produce the right amount of pounds and pence if the cashier was patient; and I discovered the difference between trousers and pants. I slid quite easily into the social scene, following the hoards of university students to the nightclub on the pier and meeting them the next night at the university bar or local pub.

At the end of two weeks, I successfully used the train to get to Cardiff and back, although I must admit that my new friends had more to do with it than I did. As I began student teaching in two classrooms—years 3 (2nd grade) and 4 (3rd grade) at the Westbourne House School, I struggled with a new school, new curriculum, new schedule, new handwriting and new accents. Now, when I say "struggled," I don't mean it was difficult, but adapting to a new culture presents its own challenges. Every day I came home with all this new information in my head and my brain said, "Hmmm, now where shall I put this? It doesn't quite fit here, so I'll put it there." I found these new experiences invigorating!

I spent the next three weeks getting comfortable. Finally, I could get through a whole day at school without asking someone for an explanation. I could tell my kids to "use a rubber" (eraser) without thinking twice, and I could chit-chat in the staff room as if I had been there for years. I always welcomed the opportunity to talk about Kentucky, but I never pressed my "American-ness." My teachers became my friends. They invited me out for "Skittles Night" and were excited for me to go "on holiday" to France.

By the midterm "holiday," my brain had magically sorted it all out. I could feel the gears turning, forcing me to adapt, adjust and carry on using everything I know combined with everything I was learning. I stopped converting every pound to dollars. I knew that the answer to "Are you all right?" wasn't "Yes, I feel fine—why, do I look sick?" but rather, "Yes, thank you. And how are you?"

A two-week Easter break gave me the opportunity to stretch my comfort zone again. Two days alone in London taught me how to protect my belongings and myself. I learned how to hop on and off "The Tube" at the right place and find my way to the hostel before dark despite my tendency to turn the wrong way when crossing the street. After using five forms of transportation, I found myself in France where I learned how to keep my mouth shut and listen. I made friends who didn't speak my language and I even learned how to salsa dance.

My last two weeks in England taught me more than the first 13 combined. I discovered that I had a life there. I learned that people cared about me and I cared about them as if they were my own family. I learned that no matter what country you're in, children still like to dance and hear different accents. They all get tired at the end of the day and they all want to know that they're important. I learned that when I don't know what they're talking about, it's okay to let them teach me.

My evaluation report says my teaching has improved, but it was one of my students that made it clear that I've gotten better. Tom, one of my year four students with a learning disability, asked me every single day if I'm with them for a certain lesson. About five weeks ago, I passed him outside on break and he said, "Miss Humbert, will you be taking us for literacy?" "Yes, Tom, I'll be with you for literacy." He looked disappointed. "Is that good or bad," I asked. "Eh," he said. "It's all right, I guess." Tom had continued to ask the same question every day. So every morning, I went to his classroom, and let him look at my timetable. On Friday, I was sitting at the teacher's desk trying to get my binder in order, and Tom came over to look at my schedule. I looked at him while he was reading it, putting one finger on the day and one finger on the time, working the plans out in his head. I sat patiently. "Hmmm," he said. "Looks like you'll be with us for literacy." I got nervous. "Oh good, and you'll be here for Maths." This is a little better. "Oh," he sounded surprised, "You'll be with us nearly all day! Hooray!" "Is that good, Tom. Can you handle having me here all day again?" "Yes, I believe that works out quite well for me," he said. And he smiled. I was relieved and very proud of myself.

Those four months in England taught me that I am independent, resourceful and creative. Student teaching abroad taught me about another culture and that teaching children in another culture is both different and similar to teaching students at home. I learned that I can be successful anywhere.

Most importantly, I learned through the COST experience that I am a teacher. I teach myself, I teach my friends and I teach my students. Every experience has added to my growing and changing perspective. My life—from my Old Kentucky Home to my English seaside town and everything in between—has prepared me for my next amazing adventure—bringing the world to the children I teach in my very own classroom.

8

WORKING WITH AMERICAN STUDENT TEACHERS: THE VIEW OF NEW ZEALAND HOSTS

Neil Andersen

I know we are the same because we both speak English [but] they speak sometimes different from us.

—Pupil, aged eleven years

We're not the same because Canada's touching America on the top of it and Mexico is touching America on the bottom of it and New Zealand has nothing—around it is water.

—Pupil, aged six to seven years

[She] learned that while there are a number of cultural aspects which may be different, at a deeper level there is less difference— family is important.

—Associate teacher

For twenty years, student teachers participating in the Consortium for Overseas Student Teaching (COST) have been introducing American culture and language—*tikanga* and *reo* in New Zealand Maori terms— to Christchurch school and neighbourhood communities. Between 1987 and 2006, 114 COST student teachers (6 male and 108 female) have been placed in schools in Christchurch, New Zealand, for their practicum placements for periods of between six and sixteen weeks, and almost all of them have been hosted by homestay families within the school's community.

The COST programme was introduced to Christchurch in 1987 by Dr. Colin Knight, the principal of the Christchurch College of Education. Dr. Knight had studied with the founders of COST, Dr. Everett Keach and Dr. Marion Rice, at the University of Georgia in 1980–1981. Since his dissertation focused on attitudes of students regarding other nationalities, Dr. Knight wanted to continue to explore ways in which to develop international understanding and world peace (Knight 1982). In a recent interview, Dr. Knight reflected on the reasons for bringing COST to New Zealand:

> With my research finding that international understanding amongst school children was affected more successfully through face-to-face meetings than through classroom instruction, Dr. Keach obviously thought that I would be interested in continuing a programme [COST] that fostered contact between individuals from different cultures.

Kissock (1997) suggested that student teaching may be the best time for teacher candidates to develop their intercultural skills, especially when they complete a placement in an overseas community setting. Studies of candidates after they return to the United States indicate that overseas school and community experience has significantly influenced their personal and professional lives (Cushner and Mahon 2002; various chapters in this volume). What has been less well documented is the situated learning experience of the homestay families, the associate teacher, and the pupils who are associated with the host classroom. In his interview, Dr. Knight noted that in the twenty years of involvement with COST, approximately 3,000 pupils in New Zealand schools have had the opportunity of contact with a "real live American," considering there are thirty pupils per class (Knight interview 2005).

This observation raises a variety of interesting questions. For example, what is the impact of COST participants on the pupils with whom they interact? Are pupils' assumptions about Americans altered as a result of the experience? Similarly, what is the impact on the associate teachers with whom these student teachers were placed for the duration of their placement? And what has been the experience of the host families? What is the outcome or impact of having hosted a student teacher from another culture in their community for a sustained period of time? This chapter addresses these questions by examining this aspect of the intercultural relationship between COST participants and their hosting communities in Christchurch, New Zealand.

THE INVESTIGATION

During the middle of the New Zealand school year in 2003 (May to August), COST placed four student teachers in four different schools in Christchurch. These four student teachers formed the cohort for this research that examined the impact of COST participants on the hosting communities—school classrooms and homestay families. The COST receiving site coordinator in Christchurch established school placements for each of the student teachers and through each school principal, homestay accommodation was found with families within each school's community. In all cases, this meant that the student teacher was living with a family that either had or used to have children attending the school of their placement. This provided the potential for the student teacher to experience the home-and-school links within the New Zealand setting. Two of the four student teachers spent their placement time in two classrooms, while the other two student teachers spent time in only one classroom.

Soon after each of the COST students returned to the United States following the completion of their placement, questionnaires were mailed to their associate teachers and host families, inviting them to record their perceptions about the experience of hosting the COST student teacher. In addition, arrangements were made with each of the four school principals for the pupils in each class to be interviewed the week after the departure of the COST student teacher. All interviews were recorded and the discussions later transcribed by the researcher.

EXAMINING ASSUMPTIONS ABOUT CULTURE AND GAINING INSIGHT ABOUT DIFFERENCE

When a student teacher participating in COST hears that he or she has been placed in New Zealand, anecdotal evidence suggests that this brings an air of calm. The COST participant and his or her caring parents and friends seem comforted by the knowledge that New Zealand is an English-speaking country, thinking there should be no problems with the language or customs when she or he goes to this southern South Pacific country. It is considered a "safe place" to go. The time taken to travel to New Zealand, with around twelve hours flying over the Pacific Ocean, is likely to generate far more concern than any possible culture clash or language difficulty, especially for those students for whom this is the first venture outside the United States. Those in the hosting or receiving roles—associate teachers, homestay families, and pupils—have a similar feeling of calm. They assume that because the student teacher, who will become part of their domestic or school life for between six and sixteen weeks comes from America, an English-speaking country, there will be no significant cultural differences.

Data provided by pupils, teachers, and homestay hosts who interacted with COST participants during the second half of 2003 suggest that initial expectations proved incorrect. For example, it appears that while no real language difficulty was anticipated by either COST participants or the hosts, language issues generated the most frequently and fondly mentioned differences recalled by hosts.

The thirst for knowledge of other countries by the antipodean pupils was another predominant finding from the research. The development of a "worldview" or a "world perspective" is actively encouraged by New Zealand teachers and the New Zealand social studies curriculum. A "good general knowledge" of things, places, and events from around the world is an admired characteristic of New Zealanders by New Zealanders. This is reinforced when the news media in New Zealand report comparisons between New Zealand students' geographical or historical knowledge and that of selected, more parochial, or local general knowledge of citizens from another country.

who may not know where New Zealand is, or, in a more "insulting" way (to the New Zealand psyche), report New Zealand to be a state of Australia! (Levstik 2001).

The pupils in the classrooms of the COST student teachers were found to have absorbed a considerable amount of specific knowledge about the United States, as well as about particular states and specific characteristics of areas of the country. The pupils' knowledge may have been encouraged by the associate teacher or the positive relationship established with them by the COST student teacher, or through the COST participant being encouraged to bring to New Zealand and share personal knowledge of their hometown and home state—its features, famous people, and interesting facts. This research established that the New Zealand pupils could recite, when interviewed about a week after the departure of their COST student teacher, detailed knowledge about the United States—its language, geography, history, artifacts, and customs.

In their written questionnaires, the associate teachers of the COST participants, while recording aspects of comparative impression of teaching styles and teaching personalities, also drew attention to the way in which hosting a student teacher from outside New Zealand required them to reflect more on their own practice and on their own knowledge of New Zealand in order to respond to questions and enquiries from the student teacher. A strong element of relative and comparative satisfaction was expressed by the associate teachers that they were living and teaching in New Zealand rather than in America!

True to the marketed reputation of New Zealanders as being hospitable and friendly, each of the host families reported that *their* COST student teacher had become an integral part of their family and not just a boarder or visitor. The enquiring minds of the COST students themselves, as well as their enthusiasm for experiencing and enjoying the newness and differences of the New Zealand culture and language, were the predominant features of their responses. The selection process through which COST applicants must pass has to be given credit for sending student teachers with these admirable personal qualities, who seem to make the most of the horizon-broadening experience they will have by just departing, even for a short period of time, from their country of origin.

Assumption of Similarity of Language

Emmitt, Pollock, and Limbrick state that

Language is seen as one of many social practices that operate interactively in a society to represent and make meaning. Language is centered on meaning: it is the most powerful and persuasive means humans have for making and sharing meaning. Because language is centered on meaning, which is shared culturally, it follows that it is rooted in the culture of the group that uses it. (1996, 6)

In an article in the *NZ Education Review*, Emma West (2003) quoted a New Zealand teacher (Shaun Howarth) who was teaching in Aurora, Colorado. He reported on his experience with English while teaching in the United States: "One of the biggest challenges is translating your [New Zealand] English to American English to be understood, especially in the classroom. . . . Out of all the countries I have worked in, I find the USA to be the most different culturally. Even though we speak the same language often things are misunderstood."

When a COST student teacher is placed for teaching practice in New Zealand, there seems to be an unspoken but mutual assumption of similarity of culture between the student teacher and the hosting associate teacher, pupils, and homestay families because both nationalities use the English language. Pupils in three of the classrooms readily declared that Americans and New Zealanders were the "same" culturally and linguistically, as was evident in such statements as "Both are related to Britain because the British explored them [but] it doesn't really relate because the Queen isn't in charge of America" (pupil, aged eight years) and "I know we are the same because we both speak English [but] they speak sometimes different from us" (pupil, aged eleven years).

After arrival, both parties found great humour and delight in experiencing differences in their assumption of similarity through the use of different language for the same things. In some settings, such differences could lead to confusion and tension between hosts and visitors, but within the setting of the COST organisation in Christchurch, New Zealand, where support networks and relationships have been firmly established and proven over many years, the differences produced delight.

Examples of these linguistic differences were evident in the responses of each group (pupils, associate teachers, and homestay families). The pupils willingly recalled their favourite differences between their use of English language and that used by their COST student teacher. The associate teachers recorded this aspect less frequently, but certainly identified it as part of the novelty within the classroom context in line with the experiences of their pupils. All five sets of pupils reported, perhaps in a culturally centric way—which shouldn't surprise us, given the pupils' ages—that their COST student teacher "talked differently," "had a different accent," "[She] doesn't speak the same as us," "They pronounce things differently." Some individual pupils (aged nine to eleven) recognized that "We have a different accent to Americans," "They've got a big accent." When asked by the interviewer "Have you [an accent]?" one pupil responded, "No. To them, we have an accent."

Many were the examples eagerly recalled by the pupils in each of the classes in response to an invitation to tell the interviewer actual examples of language differences.

"They call 'lollies' 'suckers' or 'candy,'" "We say 'biscuits' and over there they say 'cookies,'" "They call 'scones' 'biscuits,'" "She said 'whiteout' for 'twink' and she said you have to put 'periods' which are full stops,'" "There were a couple of words she said differently, for example 'Mom' for 'Mum,'" "They call 'tomato sauce' 'ketchup,'" "We call 'cherios' sausages and they call 'cherios' cereal," "She called 'books [for writing in]' 'notebooks,'" "We say 'rubbers' and she calls them 'erasers,'" "We say 'rubbish tin' and she says 'trash can.'"

Although the COST participants were known to have recorded these same language differences for inclusion in presentations about their experiences "back home," pupils in one of the hosting classrooms prepared American items for presentation at their school assembly to mark the farewell of their student teacher. The opening item was, of course, New Zealand pupils reciting "The Pledge"—complete with a well-rehearsed "Richard stands" with the explanation to the interviewer that, "In the morning the [American] children say 'Richard stands' instead of 'in which it stands' because they have memorized it and don't really know what they are saying."

Another item was entitled 'Translation Sensation" in which "What New Zealanders say" was followed by "What Americans say," with many of the examples listed above being featured.

This fun with language was also recorded within the homestay family settings.

One family reported, "Initially many words and phrases and colloquialisms were collected by the student and our family . . . [and] this leads to discussions about other areas—food, customs and so on." Another said, "The children have had fun finding out that there are different words that have the same meanings; e.g., 'blinkers' for 'indicators' and 'toboggan' for 'beanie.' Spelling and pronunciation of words caused a few laughs."

English was not the only language encounter experienced by the COST student teachers while on school placement in Christchurch. In almost all schools in New Zealand, greetings, counting, days of the week, and simple instructions (stand up, sit down, quiet please) can be expected to be communicated in either, or a mixture of, English, Maori, one or more Polynesian languages, or in the mother tongue of pupils of immigrant or permanent resident families. This multilingual setting is common in New Zealand classrooms, and the COST students' encounter with this was mentioned during the interviews with the pupils when they were asked "What do you think you have taught Miss A? What do you think she has learned from you?" One replied, "Maori language. . . . That Maori words don't have an 's' in them" and "We tried to teach her how to say 'hello' in Niueian [which the pupils could say with rhythmical alacrity], and she got it in the end."

But not to be outdone with regard to linguistic challenges, one of the COST student teachers introduced elementary Spanish words to her classroom, which was recalled with great fondness by the pupils (six- and seven-year-olds) as part of a response to a question, "What did the American teacher do as a teacher that was different from your own teacher? The reply was, "[She] teaches us how to talk in Spanish . . . taught us how to count in Spanish."

Other similarities between the cultures were recorded in the responses from the research sample. Clearly the pupils recognised that Americans and New Zealanders were similar in terms of skin colour, hair colour, and other personal features. More perceptibly, they saw similarities in terms of the same colours on our national flags—"Their flag is kind of the same because they both have stars on them and they are both red, blue, and white." And an associate teacher wrote, "Although there are differences on the surface, we all want the same thing inside—kindness, thoughtfulness, etc." And this sentiment was echoed by one of the homestay families when they said, "[She] learned that while there are a number of cultural aspects which may be different, at a deeper level there is less difference—family is important."

Celebrating Difference: Recognising What We Have and Who We Are

The responses from all parties revealed very few substantial differences of culture between the hosting respondents and the culture of their visitor—other than those related to language discussed above. Those differences that were recorded related to what could be described as peripheral cultural differences, while some few others reported the respondent's reflection on his or her own culture in juxtaposition to that of their visitor.

Peripheral differences identified by the pupils, for example, included the perennial and the obvious:

"NZ water goes down the plughole the opposite to America."

"They [Americans]—the driver in a car sits on the left not the right."

"In America they've got humungous cities like New York and in NZ we've got small ones."

"Water supply—we get our electricity from water and they get theirs by nuclear."

Other responses from the pupils were reflective of deeper comparison, borne of thoughtful identification of historical and geographical differences, the consequence of new knowledge or perception carried into their consciousness by the COST student, and/or drawn from them by the prompt question of the interviewer: "And there in America they are a lot different—how they have like civil wars going on with each other—like they are always killing each other" (pupil, aged ten to eleven years). Or, "They're not the same because Canada's touching America on the top of it and Mexico is touching America on the bottom of it and New Zealand has nothing—around it is water" (pupil, aged six to seven years). And, "Americans have fifty stars on their flag but we have got four stars on our flag" (pupil, aged six to seven years).

These observations of difference reflect the considerable amount of knowledge and understanding communicated by the pupils about the United States that had been introduced to them by the COST student teacher. The pupils of all ages were able to confidently identify that the United States of America is a country, while Minnesota, Georgia, Alabama, and Texas were states within the United States, and that places such as St. Paul, Birmingham, and Montgomery were cities within a state: "Minnesota is a state in America by the Great Lakes and St. Paul is the capital of Minnesota—its like Canterbury [NZ province] is like a big sort of state with little towns like Oxford [small town in Canterbury]—it's a bit like that" (pupil, aged nine to ten years).

Other features of the hometown/home state of the COST participants were also readily recited by the pupils—features such as "tornado alley," "Lake Superior is the biggest of the Great Lakes and the biggest lake in the world," "There is a big giant shopping mall and, um, it's called the Mall of America. . . . It's the biggest mall in the world, it's got like a roller coaster, aquariums, and parks, 500 individual stores and if you spent twenty minutes in each shop you would be there for eighteen hours."

The fascination of the NZ pupils with the elements of the stars and stripes did reveal a cultural difference, with the flag holding much less of a place in the rituals of New Zealand pupils than those of American pupils. There is no patriotic or nationalistic ritual similar to the American pupil reciting of "The Pledge" in New Zealand schools. In one of the classes, however, the pupils reported that, "We taught her our national anthem." [Interviewer: "What's our national anthem called?"] "God of Nations" (pupils, aged nine to ten years).

It could possibly be claimed that the New Zealand pupils in the host classes now know more about the features of the flag of America than the four stars and Union Jack emblems that feature in their own national flag. For example, one class of eight-year-olds knew that "the [American flag] flag's nickname is Old Glory." "On the flag there are fifty stars and these stand for the fifty states." "There's thirteen stripes—red and white—they represent the thirteen original colonies." Pupils in another class (eight- and nine-year-olds) offered information that "The white stripes on their flag stand for peace—the red stripes stand for war."

And associate teachers learned from the student teachers as well. One associate teacher recorded that hosting the COST student had led her to "clarify my knowledge of the NZ flag features and the background of these features."

Rather than note differences of the immediate, conversational, and obvious, the associate teachers noted more personal and stylistic differences in their student teachers, which they may or may not have generalised to "all Americans." "Americans are caring, supportive people," "Their families are important," "They are proud of their country but don't know much about other nations." And "They are a little more 'in your face' than New Zealanders—less aware of interrupting others and getting into people's space. This seems to be done unintentionally." Or, to put it another way, "We are a little more reserved."

Maybe mercifully, one associate teacher wrote that her student teacher was "very different to a lot of what we see on TV/media," and that her student teacher was a person "who shows gratitude very openly and publicly."

Through the hosting of their American student teachers, the associate teachers did reflect on differences and similarities of culture and approaches to teaching and wrote, on the one hand, "how lucky we are to live here" (rather than in America), and on the other hand, "how undervalued we are as teachers with our New Zealand education system compared to America."

Generally, the associate teachers felt that hosting a student teacher from America had a positive effect on their pupils. The experience of interacting with the student teacher and responding to their questions led the pupils to recognize "the uniqueness of the New Zealand culture and influence of the English [culture], foods, beaches, lifestyle, *paua* shells . . . authors, artists, TV shows coming from New Zealand . . . [and it] reinforced New Zealand traditions/*kiwiana*/language." Teachers also reported that the host parents may have learned more about the role of a teacher through hosting the student teacher in their home.

The host family respondents reported that hosting an American student had a positive effect on their households: "Learning about their country and have them see different things in us as a family we were unaware of—celebrating our Kiwi culture," "became as a big sister to our children and did a great job in helping affirm what we as parents are teaching our children," "helped with the odd U.S. question in homework," and "Our children just loved having her around, especially the younger child as they communicated so well," "We had to refer to maps a bit more. This was more in directing our student for her sightseeing travel."

The student teachers were interested in finding out about the New Zealand Maori culture. From a host parent, "quite a few questions were asked about the Maori and how they fit into society here, including differences in school systems and status of our Maori population today." From an associate teacher, "Importance of our Maori culture— songs, language, *haka* [a Maori dance of challenge to newcomers]." And from the pupils, "She asked us quite a lot of things—like how to say 'Maori.' I think she called it like 'Maaaori." "We told her some things about the Maoris—how they made flax weaving," and "We taught her about the Maori treaty," "how to use a poi," "how to do the Maori sticks," "Maori words," "Maori string games."

Perspectives on Time

From the interviews with the pupils, it is clear that they were very aware of the differences in both clock-time and seasons between the United States (northern hemisphere) and New Zealand (southern hemisphere.) Two of the associate teachers also listed the linked knowledge about time, seasons, and school holiday differences in New Zealand and the United States as one of the things their pupils had learned about through hosting the American student teacher.

Whether or not the pupils would have been able to be as precise and confident in their knowledge about these differences without having close contact with an American is a matter for conjecture, but at the time of the interviews, they could clearly and knowledgeably inform the interviewer that: "America [the place where their student teacher came from] is eighteen hours behind New Zealand in time," "If you had your birthday in New Zealand and flew to America, you could have it again on the same day," "The months are different to us—January its summer—we are in summer and they are in winter," "The seasons are opposite to America," and "The [American] children have school holidays for August–June, July and August summer break and they don't have holidays like we do."

Reports about Teaching Style

Both the pupils and associate teachers reported differences in teaching style between the American student teacher and their own New Zealand expectations of student teachers. The pupils were quick to relate things that the COST student did that they enjoyed or were to their advantage—usually in comparison to the behaviour of their own classroom teacher—and may have related similar things if they had been asked the same question about their experience of a New Zealand student teacher who had spent time in their classroom.

> "She sort of talked differently and . . . um . . . she somehow made it so that everything, even if you usually don't like it, was fun somehow. Like you enjoyed coming to school—not that we don't like coming when Miss B [regular teacher] is here!"
> "She took us out for lots of games."
> "She never got grumpy—she was like really really really nice."
> "She repeated herself a lot and talked pretty fast."
> "She gave us more worksheets than bookwork—Miss V. gives us more bookwork."
> "She let us go as soon as the bell goes—like normally we finish what we are doing before we go."
> "We did American dancing instead of fitness—the Virginia Reel."
> "She divides different from us."

In contrast, the associate teachers noted apparent differences in the expectations of the role of teacher between New Zealand and American student teachers. These differences needed to be addressed with the student teacher so that they could meet the requirements of a teacher within the context of the New Zealand school. In terms of relationships with pupils, the associate teachers noted that they felt they had to draw to the attention of the COST student teachers the following:

> "How busy our day is and how much more we take responsibility for all curriculum areas when compared with American teachers."
> "The importance of consistency for pupils."
> "NZ teachers tend not to spend as much time negotiating with children."
> "Boundaries and consequences need to be made clear at the outset."

"The fact that detailed planning and modeling is essential for any teacher to be successful—a perennial issue characteristic of the so-called teaching–practice gap."

It could be conjectured that these same issues are likely to be addressed between a New Zealand associate teacher and a New Zealand student teacher.

New Zealanders' Perspective of Americans

Although the COST participants who were the subject of the research were in New Zealand schools during the time of the start of the Iraqi war (2004), none of the comments suggest differences between the political positions regarding this issue. This is somewhat surprising, since New Zealand did not deploy troops to the initial combat in this theatre. One may have expected there to have been some comment and that this event would have had some impact on the relationship between the COST students and their host New Zealanders. By contrast, and anecdotally, there was a considerable emotional impact on the relationship between COST student teachers who were placed in Christchurch schools at the time of the September 11, 2001, New York Trade Center assault and their hosting New Zealanders.

Apart from the comment by a pupil recorded earlier about "There in America they are like having civil wars going on with each other—like they are always killing each other," and the associate teacher's comment about Americans being "a little more in your face than New Zealanders," there was only one other comment recorded about apparent differences between the national personalities that reflected a negative tone. A host parent stated, "They [Americans] are interested in us as a colony—Wakefield settlement." (Note: "Wakefield settlement" refers to the theories and plans of Edward Gibbon Wakefield [1796–1862] to sell land in the British colonies of Australia, Canada, and New Zealand to settlers who would emigrate to these colonies and work the land.)

By contrast, there was an abundance of comment about the positive elements of the personalities of the COST students as representatives of America and American culture. For example: "She catched on quite quickly. She knew a lot about New Zealand. We did an activity where we had to find out things about New Zealand and she was so quick" (pupil, eight years old); "and it was fun. And she was really nice—she sort of, um, liked to teach. She had that sort of feel when she was around" (pupil, aged ten years); "Americans are caring, supportive people" (associate teacher), and "It was like having another member of the family in the house" (host family).

CONCLUSION

This piece of research set out to establish whether there was any impact on pupils, associate teachers, and homestay families following their hosting of a COST student teacher from America. The responses indicate that, at least at the time these interviews took place (soon after the student teacher had departed for home), there was a considerable impact on the host community. Whether this impact had only an immediate rather than a long-lasting effect on the emotions and knowledge of these New Zealanders was not within the scope of this exercise. The results of this research suggest that these COST participants influenced the lives of the pupils, parents, and teachers considerably in the settings in which they were placed. They were positive ambassadors for America, for their home state, hometown, and home university.

This study opens up many areas for future research. Major among these could be a parallel investigation within a setting where there was an actual difference between the COST student's culture and language and that of his or her hosting setting. Another could be to interview the pupils, associate teachers, and hosts before the student teacher arrived, then again after he or she departed and compare the responses and establish whether there is or was an assumption of similarity. Similarly, before-and-after interviews could also be conducted with the COST students with regard to their perception of their hosting country—again to establish whether any assumption of similarity or difference did or does exist—and how they may have changed.

The impact of these COST student teachers within a setting in which there was clearly an assumption of similarity was revealed through the specific knowledge of America—or their part of it—which they had clearly communicated within their host family and classroom settings.

Through their own personalities, attitudes, and values, these student teachers were able to present a predominantly positive image of Americans and America as a nation. In all settings, the comparison between the two countries seemed to form the basis of many of the impressions and opinions expressed by the New Zealanders of America and Americans. And significantly, hosting the student teachers helped these New Zealanders become better informed about their own country and its features as well as those of America. Host families related, "There is still an English-ness about Kiwis although we are becoming Americanized" or "Our globe was used a lot to see different parts of the USA to get a better understanding of the geography of the country" and "New Zealand is a land of great contrasts—you don't have to travel far to see a wide variety of countryside." At the end of the day, however, all the New Zealanders who contributed to this study reinforced a perspective of one nine-year-old pupil who said, "New Zealand is a miniature compared to America."

Principals of schools that have regularly hosted American students in Christchurch view their placement in their schools as an opportunity for the children and staff members to broaden their own experiences and vision through the exchange of views and information about an education system from a different English-speaking country. They are positive about hosting COST students because

> They [the student teachers] are absolutely brilliant—they are superb. Bar one, we have had wonderful relationships with them all. . . . They are all different. . . . On the whole the majority that come are vivacious, bubbly, lively and really interested and they have got to be because they are paying as well! They are keen to involve themselves in the New Zealand system and with Kiwi families. . . . This is why I like the COST system because they stay with Kiwi families. (From an interview with Sue Ashworth, principal of a school that has hosted seventeen COST students between 1992 and 2006.)

When compared with the competence of New Zealand student teachers, the principals report that the COST students, while initially lacking in "know-how" and frequency of block teaching practice experiences, quickly adapt to their environment and perform most favourably. They are quick to learn the New Zealand way (teach all the subjects of the curriculum, including physical education, music, and science) and the resource base of the New Zealand school classroom (you mix your own paints for art!) and to work within these parameters.

The associate teachers who accept a request to host an American student seem to do so with interest, confidence, and positive expectation. This is reflected in the comment of one associate teacher that was echoed by others, "No anxieties—I felt privileged and extremely enthusiastic. I felt it would be a wonderful experience for myself and my class of J1's" [first year junior school—pupils aged five].

The opportunity to exchange professional viewpoints with a colleague from another country was seen as a positive motivation when accepting the request for placement. However, this positive outlook is tinged with some concern about the student teachers' abilities to become familiar enough with the New Zealand school system and a different curriculum to be able to present their best during their short experience.

On first arriving in the school and classroom, as one would expect, the COST student teachers are observed by the associate teachers to be feeling alone, a little confused by the setting and the expectations of their own institution, the associate teacher, and the observing lecturer—let alone their own personal expectations. The timing and effectiveness of the first contact with the observing lecturer, which is usually within the first week after the student's arrival, seems crucial to both the student and his or her associate teacher and to the success of the school-based part of the placement. The main element of distraction that is reported to stay with the students the longest is difficulties with living with families in the local community. According to the associate teachers, these "slow starts" at school are invariably followed by a very steep and energetic learning curve, as the students apply their considerable personal energies and innovative, creative, and positive professional characteristics to the task of becoming a competent classroom teacher in a foreign setting.

The learning curve sees the student teachers move

- from "teaching" children to being "facilitators of children's learning";
- from seeking a textbook to teach from to becoming knowledgeable about the syllabuses they are required to present;
- from treating all the children the same (and hoping they were all the same) to managing children as individuals and responding to their individual learning, social, and emotional needs;

- from being tired with all the work required of a teacher to becoming exhausted with all the work required of a teacher; and,
- from being homesick to being reluctant to depart.

New Zealand hosts find benefit in what these American students bring to their relationships with colleagues, children, and the families with whom they live. Their warmth, sensitivity, ability to receive and respond to advice, enthusiasm, ability to plan in writing, and willingness to become involved in schoolwide staff and family activities are characteristics noted and valued by those hosting the COST participants. The cultural exchange opportunity that the student teachers bring to their schools, classrooms, and host family communities is the main reason why principals, associate teachers, and host families report they are willing to host participants in the future.

Perhaps a comment by the founder of the COST experience in New Zealand best expresses the sentiment that came through in the research data and aptly sums up the value of this experience. When he was informed that 100 students had been placed in Christchurch through the COST program he had introduced to Christchurch in 1987, Dr. Knight said,

> I think it is terrific! It is very satisfying to know that what I once saw as a short-term project has been ongoing. These projects largely depend on the enthusiasm of the people associated with them and not just an institutional thing, but well-motivated people over the years. It is good to see that the project has continued because 100 students is a lot and the potential influence they will have when they go back [to the United States] and talk about New Zealand in their own schools promoting understanding of our area of the world and about what teachers do in NZ [compared to the United States] is huge.

REFERENCES

Ashworth, Sue. 2005. Interview, principal, Paparoa Street School, January 19.
Cushner, K., and J. Mahon. 2002. Overseas student teaching: Affecting personal, professional and global competencies in an age of globalization. *Journal of Studies in International Education* 6, no. 1:44–58.
Emmitt, M., and J. Pollock with L. Limbrick. 1996. *An introduction to language and learning.* Melbourne: Oxford University Press.

Kissock, C. 1997. Student teaching overseas. In *Preparing teachers to teach global perspectives. A handbook for educators*, ed. M. M. Merryfield, E. Jarchow, and S. Pickert. Thousand Oaks, CA: Corwin Press.

Knight, C. 1982. An international study of relationships between geographic knowledge of students and their attitude to other nationalities. PhD diss., University of Georgia.

———. 2005. Interview, former CEO, Christchurch College of Education, January 6.

Levstik, L. S. 2001. Crossing the empty spaces: New Zealand adolescents' conceptions of perspective-taking and historical significance. In *Historical empathy and perspective taking in the social studies*, ed. O. L. Davis, E. A. Yeager, and S. J. Foster. Lanham, MD: Rowman & Littlefield.

West, E. 2003. Learning to speak American. *New Zealand Education Review* 8, no. 40 (October): 15–21.

THE POWER OF CURIOSITY AND THE TERROR OF IT ALL: THE LIFE OF AN INDIVIDUAL STUDENT

Rosalie Romano

It is a miracle that curiosity survives formal education. It is, in fact, nothing short of a miracle that the modern methods of instruction have not entirely strangled the holy curiosity of inquiry.

—Albert Einstein

As Anatole France (1932) stated, "The whole art of teaching is only the art of awakening the natural curiosity of young minds for the purpose of satisfying it afterwards." Is there anything more compelling for a teacher than a student's curiosity? For those of us with many years in the classroom, those moments when a student *wants* to know are marked with excitement, with what some teachers call a "teachable moment." Teachers know that when they can ignite curiosity, a student will seek to understand. The energy of *wanting to know* can overcome hesitation, doubt, comfort, and more, push to energize into action. Berlyne (1960) claimed that curiosity was the motivator for exploration.

Paulo Freire argues that the basis of a critical classroom is for teachers to understand the primacy of curiosity. Before teachers can entertain methods or pedagogical approaches for an engaging classroom, "the teacher must be clear and content with the notion that the cornerstone of the whole process is human curiosity" (1998, 74). Curiosity drives us to question, states Freire, "and to know, act, ask again, recognize" (81). Curiosity, then, motivates us not only to want to know but also to reflect and to act upon that reflection. Curiosity moves us to action. "There could be no such thing as human existence without the openness of our being to the world" and what more important disposition or quality can any teacher have, but "openness to the world" through the portal of curiosity? (82)

For those of us who have committed ourselves to the education of new teachers, the task of fostering curiosity is complex. Many times we must reacquaint the adult student candidate with his or her curiosity, sometimes simmering longingly beneath the academic surface of the spirit or lying deeply dormant from years of schooling that taught the importance of "other people's questions" rather than one's own. "Banking education," the transmission of information by the teacher to passive students who receive and are expected to regurgitate back that information, is forming the backbone of No Child Left Behind initiatives, particularly for poor, working-class, and frequently, middle-class students. If and when these students reach college and choose teacher preparation, the invisible framework, powerful because it is a dominant experience, is this transmission model. An overseas or intercultural student-teaching experience, with its opportunity to see the world through a teacher's eyes, ignites the curiosity of some of these students, and increases the potential of questioning this dominant experience.

This chapter explores the impact of the power of curiosity in new teachers, ignited by a moment's imagining or a lifetime dream of going overseas, and the terror of it all once they are set to embark across the pond. The glittering carrot, in this case, that arouses their curiosity is the Consortium for Overseas Student Teaching (COST) Program. In another chapter, Mary Anne Flournoy explains how we at Ohio University prepare COST students for their overseas experiences. In this chapter, I explore the space between the act of applying, the act of flying away, and particular COST students' responses to their overseas experience. The undercurrent of terror meets the wave of curiosity to sometimes produce their extraordinary growth into remarkable teachers or the defeat of curiosity for the safety of the road well traveled. First we will turn to the context of teacher preparation and what student teaching overseas enhances in our aims for teaching.

BACKGROUND: WHY GLOBAL
EDUCATIONAL EXPERIENCES?

Today, teacher preparation is moving increasingly toward mechanistic, technocratic "training" for candidates. Prepackaged, determined education programs must align with state and national accreditation bodies that base their acceptance or rejection on evidence provided by the institution as to how it meets accreditation goals. Out of this frequently disembodied program, the candidate is supposed to "learn" how to teach. Emphasis on methods, increased content knowledge, and other requirements for accreditation leave little or no space for the contextualization of teaching students. Kincheloe, Slattery, and Steinberg (2000) argue for teacher preparation to emphasize contextualization, particularly as it relates to the global issues. Without understanding that one size does *not* fit all, as the norm is today, teachers may enter into classrooms with the best of intentions but fail to be aware of the social and economic milieu that affect the learning of their students. Raising this awareness, this consciousness, must be at the preparation level, argue Kincheloe and co-workers (2000) so the new teachers come to critically assess attitudes, pressures, and beliefs students bring with them into the classroom. They argue, what good is passing "the test" when we pay no attention to the actions and behaviors that give rise to racial prejudice, homophobia, and the injustices everywhere that have an impact on us or on those around us? To teach as if you are touching the future requires that teachers pay attention to the world at large, because we are not alone in the world. The connections between and amongst nation-states are tightly woven, not only through economics but through culture as well.

Kincheloe, Slattery, and Steinberg (2000) offer us a framework for exploring the potential influences and impacts that overseas teachers can have on a new teacher. These themes emerge from the reflective journals and interviews with many of the Ohio University students who participate in COST, but with four cases outlined in this chapter in particular. To illuminate the experiences of these students, I have interpreted and restated Kincheloe and co-workers' frameworks into four dispositions to use to light our way: worldly connections, a tolerance for ambiguity, curriculum making, and a hopeful view of the future as a global actor (2000, 40–45).

THE COST STUDENT TEACHERS FROM OHIO UNIVERSITY

Nestled in the foothills of Appalachia, Ohio University is the oldest university beyond the original thirteen states. Founded in 1804, Ohio University enrolls about 10,000 undergraduates and as many domestic and international graduate students for its many programs. Ohio University's geographical location in the southeastern corner of Ohio, amongst the Hocking Hills and Hocking River, attracts undergraduates from primarily middle-class families from the Midwest region states. Many attend OU because of its undergraduate teacher-preparation program in the College of Education. Beginning in the sophomore year, education majors take a program of study that is NCATE accredited. As part of their requirement for licensure, education majors can opt to go overseas to student teach through the COST Program. Currently, the College of Education yearly sends approximately twenty education majors overseas to satisfy their student-teaching requirements through the COST Program.

The COST teachers you will learn about represent the potential of students to step across the threshold—or not—to face the terror of it all. In each case, the student was propelled by curiosity toward the finality of action and of choice, and faced his or her potential for being changed, indeed transformed, as a person and as a teacher.

Stan

Stan came bounding into my office, holding the COST brochure in his hand, and pulled up a chair. Looking me straight in the eye, he asked, "What would I have to do to go student teach overseas?" Stan was in the partnership program I coordinate, and I had come to appreciate his usually deliberate, shy demeanor that he displayed during the partnership interview in the spring of his freshman year. Now entering his junior year in the partnership, Stan was respected by cooperating partnership teachers for his engaging lessons with middle-schoolers. But I was not prepared for this enthusiasm he brought into my office that day. He had seen the brochure and for an instant had imagined himself in another country, teaching in a school. "How do I get to do this?" he asked me again. Since our process for COST requires two additional courses on cross-cultural understanding and communication, plus a five-week practicum in a classroom, the commitment is a large one, in terms of time particularly. Stan had been raised in a small Midwestern town, with little ethnic or cultural diversity, and in schools that reflected this homogeneity. Yet here he was, bristling with energy ignited by a moment's imagination of what it might be like to go abroad. I asked him (as I do each prospective COST student), "Where in the world do you see yourself?" And, predictably, without hesitation he chose "Australia." And, as I always do, I asked, "Why Australia? What would you want to learn about yourself as a teacher by going abroad in general, and to Australia in particular? Why not, say, South Africa or Japan, I wonder?" And that was the moment that I saw the beautiful light of curiosity shine upon his face, and his response back to me confirmed it. "But I don't speak Japanese," he responded. "So why not learn how?" I replied.

Stan turned in his COST application with Japan as his first choice, and turned his full attention to learning everything he could about Japanese culture and society, geography, history, and language. He audited Japanese I, and by the end of the quarter, the instructor encouraged Stan to take Japanese II for credit, and then a compressed Japanese III course during the winter intercession. And Stan did! He lived and breathed and absorbed the language, which led to learning even more about the culture and society. By the time Stan stepped onto the plane for Kobe, Japan, to his student-teaching assignment, he was thinking lessons and units, trying, as a social studies teacher, to discover ways ahead of time to connect the place with the pupils.

Janice

I'd met Janice in the start of her sophomore year, a young woman from a tightly knit family who lived all of her life in a suburb of Cleveland, Ohio. I'd actually met Janice and her parents when they visited the College of Education as a potential school for their daughter. Janice was extremely quiet, thoughtful, and deeply committed to becoming a teacher. So when she was a student in my education course, I recalled our meeting and subsequent discussion about her desire to teach in her hometown once she completed her degree and obtained licensure. As the quarter progressed and the class became more of a community, our discussions around issues of diversity and education became more lively and challenging. Janice especially was writing more each week in her reflective journal, asking at one point how teachers could teach what they have never experienced, in this case, cultural diversity. I brought up the question in class the next week, asking what others thought about their own experiences with diversity and how they thought they would teach about diversity with their future students.

A few weeks later, Janice stayed after class to ask about programs at OU that exposed students to different cultures. Among the programs I told her about was COST. She wondered if she would be able to student teach in a school, even though English speaking, but having no other experiences with other cultures. What would it be like for her or for those students to have an American with no travel experiences? Janice eventually applied to student teach abroad in South Africa, where her experiences led to the answer to her question.

Frieda

Frieda e-mailed me and called repeatedly to find out more about the COST program. An early childhood education major, she was determined to go to Australia to student teach because she had always wanted to go "down under." From the beginning, she had set her mind to go to Australia and kept her choices of COST sites exclusive to Australia. She was a conscientious student throughout the application process, the two required COST courses, and the practicum. Frieda, however, was the COST student whose curiosity could not sustain and propel her through the threshold. As her plane was loading for Australia, Frieda froze and felt only the terror of it all. She did not board, but called her parents to come back to the airport to take her home. She informed me the next day that she was still in the States.

Erin

Erin's case does not stand out, initially, as did the other three, which I would call extraordinary examples of our COST teachers. Erin situates herself as an example of a good student, and who had a good enough dose of curiosity to do well in the COST courses and the practicum. Her experience overseas in the particular site was actually the factor that distinguishes her from the others. Her overseas supervisor was involved with too many obligations at his university that term to provide the support Erin could have used in her school setting. However, Erin realized she would be supported in her situation through the weekly reflections that we require of all our COST students. She wisely developed a system where pedagogical and academic questions were discussed between us, taking the place of what would normally be the responsibility of the on-site coordinator.

WORLDLY CONNECTIONS

In our post-9/11 world, contradictions and irony abound. We are at once a global village in that what happens anywhere is brought by media to be seen or heard in our homes wherever we live. Yet this media information on world events also fills us with suspicion or dread. We struggle with understanding the world and our place in it. And for parents of youth—everywhere—we are wont to "protect" them from the unpredictability of the world today. It is understandable, then, when COST students tell us that their parents are reluctant or concerned or against their going abroad. At a time when the world is begging for understanding between people, one way to increase this understanding is for teachers to bring worldly connections into their classrooms. Much of what new teachers learn about in their preparation programs can be divorced from actual lives of their pupils in the classroom. The child psychology, content, methods, instruction, and curriculum that make up a teacher-preparation program are difficult to weave into practice. If students are placed in schools, even then there must be guidance in seeing the contextual and complex nature of the classroom. The link between the context of the classroom (meaning students' lived experiences) and the new teacher's beliefs about what it means to teach is significantly important. When a new teacher recognizes this link, awareness of the richness of his or her pupils' conceptual understandings can be used to develop curriculum that becomes alive and engaging.

New teachers who are interested in overseas student teaching may be motivated by curiosity but must negotiate the same terrain and challenges of learning to contextualize teaching as do those who will student teach at home. Nowhere is this more dramatically demonstrated than when the COST student enters the school and classroom that will be his or her laboratory for the term. In the case of Stan, his classroom in Japan was filled with pupils from across the world. This is an international school for those who are working or visiting Kobe for extended periods and wish their children to be taught in English. Although English is the common tongue, the assumption that cultural understandings are the same is false. Stan entered a secondary social studies classroom and realized immediately that before he could teach, he would have to learn about his pupils and their backgrounds. His first lesson on geography was met with silence, as his pupils tried to figure out his instructions. English language as it is spoken across the world carries with it unexamined meanings. When Stan was asked by the school to be a bus monitor, he saw it as a chance to perhaps know his pupils in a different way outside the classroom: "The school asked me to ride the bus a few days in the morning and after school just to make sure everyone gets on and off all right. This works out fine for me because we have plenty of time to plan and set up during day, and also I get to see more of Kobe and practice my Japanese with the driver!"

Stan made the decision to put aside the formal lesson, and instead, try to get to know who his pupils were, where they came from, and what they knew already about geography (since most had traveled from many different parts of the globe before they arrived in Kobe). As he developed over time a relationship with his pupils, he began to understand how to motivate them to learn. What this meant for Stan was that geography came alive for both him and his pupils when he put a human face on a lesson. Che came from a Latin American country, but that country is distinct from those countries that surround it, including different customs and dialect. Che became the expert resource for the weeks that Latin America was studied. Stan reflects, "Connecting to my students' learning meant I had to connect to who they are as human beings. I had to be curious about who they are, but also be aware of how we are connected, even though from different parts of the world."

Stan brought with him to Japan a curiosity to know about the world in a new way. He put forth extraordinary effort to acquire a fluency in Japanese so he could travel on his own and also be able to converse with other Japanese teachers or pupils in their own language. His awareness of culture expanded from the classroom into the community. In this reflection, Stan reveals this heightened consciousness:

> I have learned quite a bit in the short time that I have been here. One thing that I have noticed most of all is that I have become very aware of myself because of how different I am than those with whom I interact. Before I arrived, I knew this was something that would happen, but I had no idea to what extent it would be. In watching the people around me, I see that I differ in my physical appearance, the way I eat, the way I interact with people, the way I stand on the train, and even the way I buy something at the store. Along the lines of interacting with people, I knew that the Japanese are friendly, but I have been amazed at how kindly I have been treated by complete strangers. For example, each time that I have asked someone where something was, they would actually go out of their way and take me there themselves. Also, I noticed that when I would ask a question in Japanese, the person would almost always attempt to use some English in their answer, although the conversation was a bit more comprehensible in Japanese. I know at home, when a foreigner would ask an American a question, very rarely would that person attempt to respond in any other language than English.

Note the way Stan seems to be looking at himself through the eyes of others. It is not others he sees as "different." He is the "foreigner" and he looks at himself as others might see him. His location has shifted, and at the last sentence he sees how someone like him might be treated if he were in the United States, noting how the people who have stopped to help him try to speak English, even though he is in week three of his experience and is trying to speak Japanese exclusively outside the school.

This sense of connectedness is an outgrowth of being open to other ways of being in the world. Such a critical disposition is a direct outgrowth of the Freirian curiosity that leads one to be open, to reflect, and to act. This is not passive experience. In Stan's case, exposure to being an outsider pushed him toward a deepening consciousness that included a sympathetic view of what it must be like for an outsider in the United States. This wide-screen awareness changes one's perspective, and colors what you teach, how you teach it, and who you are as a teacher. This is the global connectivity that the COST experience has the potential to foster in new teachers.

TOLERANCE FOR AMBIGUITY

"When will I know where I am going to be placed?" is the most frequently asked question of all COST student teachers. We respond by
pointing out that waiting, not knowing, is part of the cross-cultural experiences of COST. The U.S. society wants to know immediately, wants
to know all details as fast as possible, wants to plan ahead for all contin-
gencies, and wants all this information yesterday. Of all the challenges to
going abroad, the not-knowing causes the greatest discomfort. In
Freida's case, the work she did in her COST courses, *Learning from
Non-Western Cultures* and *Cross-Cultural Understanding*, prepared
her intellectually for the experience. As an excellent student, Frieda did
all of what she was asked, and then some. Her written essays and reflections on class discussions were clear and open; her report on her
country was enlivened by details and interesting facts about the school
system; and her interactions with other COST students in class gave no
indication (at least that we picked up on) that at the eleventh hour, she
would, while waiting to board her flight for Australia, phone her parents
to come pick her up and take her home.

A new culture, a new way of being in the world, was waiting for her
as a teacher. If she boarded that plane, her sense of self as she knew it
would be changed. Freire stresses that education is not neutral. He argues for an education that fosters our capacity to transform the world,
"of naming things, of deciding, of choosing, of valuing, and finally, of
ethicizing the world." But transformation is not a one-way process. We
must also become transformed to a deeper relational and respectful appreciation of the multiple expressions of what it means to be part of a
complex, globalized community. This requires an ability to tolerate the
ambiguity that is involved in relating across differences, a move that is
not easy and certainly not comfortable. But, I think, we as educators
must enter this new terrain; we ignore it or turn our backs on it to our
own peril.

We cannot force new learning and new ways to be in the world but
must invite and coax. It is, however, a person's choice, often motivated
by a strong dose of curiosity and sense of adventure, that will assist in his
or her journey. But in this one case, curiosity could not stand up to the
terror of it all—the terror of ambiguity, of complexity, of transformation.

John Greenleaf Whittier wrote, For of all sad words of tongue or pen, The saddest are these: "It might have been!" Yet I also understand how courage can fail, and the safety of home, of the familiar, will in the moment seem like this is all you ever want or have wanted in all your life.

CURRICULUM MAKING

The significant part of student teaching overseas is learning about different perspectives on the curriculum, and then developing reflective skills to become a curriculum maker. Since teachers are historical and cultural beings, they bring particular beliefs and paradigms into the classroom that influence how they relate to pupils and how they think about knowledge. Standard forms of curriculum are the silent partners in teaching worldviews, often reinforcing and reinscribing exclusionary Western worldviews. Classrooms across the United States have children of diversity trying to negotiate between what they know and experience and the requirements of the dominant paradigm.

When students go abroad to student teach, they glimpse this exclusionary paradigm for themselves, because they now must negotiate between what they know and experience and the requirements of the dominant paradigm of the culture they are entering as new teachers. They discover what it means to be on the other side of an exclusionary worldview. When Stan is asked to teach social studies to his pupils, the map, quite literally, went upside down. Maps in his classroom highlighted Asia; he had to look twice to locate the United States on one map. Teaching history now means the history of the country, and oftentimes there is a distinctly different portrayal of the United States than what is portrayed in U.S. social studies texts. COST social studies teachers comment on how much information is provided about the United States and, even more significant, just how much young people are aware, often acutely so, of U.S. current political stances and decisions. In fact, one of the first questions pupils have of the COST teacher is about U.S. international policy—and the COST teacher finds he or she must answer for the current government, which requires some understanding and knowledge of current events and governmental decision making.

Instead of being secure in their own culture and relying on cultural assumptions, the COST students find themselves pushed to understand and empathize with a diverse range of people and their social and political context. This experience challenges deeply held and often submerged beliefs and attitudes about U.S. culture and government, taken for granted until faced with a different way of looking at the world. Stepping out of their comfort zone to meet and understand—even accommodate—their pupils' ideas and beliefs disrupts those submerged beliefs and enlarges the COST student. It is our intent to support this experience, which has the potential to enlarge understanding and vision so they develop a deeper self-understanding of themselves, their culture, and others.

Here is a COST student teacher's emerging awareness of different approaches to secondary math. This COST student teacher's predilection is for the structured instruction she had been taught both in her high school and in her university math courses. She was teaching a high school math class in South Africa and reflected: "I have noticed that the mathematics curriculum and textbooks are more discovery-based, having students work out proofs and patterns instead of just showing them 'this is how it is.' However, I also don't think there is enough direct instruction: there should be a balance, and I think this may be why the students sometimes struggle to grasp concepts."

What makes this intriguing is this thread of expectation and comparison that ran through her weekly reflections from start to the end of the term. Guided questions that asked her to examine her pedagogical beliefs were answered to a limited extent, and in the next week, her beliefs would manifest in another topic. The issue of discovery learning was one that made this student teacher uncomfortable. Yet, there were some glimpses of her growth in understanding that degrees of curricular freedom might have some advantages. In an eleventh-grade class, she noted:

They [math books] are also not set up into nice little units like our texts in America are. In America, each section has an explanation followed by exercises, all in a perfect size to teach one per day. Here, there is a little explanation followed by either very little or a lot of exercises. It's up to the teacher to judge how much to do that day. It's kind of nice when you have to plan for shorter or longer periods.

Here, this student teacher continues to look at the structure rather than the concepts of the standard curriculum. Note how she responded to this same curriculum a few weeks earlier: "I'm not quite certain what the math curriculum is like yet. I glanced through a few of the textbooks (Grade 9, 11, and 12), and it seems to be pretty similar to what we do, although it goes a little more in depth. There are not incredible amounts of exercises (they call them 'sums') in the book, like we have. There are only a few examples."

Curriculum making in the United States seems to be moving toward a prescriptive approach, and new teachers may have little or no experience with different instruction methods other than tell and show. However, in other countries, students find out that standards are in place, but teachers are expected to be the designers of their own curriculum, making lessons that match their pupils' academic needs. The identity of a teacher is at stake here. If a teacher sees herself as the curriculum maker, perpetual need to research topics becomes an integral part of this role. Constantly reading and learning, the teacher thinks about how to structure a lesson around specific concepts and design activities to illuminate those concepts, and to build on whatever learning emerges to create the next series of lessons. The aim is for the classroom of pupils to attain understanding of specific concepts.

Where textbooks are ready-made, with exercises at the end of each lesson, answers in the back of the text, and a teaching guide set out day by day, lesson by lesson, a new teacher may come to rely on someone else's ideas, someone else's plan, never making the curriculum match pupils' needs and pace. (I tell my teacher candidates who are in my curriculum development class that to learn how to design curriculum is like learning to drive a stick shift rather than an automatic.) However, in almost all placements in schools where COST sends teachers, standards and benchmarks guide the lessons, but it is expected the student teacher, like the teachers, will create their own curriculum.

And it is in the exercise of curriculum making that the richness of being a teacher is enhanced. Like an artist, crafting a lesson using the raw materials of primary sources, references, and other research materials helps link the teacher as agent in the understanding of her pupils. She is the mediator and creates a medium that she can adjust and adapt as her pupils need, allowing them to answer the questions they have about a topic, rather than providing answers to someone else's questions. Sometimes the spark is ignited in a COST student teacher and a synergy occurs, as in this case of a secondary math teacher:

> I taught a lesson in probability in an effort to prepare students for the probability section of their CTA. (Most of the students have had very little exposure to probability, so the lesson was mostly an introduction to sorting, charting, and interpreting their data from their candies). Soon enough, word got around to the math department that I was doing a lesson in probability (which the teachers are not very familiar with either).
>
> So far, I have visited and taught the lesson in two other math classes and am scheduled to teach two more next week! Even after I finished my lesson in one class on Wednesday, the teacher of the class I taught said that he even understood probability better after the activity.

Such confidence in one's capabilities to teach—and to teach teachers, no less—is invaluable. This COST student teacher acquired a strong sense of self as a curriculum maker, practicing teaching the concept of probability to her pupils and their teachers in the school. The overlay here is that this COST student teacher moved from student to teacher during her time abroad. The school lauded her efforts with the pupils, and appreciated her willingness to share her knowledge with her teacher colleagues, who, I might add, were inclined to share their best lessons with the COST teacher. What a sense of professional collaboration and sharing!

HOPEFUL VIEW OF THE FUTURE AS A GLOBAL ACTOR

As teacher educators, most of us have made deep commitments to the profession for many different reasons. I believe in the power of education to sustain a free, just world for all, and this requires an acknowledgement at some level that we are all connected as a human race. Education for the flourishing of human lives is an expression of *ubunto*. As Bishop Desmond Tutu describes,

> Africans believe in something that is difficult to render in English. We call it *ubunto, botho*. It means the essence of being human. You know it when

it is there and when it is absent. It speaks about humaneness, gentleness, hospitality, putting yourself out on behalf of others, being vulnerable. It embraces compassion and toughness. It recognizes that my humanity is bound up in yours, for we can only be human together.

This is the global connection that means the humanity of all, the connection of spirits. But to come to understand one's humanity, one's *ubunto*, requires moving beyond the parochial, walking away from the comfortable community of one's place, and entering another place, perhaps in its own way, as parochial as the one you left behind, but now different, nuanced and textured in new ways. COST student teachers step out of the confines of their comfort zones and we hope they allow themselves to be another way in the world, to see the world anew, to forever shift their perspective of who they are and what they will do in the world.

Sometimes, as in the case of Frieda, the step is never taken, and a retreat back to the familiar is chosen, but the majority of COST students take that crucial step and enter a new way of seeing, of living, of teaching the world. This is the aim of the COST program, to provide opportunity to be part of the larger world in ways that are particular to being a teacher in a classroom in a school in a culture in a country not one's own.

Janice had never left the United States and had always traveled with her family. She was placed in South Africa as a math student teacher and left as a global citizen. Janice was working with a group of pupils in Math Olympiad, and they won the regional competition, allowing them to compete in the nationals, in Cape Town. We received this reflection from Cape Town later that week:

> One other VERY exciting event has also happened within the last few days. I have been invited by Mrs. R. [cooperating teacher] to attend the Math Olympiad international competition with her and at least nine other students. The most exciting part? It will be in India! For R10,000 she has arranged a 10-day trip, four of which will be travelling in Dubai, Jaipur, Agra, and Delhi, with the other four days at the competition in Lucknow (the other days are lost in travel).

Janice was excited and looked forward to travelling with her pupils to India. In the above reflection, she gives no hint of hesitation to travel for the ten days on their way to Lucknow. The decision had to be made quickly, as arrangements and confirmations were necessary, and Janice never looked back.

> We will be the students' "coaches" and there is also a seminar for teachers that I will be attending as well. The students will have just finished taking their final exams and I will be without much to do (seeing as the teachers will be solely working on turning in final grades for the students). Hopefully this will be ok and I can continue my reflections while at the competition. Let me know if you see a problem with this, but the opportunity came about suddenly and I had to make a quick decision. I am incredibly excited about this and had no idea I would have this opportunity. It's hard for me to believe I will actually be going to a totally different country, while visiting one!

But Janice's adventure was only beginning. Because of her high involvement in school extracurricular activities, one of the teachers invited Janice to join her husband and children in Mozambique for the school holiday, and Janice accepted this invitation. She wrote,

> Wow! Mozambique—what an experience. I don't even know where to begin with all of the stories I could tell. I feel like such a seasoned traveler after doing so much of it by myself. I learned a lot about myself and communicating in far different cultural environments than I am used to—with language barriers! I truly felt like I got a more "African" experience in this excursion to Mozambique and got to see more of the third world side on a whole, than I have in all my experiences so far. It was good preparation for India, I think, as far as the merchants and learning how to deal with them. I am slowly improving my bargaining skills.

To be a global citizen requires an openness to other ways of living, of speaking, of interacting. Without judgment or comparison, Janice enlarged her sense of self and her attachment to the world. Freire argues that such a step is indicative of one who understands her (or his) incompleteness, that is, a person who senses there is more beyond one's self, and is propelled to be curious about it and then to search. "Men and women are capable of being educated only to the extent that they recognize themselves as unfinished. Education does not make us educable. It is our awareness of being unfinished that makes us educable" (1998, 58).

Educable means here one who can and does open oneself to the world beyond self, beyond the comfort zone of the familiar. And while taking this step is fraught with terror, those who have the courage to do so are transformed that they will spread this to their future pupils. They become teachers in the world. As Stan shared,

> For me, learning about myself, my own culture, and how it is viewed by others is something that has been very interesting to me because up until now, I had not been exposed to this perspective. When I am by myself in the city, and I look around and everyone else is Japanese, I can't help but to become aware of how different I look and act, and this has all made me really think a lot about my place in the world.

We who educate are engaged in an endeavor at once moral and humble, a creative expression of what it means to be human. We touch lives, and can make an impact upon another, who carries that impact into their lives, touching, perhaps, their students' lives. Keeping alive the spark of curiosity that would propel a student to ask, to seek, to question, to step out of the familiar and embrace the unfamiliar—until it becomes familiar and part of one—is worthy of effort and commitment. As Mark Twain reminds us, "Travel is fatal to prejudice, bigotry, and narrow-mindedness, and many of our people need it sorely on these accounts. Broad, wholesome, chartable views of men and things cannot be acquired by vegetating in on a little corner of the earth all one's lifetime." The COST Program consciously cultivates the curiosity of new teachers to student teach abroad that they may become teachers who are broad, wholesome, and charitable to all they meet, whether it is in Africa, Asia, or their middle-school math students right here in the United States. Once one has allowed the world to expand his or her view, he or she becomes a citizen of the world. For teachers, they become ambassadors of a global community to their pupils. I think this is one way to fulfill Bishop Tutu's eloquent plea for *ubunto*.

REFERENCES

Berlyne, D. C. 1960. *Conflict, arousal, and curiosity*. New York: McGraw-Hill.
France, Anatole. 1932. *The crime of Sylvestre Bonnard*. New York: Modern Library.
Freire, Paulo. 1990. *Pedagogy of freedom: Ethics, democracy, and civic courage*. Lanham, MD: Rowman & Littlefield.

———. 2004. *Pedagogy of indignation.* Boulder, CO: Paradigm

Kincheloe, J., P. Slattery, and S. Steinberg. 2000. *Contextualizing teaching: Introduction to education and educational foundations.* New York: Longman.

Twain, M. (1966). The Innocents Abroad, Mark Twain. New York: Signet Classic, 1966

John Greenleaf Whittier (1807–1892), U.S. poet. repr. In *The Poetical Works of John Greenleaf Whittier,* ed. W. Garrett Horder (1911). Maud Muller, l. 105–6 (1856).

10

REFLECTIONS ON THE IMPORTANCE AND VALUE OF THE OVERSEAS STUDENT-TEACHING EXPERIENCE

Rosalie Romano
Kenneth Cushner

Oliver Wendell Holmes argued that "a mind that has been stretched by a new experience can never go back to its old dimensions." The various programs reported on in this volume build upon the value of being stretched and the aim of fostering new dimensions in what it means to teach and to be a world-class teacher. Those who have participated in an intercultural student-teaching experience and have opened themselves to being teachers within another country or culture have been exposed to new ways of looking at the world, not only in a curricular and pedagogical sense but equally in a cultural sense. In the attempt to influence one's cultural identity, the orientation most students receive prior to going abroad explicitly aims to sustain an openness to ambiguity, to difference, and to self-reflection. These characteristics are a form of cultural capital for any teacher, but for a new teacher, they are invaluable. Central elements in this chapter are the Freirian concepts of identity and teacher as cultural worker that frame how we see the importance and value of the overseas student-teaching experience. These aspects of intercultural student teaching have significant potential to be cultivated in a student, so embedded by the experiences that the seeds continue to grow and live fully in the future interactions of these teachers and their students. Through the cultivation of identity and becoming a cultural worker, these teachers can touch the future generations in the hope of knowing the connections we all have as human beings upon this Earth.

A primary goal of an international student-teaching experience is to enhance global and intercultural understanding among teachers who will ultimately transfer this orientation to the students in their charge. Understanding the manner in which people learn to be effective living and working across cultures, and thus how to successfully teach toward this, is fundamental to teacher educators. Stachowski, Richardson, and Henderson (2003) report on the value that cultural study and immersion have on the development of culturally responsive teachers. They reflect upon Blair and Jones' concern that the study of culture has an essential role in the preparation of teachers, although this is not always the case. Blair and Jones state,

> It is common for education majors to focus on classroom management, information giving, school routine and daily survival to the exclusion of fresh and careful reflection on the daily life, values, history, and aspirations of the school community. Yet, today's teachers must be students of human behavior, social events and their causes, and the characteristics of the citizens they serve. (1998, 77)

And Merryfield (1997), who repeatedly calls for teacher-education programs to prepare teachers to teach toward diversity and equity within a globally connected world, argues that methods and materials must encourage students to reflect upon their experience while they explore, analyze, and participate within global and local communities.

This is where international and domestic intercultural student-teaching experiences such as those reported on in this volume come into play. Students learning to teach in other cultural settings go well beyond the level of being a tourist, in most cases living on their own without the support of others who are culturally like themselves. The experience abroad, regardless of the level at which it takes place, engages the student holistically, involving both physical as well as psychological transitions that have an impact on the cognitive, affective, and behavioral domains. And these transitions occur twice, once during entry into the host culture and then again upon reentry into the home culture.

Such is the basis of experiential learning—it involves experiences that are both affective and personal in nature, and it is critical to cross-cultural learning. While we can transfer a significant amount of culturally appropriate information to learners through a cognitive approach using scores of books, inspiring speakers, and insightful films, this has, unfortunately, little impact on people's affect and subsequent behavior (Cushner and Brislin 1996). Experiential learning involves both the right and left hemispheres of the brain holistically, linking encounter with cognition. The lived intercultural teaching experience, thus, plays a major role in the success of this effort—there is just no substitute for the real thing.

Two other characteristics often associated with experiential cross-cultural learning are important to consider at this point. Distinct from simple cross-cultural encounters or tourist ventures, intercultural experiential learning experiences, as Angene Wilson (1987) described, are planned and reflected upon. And it is this reflection that becomes critical to the learning process. Teachers can be a critical link in structuring educational experiences that assist students to reach out to the international community, both at home and abroad, with the aim of forging relationships based on deep and meaningful understandings of peoples' similarities as well as differences. But teachers must have these experiences themselves if they are to subsequently transfer this knowledge and skill to their students.

CULTURAL IDENTITY OF A TEACHER

An identity emerges out of one's cultural upbringing that is carried throughout one's life and relations with others. For a teacher, identity motivates and colors the social dynamics of teaching, as well as the pedagogical approaches used to teach. If a teacher does not reflect on the impact of culture upon his or her identity, the ramifications for students can be immense. Freire (1998a) argues that a teacher's cultural identity is the engine that moves whatever happens in the classroom. If a teacher is critical in the Freirian sense, that is, has a depth of awareness of herself as in reciprocal relation to her students, an awareness of connection and justice, then the teacher will work toward the well-being and critical consciousness of her students—on their behalf, not hers. Their work together in the classroom can raise their consciousness of their place in the world, of themselves as actors and agents, rather than passive recipients. To teach in the Freirian sense of critical educational practice is to question, to challenge, to become aware of possibilities in life, not to accept the status quo. As Freire states,

> Critical educational practice is to make possible the conditions in which the learners, in their interaction with one another and with their teachers, engage in the experience of assuming themselves as social, historical, thinking, communicating, transformative, creative persons; dreamers of possible utopias, capable of being angry because of a capacity to love. (1998a, 45)

For Freire, the aim of educational practice is to foster a sense of efficacy and action in students, rather than place them in the position of being the object of a teacher's work. The students are the center of learning—and learning leads to action in their self-interest. Contrast this with the traditional paradigm of teacher-centered classroom, where the teacher practices a banking method of teaching, where students are repositories for teacher content, a classroom where students must answer other people's questions.

To shift this paradigm and move into critical educational practice requires of a teacher a willingness to be part of her students' learning, where learning is reciprocal and active on both parts. The teacher in this situation has authority, but this is used to set conditions of learning that engage students in understanding themselves and others, in identifying issues that affect their lives, in naming that which inhibits their educative, social, and creative growth as persons and dreamers. The teacher must be predisposed to turn toward her students as co-workers, as well as guide them in their learning to name their world.

To move into this paradigm, a teacher must be aware of her differences with her students, as well as her connections with them. Both teacher and students are subjects; students are not objects, as in the banking method, but subjects who act upon their world. Subjectivity, the human interaction between people, must be predicated upon respect: respect for the agency of the student, and a teacher's respect for herself as critical practitioner. She cannot view her role as a teacher to impose or to control her students. Rather, she must work with and alongside them, listening to their questions and constructing the learning of topics around those questions. And one can only listen to another if it is grounded in respect for that person. Respect changes all relationships, and is, according to Freire, fundamental to being a critical practitioner.

Through respect, students grow into their own agency, their own self-assumption of who they are and how they might influence their conditions. When an overseas student teacher enters a new school in a new cultural environment and classroom, a singular opportunity to become or enhance a critical practitioner stance is given. Sometimes teacher candidates have been prepared in a program that ignores the sociopolitical context of education, where the technical approach is privileged with no questioning as to the teacher's authority to know what and how to teach. Such unexamined assumptions can wreak havoc upon the new teacher who happens to be placed in a classroom with pupils of different ethnic, linguistic, or cultural backgrounds. Unless the teacher is predisposed to question herself, to see her pupils as subjects rather than objects, and to desire to work with them rather than impose upon them, the classroom cannot become a transformative space where learning and engagement can thrive. Freire warns us that "Purely pragmatic training, with its implicit or openly expressed elitist authoritarianism, is incomparable with the learning and practice of becoming a 'subject'" (1998a, 46).

An international student-teaching experience provides opportunities for new teachers to become critical, to assume their subjectivity within classrooms through meeting new cultures and learning to navigate as part of that culture. We do not presume to think that critical practice and consciousness occurs on its own simply by exposing a new teacher to a new cultural environment, however. Rather, consistent guidance and exposure to new ideas and skills set conditions for a new teacher to question her identity without resistance and fighting for control. The key is to cultivate an appreciation for difference, and to help the new teacher situate herself as a subject, unfinished and changing, willing to learn new ways of seeing not only teaching but also the world as well. Respect must be made explicit and specific as a disposition to be fostered prior to going abroad and then during the student-teaching experience overseas.

Respect is one of those values that manifests itself in a classroom in its own language and attitude. When a student teacher stops and listens to a pupil's ideas, and responds to those ideas seriously, pupils can see how she respects who they are as people. An international student teacher who participates in after-school activities with her students, who coaches or teaches or attends their club or team meets, places herself in the position of acknowledging her pupils outside of the classroom. Relationship building is the glue of respect, and for teachers it is accessible. And this teacher exposes herself to all the cultural nuances and knowledge available in the new setting. All a teacher has to do is show up, and pupils take note.

Overseas student teachers are drawn into the life and activity of school, in part, because their life is centered around school and teaching—at least at the start of their experience. Encountering pupils in extracurricular activities shifts the perspective of these teachers to see their pupils as people with complex interests and lives. Stories about families are exchanged, views on sports events are ongoing conversations, and meeting family members who attend a competition increases the experience of the student teacher to better understand the pupils in the classroom. Such a student teacher in Guadalajara, Mexico, for example, was an outstanding chess player. He joined the school chess club, and soon discovered that a third-grader and the school custodian were excellent chess players, quite advanced. Not only did this tournament reveal unexpected talent, but his obvious enjoyment of playing chess allowed others to see him in a different way, too. "Sometimes a simple, almost insignificant gesture on the part of a teacher can have a profound formative effect on the life of a student" (Freire 1998a, 46).

We encourage international student teachers to actively participate in all areas of school life for this very reason. Such a student is a stranger in a strange land; her pupils are only too willing to guide her into their culture. This extracurricular opportunity weaves a web that is carried into the classroom and in teaching. Respect emerges in significant forms as the student teacher begins to see pupils in new surroundings, demonstrating their prowess in sports or games or drama. Recognition of pupils' talent, or oftentimes simply their efforts, is enough to provide incentive for learning and increased participation in the academic classroom. While most experienced teachers know this and do try to get out to school events, the new teacher frequently is unaware of the kind of understanding gained by participating in these important socializing activities. The act of participating, of recognizing a pupil from class who is playing soccer or chess, for instance, enhances education into what it should be—an experience of the whole person, rather than a solely academic task.

International student teachers see everything about a school as "new" or "different," even as they describe what is common to most schools: teachers, classrooms, clubs, pupils, and their behaviors. In another culture and country, even the familiar is made unfamiliar, providing an invaluable opportunity for the new teacher to really see, to become consciously aware of the physical, the social, and the academic manifestations of the life of a school.

Freire argues it is the hidden curriculum of school life that we should pay attention to when he says, "What is important in teaching is not the mechanical repetition of this or that but a comprehension of the value of sentiments, emotions, and desires" (1998a, 47). Critical educational practice is linked to a teacher's capacity to see pupils as exciting, complete, vivid human beings, who have skills, knowledge, and understandings about themselves and the world. A teacher who can tap into pupils' prior knowledge and skills can foster their curiosity about new ways of thinking and different ways of being through their teaching. What a powerful pedagogical lesson this is for a new teacher, to come to glimpse the world through the eyes of her pupils, and to recognize how much they know and can teach her about their world, their country, their culture. This awareness is all the more memorable and acute because this student teacher is in a new culture where she is pushed to suspend her cultural as well as her educational paradigms.

TEACHER AS CULTURAL WORKER

For Freire, the concept of cultural identity is a "dynamic relationship between what we inherit and what we acquire" (1998b, 69). When student teachers travel abroad, they are stretched to interact with all manner of differences as they navigate airports and ground transportation, and find their ways to their school community. While it is common for the overseas supervisor to meet the student when he or she lands, with the first breath of air in the new country this student rapidly must adjust to light and sound, geography, and road systems. The accents, signage, building organization, and so forth urge the student to keep alert. In fact, this is a necessary disposition to being a teacher in the classroom, to see and to sense the nuances of change and difference that young people bring into the classroom each day. If a teacher is to be responsive and respectful to her pupils, she must always be "wide awake," alert to subtle shifts in mood or behavior in them.

Sometimes what we acquire ideologically from our sociocultural upbringing challenges the student (and all of us, really) when we travel abroad and live in another culture. Each time we relate to another, we interpret from our cultural foundation, which can sometimes be tension filled. A solicitous host mother can "feel" hovering and too confining to a student teacher, which the student must somehow deal with. While we may be conditioned by our culture, we are, however, not predetermined by it, and with new cross-cultural knowledge, we can better understand a situation and learn to make alternative attributions. We can reason our way through the cultural tension. We urge our students to think about how to broach the topic of what they feel with their host mother, for example. Or to reason through what they perceive to be a particular attitude on the part of their cooperating teacher. The "wide awakeness" assists in this process because the sense of cultural balance has shifted within the student teacher to allow an openness to consider another point of view. When a person is within one's dominant culture, rejecting difference or thinking (subconsciously) that her culture is better than another becomes the normative way of looking at the world. Living abroad shakes a normative view so the student becomes aware of his or her ethnocentric way of viewing the world. In a wonderful irony, the international student teachers' attempts to understand another culture frequently awaken their awareness of their own culture and beliefs. And out of this emerges an appreciation for the culture and the beginnings of understanding. These pathways of understanding guide the student teacher towards a new openness that increases with each experience. Over the weeks of student teaching abroad, the student begins to "feel" at home in the new culture, and the texture of the reflections they write reveals this disposition. The student teacher is a cultural worker—that is, one who can live in multiple cultures, navigate with acceptance through the new channels of cultural perspectives. It is in the experiencing of difference that we experience who we are (Freire 1998b). In our awareness comes knowing; and with knowing, growth.

Many students who have chosen to student teach abroad have returned to the United States as teachers who are cultural workers. They have lived in another culture, as a different cultural being, and learned to be part of their new culture while at the same time becoming aware of their own. They return enhanced. For some, they have transformed the vision of themselves as educators. Walking into their own classrooms in the United States, they bring with them a "wide awakeness" that allows them to see and respond to their pupils. While they share their experiences abroad with their pupils, these teachers also have a confidence about themselves that distinguishes them from other first-year teachers. This confidence has been earned by living with and among different cultural beings, and working to understand themselves in relation to those who at first are deemed different.

One former student teacher wrote to share how each year he sees his pupils as a new culture to be discovered, to learn from as much as to teach. He takes nothing for granted, he says, which tends to annoy his colleagues, but reaps invaluable results in the relationships with his pupils and their academic progress under his guidance. While he brings in stories and artifacts to share with his pupils, he also teaches them about how we live in our U.S. society. He builds on his stories to help his pupils become "wide awake" as well to their social consciousness, especially around issues of race and class. This teacher's enlarged vision and understanding of others he attributes directly to his experiences as an overseas student teacher. Such teachers are, at their best, cultural workers who model to their pupils year after year what it means to be a world-class teacher, a global citizen.

IN CONCLUSION

Merryfield (2000) reminds us that most teachers have not been prepared to understand the impact of globalization or domestic diversity in the lives of their pupils and communities, let alone on themselves. In her study of eighty teacher educators recognized by their peers for their success in preparing teachers in both multicultural and global education, Merryfield discovered something of critical importance to those concerned with the intercultural development of their pupils. She found there to be significant differences between the experiences of people of color and European Americans that reflect the importance of insightful, experiential learning. Most American teachers of color have a double consciousness (DuBois 1989), having grown up conscious of both their own primary culture as well as having experienced discrimination and the status of being an outsider by encountering a society characterized by white privilege and racism. Middle-class white teacher educators who are effective at teaching for diversity had their most profound experiences while living outside their own country. These teachers had encountered discrimination and exclusion by being an outsider within another cultural context, and they had found ways to bring this to their teaching.

Those who leave the comfort of their home society for an extended period of time come to understand what it is like to live outside the mainstream and to be perceived as "the Other." It is the impact of an intercultural experience, like that provided by overseas student teaching, that has facilitated many European American mainstream teachers to become more ethnorelative in their understanding of others, more skilled at crossing cultures, and committed to bringing about change through their work. A significant international experience, thus, leads to new, firsthand understandings of what it means to be marginalized, to be a victim of stereotypes and prejudice, and how this might affect people. Thus, the international lived experience sets the stage for developing a consciousness of multiple realities and serves as the stimulus that prompts new learning.

The lived intercultural experience thus becomes the critical element in gaining a meaningful understanding of other cultures as well as one's own place in an interconnected world, especially for those who typically are not experienced in cross-cultural matters. Intercultural teaching practice can be the catalyst that starts teachers on a path of learning from others as well as forging relationships based on deep and meaningful understandings of peoples' similarities and differences. Schools of education should strive to make this opportunity available to an increasing number of students as a way to increase the skills that we know they will need as they enter classrooms of the twenty-first century.

REFERENCES

Blair, T. R., and D. L. Jones. 1998. *Preparing for student teaching in a pluralistic classroom*. Boston: Allyn & Bacon.

Cushner, K., and R. Brislin. 1996. *Intercultural interactions: A practical guide*. 2nd ed. Thousand Oaks, CA: Sage.

DuBois, W. E. B. 1989. *The souls of black folks*. New York: Bantam Books.

Freire, P. 1998a. *Pedagogy of freedom: Ethics, democracy, and civic courage*. Lanham, MD: Rowman & Littlefield.

———. 1998b. *Teachers as cultural workers: Letters to those who dare to teach*. Boulder, CO: Westview Press.

Merryfield, M. 1997. A framework for teacher education in global perspective. In M. M. Merryfield, E. Jarchow, and S. Pickett (Eds.), *Preparing teachers to teach global perspectives: A handbook for teacher educators*, edited by M. Merryfield, E. Jarchow, and S. Pickert, 1–24. Thousand Oaks, CA: Corwin Press.

Merryfield. M. M. 2000. Why aren't teachers being prepared to teach for diversity, equity and global interconnectedness? A study of lived experiences in the making of multicultural and global educators. *Teaching and Teacher Education* 16:429–43.

Stachowski, L., J. Richardson, and M. Henderson. 2003. Student teachers report on the influence of cultural values on classroom practice and community involvement: Perspectives from the Navajo reservation and from abroad. *Teacher Educator* 39, no. 1:52–63.

Wilson, A. 1987. Cross-cultural experiential learning for teacher. *Theory into Practice* 26:519–27.

INDEX

ABOUT THE AUTHORS

Cristina Alfaro is the California State University (CSU) chairperson for the International Teacher Education Consortium (ITEC), and director of the CSU International Teacher Professional Development Program. She is also a critical literacy assistant professor in the Department of Policy Studies in Language and Cross-Cultural Education at San Diego State University. Her research interests center on home/school cross-cultural languages and literacy practices. As a teacher researcher, she has examined the role of teachers' ideological and political clarity related to teaching practices with language minority student groups.

Neil Andersen has spent his working life in the field of education in New Zealand, serving as a primary school teacher, a teacher recruitment officer, a teacher educator and trainer, a university lecturer, a professional leader in a NZ Polytechnic, a visiting professor in Japan (at the time of the Kobe earthquake in January 1995), and is currently campus principal of a private vocational education provider in the area of digital technology. For twenty years, he has filled the role of COST receiving site coordinator and during this time has been responsible for the school placement of 120 preservice teacher-education students from consortium institutions. Neil is keen on sports and following regional representative participation in swimming, softball, and soccer in his younger days, he remains an active soccer player.

Sharon Brennan is an associate professor in the Department of Curriculum and Instruction at the University of Kentucky. She currently serves as director of Field Experiences and School Collaboration in the College of Education at the University of Kentucky. Dr. Brennan's interests include global education, teacher mentoring, and program development in teacher education. She has a long-standing commitment to international education, teacher development, and university/school partnership initiatives. She served as executive director of the Consortium for Overseas Student Teaching from 1987–1995.

Julie Cleary is program coordinator and overseas student-teaching advisor in the College of Education at the University of Kentucky. She also coordinates activities associated with a statewide teacher internship program for the university. Her interests include intercultural learning, student development, and teacher assessment. She has been involved in teacher education initiatives for almost two decades.

Kenneth Cushner is executive director of international affairs and professor of education in the College and Graduate School of Education, Health and Human Services, at Kent State University, Kent, Ohio. Dr. Cushner is author or editor of several books and articles in the field of intercultural education and training, including *Human Diversity in Education: An Integrative Approach*, 5th ed. (2006); *Human Diversity in Action: Developing Multicultural Competencies in the Classroom*, 3rd ed. (2006); *Beyond Tourism: A Practical Guide to Meaningful Educational Travel* (2004); *International Perspectives on Intercultural Education* (1998); and *Intercultural Interactions: A Practical Guide*, 2nd ed. (with Richard Brislin, 1996). He is a past director of COST, the Consortium for Overseas Student Teaching. In his spare time, Dr. Cushner enjoys music (percussion and guitar), photography, and travel. He has developed and led intercultural programs on all seven continents.

Gretchen L. Espinetti received a bachelor's degree in elementary education with majors in French and Spanish from American International College, and a master's degree in educational administration with a focus in TESOL at George Washington University. She has taught in a bilingual HeadStart program in Massachusetts, with Department of Defense Schools in Japan, the Philippines, and Korea, as well as Arlington/Fairfax, Virginia, and in San Diego, California. Currently, she is the full-time director of the Office of Clinical Experiences at Kent State University and serves as COST coordinator while pursuing a PhD in cultural foundations. Her research interests include third culture children (TCKs) and the impact of this multicultural phenomenon on their schooling in the United States. During the academic year, she teaches in the early childhood program and has taught courses in multicultural practices for preservice and in-service teachers in the Education Foundations and Special Services Department.

Mary Anne Flournoy is associate director emerita of the Center for International Studies at Ohio University in Athens, Ohio. She founded the Ohio Valley International Council, the university's international outreach arm. She is currently adjunct assistant professor of educational studies, co-coordinator of the Consortium for Overseas Student Teaching, and a faculty fellow in the Office of Nationally Competitive Awards as well as a former social studies teacher in Maryland, Texas, New York, Ohio, and Indonesia.

Jennifer Mahon is an assistant professor of sociocultural education at the University of Nevada, Reno. Her research interests include international education, critical pedagogy, and intercultural sensitivity. Currently she studies the development of intercultural sensitivity across the lifespan, especially as it is influenced by intercultural conflict. Dr. Mahon has worked in the field of overseas student teaching for nine years. In addition to her research with returning students, she has handled many aspects of facilitating exchanges including programmatic setup, placement and advisement of student teachers, as well as recruitment and support of host sites. Dr. Mahon is a junior fellow of the International Academy of Intercultural Research, and a board member of the Northern Nevada International Center. Dr. Mahon has a graduate diploma in multicultural education from the University of New England in Australia, which she completed as a Rotary Foundation Scholar. She earned her doctorate from Kent State University, double-majoring in curriculum and instruction, and cultural foundations of education. She is certified to use the Intercultural Development Inventory and has

completed the one-year training program of the Gremlin Taming Institute. An experienced secondary English and ESL teacher, she has lived
and worked in Australia, England, and Costa Rica.

Laura L. Stachowski is the director of the cultural immersion projects
in the School of Education at Indiana University, Bloomington. She is
also a faculty member in the Department of Curriculum and Instruction. She prepares and places cultural projects participants for student
teaching and community involvement experiences in the national
schools of Australia, China, Costa Rica, England, India, Ireland, Kenya,
New Zealand, Russia, Scotland, Spain, Turkey, and Wales, and in Navajo
Reservation schools in Arizona, New Mexico, and Utah. Dr. Stachowski
also offers the Overseas Practicum for Experienced Teachers, which
provides in-service educators with overseas school experiences during
the summer. She earned her PhD at Indiana University in 1994.

Rosalie M. Romano is associate professor of educational studies, Ohio
University. Her research is centered in critical theory/pedagogy in
teaching and learning and she directs the CARE program, Creative Active Reflective Educators for democratic education. Additionally, she is
the COST coordinator at OU. She is the author of *Forging an Educative
Community* (2000) and *Hungry Minds in Hard Times* (2003).

Reyes Quezada is associate professor in the School of Leadership and
Education Sciences, Learning and Teaching Program at the University
of San Diego. He has been on the faculties of the University of Redlands
and California State University, Stanislaus. He has taught undergraduate and graduate degree courses in multicultural education and bilingual education, family-school and community partnerships, physical education for elementary school teachers, outdoor and adventure-based
leadership, and student-teaching seminars. His area of publications includes recruitment, retention, and promotion of faculty and teachers of
color, effective parent involvement of ethnically diverse families, adventure-based education, and international teacher-education programs.
He received his EdD from Northern Arizona University.

Angene Wilson retired in 2004 after twenty-nine years as professor of secondary social studies education at the University of Kentucky. She was also associate director of international affairs at the university from 1990 to 1996. Among early Peace Corps volunteers, she taught history in Liberia from 1962 to 1964 and later taught at teacher-training colleges in Sierra Leone and Fiji. In 1997 she was a Fulbright Scholar in Ghana. She led teachers to Nigeria in 1980 and to Ghana in 2004.